STRATEGIC ATLAS

The policy of a state lies in its geography.
—NAPOLEON

STRATEGIC ATLAS

A Comparative Geopolitics of the World's Powers

THIRD EDITION

Gérard Chaliand and Jean-Pierre Rageau

Translated from the French by Tony Berrett

Maps by Catherine Petit

HarperPerennial
A Division of HarperCollins*Publishers*

THIS ATLAS IS DEDICATED

- to the British geopolitical analyst Halford J. Mackinder (1861–1947);

- to the theorist of sea power, the American Alfred T. Mahan (1840–1914);

- to the pioneer of geopolitics, the German Friedrich Ratzel (1844–1904);

- and to the French geographer Pierre Vidal de la Blache (1845–1918)

This book was originally published in France under the title *Atlas Stratégique*, © Librairie Arthème Fayard, 1983.

HarperCollins books may be purchased for educational, business, or sales promotional use. For information please write Special Markets Department, HarperCollins Publishers, Inc., 10 East 53rd Street, New York, N.Y. 10022.

FIRST EDITION

Library of Congress Cataloging-in-Publication Data
Chaliand, Gérard, 1934–
   [Atlas stratégique. English]
   Strategic atlas : a comparative geopolitics of the world's powers
 / Gerard Chaliand, Jean-Pierre Rageau ; translated from the French
 by Tony Berrett ; maps by Cathering Petit.—3rd ed.
     p.   cm.
   Translation of: Atlas stratégique.
   Includes bibliographical references.
   ISBN 0-06-271554-2—ISBN 0-06-273153-X (pbk.)
   1. Geopolitics—Maps. 2. World politics. 3. Great powers—Maps.
I. Rageau, Jean-Pierre. II. Vallet-Petit, Catherine. III. Title.
G1046.F1C513 1992 <G & M>
327.1′01′0223—dc20   91-58286
                                    MAP

93 94 95 96 97/RRD 10 9 8 7 6 5 4 3 2 1
93 94 95 96 97/RRD 10 9 8 7 6 5 4 3 2 1 (pbk.)

CONTENTS

SECURITY PERCEPTIONS OF WORLD AND REGIONAL POWERS

NATURAL CONSTRAINTS

ECONOMIC DATA

POPULATION FACTORS

NORTH–SOUTH

THE MILITARY BALANCE

PREFACE

This atlas is not a mapping of past or future battles, or a graphic depiction of opposing military forces. Strategy, like politics, embraces war, but is more than war. What is provided here is truly a geopolitics of the relations of force in the contemporary world. In order to portray as accurately as possible realities that are at once multifaceted, complex, and sometimes impossible to represent at all (how, for example, to measure determination, which is of course a key factor in conflict situations? Can one predict surprise?), we have sought to be as global as possible.

From the outset, our perspective on our planet breaks with the Mercator projection, with its horizontal and almost pre-Galilean world, in which the land masses appear to cover a larger area than the seas. The modern perspective should give a more faithful picture of a globe on which the poles, the axes of the world, have been, at least until recently in the case of the Arctic, a decisive area that does not appear on the usual maps. We have therefore favored a multiplicity of projections, and these have been selected solely for the purposes of our demonstration, and to show every aspect of the world.

Thus, geographically our atlas gives considerable space to the oceans, which cover the larger part of the planet, on which sea power is engaged, mastery of which has ensured Anglo-American hegemony for almost two centuries: the Arctic Ocean, whose frozen surfaces do not prevent the passage of nuclear submarines underneath; the Pacific, whose strong points are all controlled by the Anglo-Americans and the French; the Atlantic, both North and South; and the Indian Ocean.

We have also sought to show, in addition to the usual views and projections used by Europeans and Americans, the world as it is—or was—seen by the Chinese, the ex-USSR, and the Arab Muslims. We have sought to show the great cultural and religious domains, which are the matrices of world views, and in this way to complement our strategic approach with the historical background that shapes collective behaviors and that may determine external decisions to fight, or provoke imbalances within a society.

No attempt has ever been made, for example, to compile a map of the major traditional enmities that have determined conflicts in a given historical epoch. How, for example, can we understand Poland without alluding to its dual rejection of the Russians and the Germans? Our atlas also includes considerable material depicting the at least militarily bipolarized world that emerged from World War II and lasted almost up to the present. It shows the current world strategic situation while at the same time indicating the changes that have occurred over the course of the Cold War.

This strategic atlas also looks at a dimension that is not treated in the usual works: states' perceptions of their security—not only those of the world powers, but also those of the lesser-known regional powers such as Saudi Arabia, India, South Africa, Brazil, Japan, and

Israel. It is, for example, not sufficiently appreciated that the security perceptions of a state such as Saudi Arabia have been a function of its hostility not only to the Soviet Union and Israel, but also to the former Soviet presence in Afghanistan, Ethiopia (an obstacle to Arab control of the Red Sea), and the Democratic Republic of Yemen on its southern flank; of its rejection of a regional hegemony by Shiite Iran; and finally of its own military and demographic weakness, half its working population being foreigners.

We have also tried to present a multiform world with very different perceptions*. Of course, our work includes a number of more conventional maps concerning agricultural, industrial, mineral, and energy resources, as well as demographic data and information making it possible to grasp the nature of North-South relations. Wherever it seemed useful, we have provided statistical projections up to the end of the century. Finally, our atlas includes a strictly military section, partly centered on nuclear questions. In short, our conception of strategy attempts to embrace the totality of human, material, and cultural factors that make up a global balance of forces.

As such, our atlas does not claim to be free of all shortcomings. But we are nevertheless certain that we are taking a novel approach to revealing the political realities of the contemporary world.

We would like to thank General Pierre Gallois, who looked at our military maps and generously provided two that he had drawn himself; Catherine Petit, our cartographer, for her work; and Claude Durand, who was from the beginning convinced of the novelty of our project and took on the risks involved.

Gérard Chaliand
Jean-Pierre Rageau

---

*Perhaps we have been helped in this by the fact that we both studied at the Ecole Nationale des Langues Orientales, one of the very few institutions where it was possible in the 1950s to acquire a view of the world that was not Western-centered.

INTRODUCTION

When the Berlin Wall came down on 9 November 1989, symbolically marking the end of the Cold War, the 45-year-long period since the end of World War II came to a quite unexpected and abrupt close: the West won the fruits of war without war.

When Mikhail Gorbachev came to power in 1985 and then began to talk about *glasnost* and *perestroika*, there was not the least inkling to suggest the imminent collapse of an order based on the hegemony of Communist parties in central and southeastern Europe. From the beginning the regimes installed by Moscow had used the Party, the police, and the army to keep a grip on increasingly dissatisfied populations. But from 1953 (Berlin) to 1981 (Poland) by way of Budapest (1956) and Prague (1968), force was used to put down any attempt to challenge the established order. Under Brezhnev in the 1970s and up to his death (1982), the USSR itself, although notoriously backward economically, nevertheless continued to make progress in the conquest of space and in military affairs while conducting an aggressive foreign policy. In the aftermath of the American withdrawal from Vietnam in 1973, the Soviet Union chalked up advances in Angola (1975) and in Mozambique, and Ethiopia (1978), and in Afghanistan in 1979 it intervened militarily for the first time outside the Warsaw Pact countries. Its allies also made advances with the fall of Saigon (1975), the invasions of Laos and then Cambodia by the Vietnamese (1978), and the Sandinista victory in Nicaragua in 1979, while guerrilla war engulfed El Salvador.

Meanwhile, the crisis over the installation of U.S. nuclear missiles in Europe (which began in December 1979) reminded Europeans of their vulnerability. It was only after several years of indecision that the Pershings were installed, thus restoring a military balance in the European theater. When the president of the United States launched the Strategic Defense Initiative, better known as "Star Wars", in March 1983, few observers could imagine that soon the new financial effort demanded by the arms race would help to alter Soviet views and that a section of Soviet ruling elites might have a new perception of their own future in East-West competition.

No sooner had he been elected secretary-general of the Party (March 1985) than Gorbachev launched the slogans of *glasnost* and *perestroika* (October 1985). U.S.-Soviet summits became more frequent: in Geneva (November 1985), in Reykjavik (October 1986), in Washington (December 1987). A reduction in the arms race got under way, as did a significant reduction in the quantity of military hardware in the Central European theater (an indication of the importance of the December 1987 INF agreement).

Meanwhile, Andrei Sakharov returned from Gorki (December 1986). Most Soviet political prisoners were freed (February 1987). But the "national question" soon reared its head; demonstrations in Moscow (July 1987) by Crimean Tatars who had been collectively exiled by Stalin; demonstrations in Estonia and in Armenia (February 1988) demanding democracy and the, in the case of Armenia, reattachment of Nagorno-Karabakh, a region whose population is Armenian but which is administered by Azerbaijan; and, in quick succession, pogroms at Sumgaït (February 1988).

And before long in the "people's democracies":
- The first big opposition demonstration occurs in Budapest (March 1988).
- A wave of strikes by workers all over Poland begins (April–May 1988).
- A demonstration takes place in Prague for the 20th anniversary of the crushing of the "Prague spring" (August 1988), followed by a second massive demonstration in October for the 70th anniversary of Czechoslovakia's independence.

All this was happening against a background of a staged Soviet withdrawal from Afghanistan between May 1988 and February 1989.

The earthquake in Armenia (55,000 casualties) saw for the first time the arrival in the USSR of international aid workers who observed Soviet incompetence and the outdatedness of the health infrastructure.

Events accelerated in Central Europe after Lech Walesa formed a shadow cabinet in Poland in December 1988. While the dissident Vaclav Havel was arrested in January 1989, a roundtable meeting was held in Warsaw between the government and the opposition. In Budapest in February 1989 the principle of the single-party state was abandoned.

Over the six months between April 1989 and the opening of the Berlin Wall, each month brought unbelievable changes:
- In April, Solidarity is legalized in Poland.
- In May, the Iron Curtain between Hungary and Austria is dismantled. East Germans are soon leaving the GDR in droves.
- In June, Solidarity is victorious in parliamentary elections. Reformers take power in Hungary.

- In August, the three Baltic countries form a human chain to protest at the time of the 50th anniversary of the Nazi-Soviet pact. T. Mazowiecki becomes the new head of the Polish government.
- In October, Erich Honecker is replaced as head of the East German CP. The Republic of Hungary is proclaimed, and the Hungarian CP is no more.
- In November, the Berlin Wall is opened. The secretary-general of the Bulgarian CP, Todor Zhivkov, is overthrown. Vaclav Havel becomes president of Czechoslovakia.
- In December, Ceaucescu is toppled in Bucharest.

During the first half of 1990, three processes began to crystallize:

1. The process of German reunification, with Germany remaining within NATO, 1 July 1990; economic, monetary, and social union between West and East Germany.

2. The virtual disappearance of the Communist parties in Hungary, Poland and Czechoslovakia, with a series of reforms transforming the economies of these countries into market economies. But the Bulgarian and above all the Romanian CPs continued to control political life and the pace of reforms.

3. A very different unfolding of events in the USSR, torn between more and more pressing national questions, growing economic difficulties, and a pursuit of constitutional and economic reforms with no visible success:

Intervention of the Red Army in Baku (January).

Interethnic conflicts in Dushanbe, Tajikistan (February).

Declaration of the independence of Lithuania (March).

Declaration of the sovereignty of Estonia (March).

Election of Gorbachev as president of the USSR (March).

Declaration of the sovereignty of Latvia (May).

Declaration of the sovereignty of Russia, with Boris Yeltsin at the head of the newly elected Supreme Soviet (June).

These events disproved the axiom of experts on the USSR and/or Marxism-Leninism who had argued that no Communist regime could cease to exist except by force. Willy-nilly, by its refusal to use armed force to halt the process of reform in Central Europe, Gorbachevism made possible an unprecedented revolution. This made it possible, at least for some, to believe in the advent of a new era, or the "end of history." But after the euphoria of victory—for a peaceful victory is what it indeed was—the problems are still there, in a new form, and, as usual when a new situation appears, with the anguish of the unknown and *new imbalances*.

- The United States appears to be in relative decline, with its economy's loss of competitiveness, its need to modernize large sectors of industry, and its debt burden. But it remains the military guarantor of the international order provided that it is not afraid to pay the human cost of *imperium*. The Gulf War strikingly confirms its preeminence.
- Reunited Germany inspires some concern because of its economic weight; will it not be *primus inter pares* in the EEC in a Europe lacking political cohesion?
- In Central Europe an old cleavage is already reappearing between, on the one hand, Poland, Hungary, and Czechoslovakia (Catholic) and, on the other, Romania and Bulgaria (Orthodox and long ruled by the Ottoman Empire). The first three appear likely to be flexibly associated with the EEC while the latter

will be relegated, in the medium term, outside the Western zone.

In the Soviet Union, meanwhile, the abortive putsch of August 1991 turned into a revolution. This revolution, heralded by Sakharov's creation in 1989 of an as yet very small-scale democratic opposition, and reinforced by the election of Yeltsin as president of the Russian republic in June 1991, put an end to the dictatorship of the Bolshevik Party instituted by Lenin following the October 1917 revolution.

Russia, and the republics that had already ended the grip of the Communist Party two years earlier (the Baltic countries, Armenia, and Moldavia), joined the movement for democratization that had appeared in Eastern Europe before the great turning-point of 1989. This, it will be recalled, was the case with Hungary, Poland, Czechoslovakia, and East Germany.

The situation remains ambiguous, to say the least, in countries where Communist governments managed to adapt in order to survive, such as Romania and to a lesser extent Bulgaria. This is also the case in Serbia where ultranationalism allowed Slobodan Milosevic, a Party member, to remain in power and enjoy popular support.

The end of Leninism and the dictatorship of the Party in the ex-USSR is an event that is all the more important because the Soviet Union was the model for all the other experiences of the same type. The few that survive are surely bound to disappear in time: Cuba, North Korea, Vietnam, and China.

At the time some appeared to believe the putsch would succeed, although the fact is that a coup d'état is not at all certain of success if it does not control the situation from the first day. Gorbachev was the only major figure to have been arrested. Yeltsin remained free to lead the opposition. Compared with the military coup d'état of General Jaruzelski in Poland in October 1981, the unorganized character of the August 1991 coup in Russia is glaringly apparent. In Poland, right from the very first morning all the leaders of Solidarity were arrested, telephone communications were cut, and censorship of information was total. In Russia strike calls could be sent from the Russian parliament to the miners. The Western press and television were able to continue their work unhindered. The coup-makers could not or would not use violence, in stark contrast to the intervention of the Black Berets in Vilnius in January 1991 when they moved to seize the Lithuanian television building. Among the republics the coup was supported only by Azerbaijan and Uzbekistan. The miners' strike quickly spread to much of the country, while Yeltsin courageously took a stand in defense of legality. The situation, momentarily undecided, turned rapidly on the second day in favor of Yeltsin when divisions became apparent among senior military officers and popular opposition to the putsch in both Leningrad, whose mayor, Anatoly Sobchak, played a key role, and Moscow could be put down only by a bloody repression. On the morning of the third day, the fact that no order to attack the parliament had been given sounded the death knell for the coup leaders.

The failure of the coup did more than precipitate things; it led very rapidly to the collapse of the Soviet Union as such.

The failure of the coup was also an opportunity for other individuals, apart from Yeltsin, to emerge as leading figures: Sobchak; Edvard Shevardnadze, the former foreign minister who had left Gorbachev's government after warning of the growing risk of dictatorship; Gavril Popov, the mayor of Moscow; and Alexander Yakovlev, who contributed enormously to glasnost (the last two being the leaders of the "Movement for Democratic Reforms)". In a way the Communist Party committed suicide, as the Armenian president Ter-Petrossian said. As for Gorbachev, consummate tactician that he is, after a brief period of indecision, he realigned his position taking into account the continuing upheavals. But ultimately, after trying to keep the Union together, Gorbachev in December 1991 had to resign as president of a Soviet Union that no longer existed.

The republics were decisive elements in the collapse of the Soviet political system over the three years between 1988 and 1991—particularly republics such as Lithuania, Latvia, Estonia, Armenia, and Moldova, which held free elections long before Russia and which removed their local Communist parties from power. Of course, universal suffrage and the intention of achieving independence are not in themselves a guarantee of democracy, as the case of Georgia illustrates: the former president, Z. Gamsakhurdia, oppressed Georgia's minorities and arrested his political opponents.

Given its economic situation and its historical traditions, the ex-Soviet Union, which at present calls itself a "Commonwealth of Independent States" (CIS), will never re-experience Bolshevism. In that respect, the failed coup proved to be more than useful. The origins of the coup probably go back to the autumn of 1990, when Gorbachev rejected the 500-day economic plan and began to rely increasingly on conservative elements in order to maintain the Party's monopoly of power, which the introduction of a market economy and the privatization of state enterprises jeopardized. Gorbachev in fact believed in the monopoly of the Party and the maintenance of the Union; the results of the failed putsch—the destruction of the Party monopoly and the dissolution of the Union—clearly went against his political interests. His adaptation to the new situation was in a way forced on him.

After the failure of his reformist approach Gorbachev continually maneuvered by setting himself up as the indispensable figure balancing opposites. His strategy, as a leader with no social base, consisted in attempting to reform the country by modernizing it through a limited democratization and hoping that Western aid would be significant. And he sought to do this while retaining the political monopoly of the Party (with some minor reforms), socialist ownership (manager of the power of the bureaucracy and the privileged strata), and finally the Union, with some modifications. That project failed.

Without exception, all the republics have separated themselves from what was the center, Russia. The most unexpected secession was certainly that of the Ukraine. Russia, nonetheless, still represents more than two-thirds of the total surface area of the ex-USSR and has half of its population. Its resources, economic potential, armed forces, and nuclear capacity are considerable.

On the international level a page has finally been turned. President Bush endorsed it in September 1991 when he announced a very substantial reduction in short- and medium-range nuclear weapons. The Russians followed suit. Not since 1947 has the prospect of war been more remote. The 20th century—1914–1991—has symbolically come to an end.

But at present, the main problem in the CIS is economic. Inflation is soaring, and production is at its lowest. In fact growth in 1990 and 1991 was negative, with production falling at a rate of close to 15 percent in 1991. At the same time as crash reforms, it is going to be necessary to embark on an overhaul of the communications and transport insfrastructure. Overall the question of nationalities and minorities has to be solved.

In the spring of 1992, Russia embarked on the boldest, most risky privatization program ever attempted. About 100,000 shops and most of the country's light industry are expected to be sold at auction by the end of the year. In the next two years, assets representing about 60% of Russia's GNP are due to be sold.

The chance of success of a reform plan that relies on the existing bureaucracy is slim. Russia and the other CIS states are heading into their most difficult years. Their precarious democracy will be very much at stake as economic difficulties worsen.

While the situation was changing radically in Europe, the Gulf crisis following Iraq's intervention in Kuwait on 2 August 1990 drew attention to other contradictions.

The Jungle of Nations

From 1988 onward a series of local or regional conflicts in which the United States was directly involved were settled; the independence of Namibia, withdrawal of the Cubans from Angola, dismantling of the United States-backed "contras" in Central America while the Sandinistas ceased to hold power in Nicaragua. Even in Cambodia, where the situation is particularly complex, the withdrawal of the Vietnamese and the United States' acceptance of talks with the Phnom Penh government opened up the possibility of a settlement.

But however important East-West rivalry was, it did not involve all conflicts. Not to mention the fact that in the south of the planet there is little reason to be content with the status quo. Much of the south is in a state of instability and chronic subversion.

In fact, the growing economic interdependence over recent decades has gone hand in hand with an ever greater political multipolarization, making the world less and less predictable and the consequences of crises more and more serious. The oil crises of the 1970s and the Gulf war are illustrations of that.

One has only to recall the extent to which the Suez crisis following Nasser's nationalization of the canal in 1956 heralded the achievement of political autonomy by the Third World at the time of decolonization. Not only did this crisis occur outside the East-West conflict, but the United States and the USSR were in agreement to force the Anglo-French coalition to call a halt to its military intervention. Already, symbolically, the Bandung conference (1955), held in the presence of Chou En-lai, Nehru, and Nasser, had marked out a North-South cleavage. The colonized wanted to take their destiny back into their own hands.

With the Sino-Soviet split and Gaullism, political autonomies became more and more marked and helped to transform a militarily bipolar world into a politically multipolar one. Once decolonization was completed, largely by the mid-1960s, many states that had once been regional powers gradually rediscovered their own dynamism. Old geopolitical ambitions resurfaced:
• Indonesia has systematically built up its drive to the east and southeast over the last twenty years; the Moluccas, East Timor (1975), and soon Papua New Guinea.
• Morocco annexed the former Spanish Sahara (1975).
• Somalia took advantage of the disorders in Ethiopia to attempt to seize the Somali-inhabited Ogaden in 1977.
• Syria intervened in Lebanon (1975) and stayed there, gradually stepping up its presence.
• Libya several times attempted to move into Chad and was kept out only by French interventions.
• Vietnam, barely reunified, brought Laos within its orbit and invaded Cambodia (1978), recovering a century later its old dynamic, one of whose aims was to counterbalance the weight of China. China for its part attempted to teach a lesson to its southern neighbor (1977), which it regarded as an "arrogant tributary".
• In 1980, imagining it could seize the oil-rich Iranian province of Khuzistan without too much difficulty, Iraq launched a war which it only just managed to win after receiving almost universal support.
• In 1982 Israel embarked on an operation in Lebanon which went beyond the defensive character assigned to it by Menachem Begin, who was outmaneuvered by General Sharon.
• Argentina, under the rule of generals, invaded the Falklands thinking to capitalize on nationalism. Britain's reaction and capacity to respond came as a bitter surprise (1982).

Saddam Hussein's invasion and then annexation of Kuwait obeyed the same logic of increasing power and ran into the same rejection of the fait accompli as Argentina.

In the shadow of the East-West conflict, regional powers with more or less declared designs for hegemony were reinforced and now play a role in the world balance.

By annexing Kuwait, Iraq altered the status quo in the Middle East and laid claim to becoming the dominant power in the region, both economically and militarily. By providing itself with a nuclear capability, Iraq soon would have become very menacing for Iran, Syria, Saudi Arabia, Egypt, and Israel, which explains the hostility of those states toward it. Furthermore, with Kuwait, Iraq had control of 20 percent of the region's oil production and could play a considerable economic and political role.

Beyond questions of law—countless United Nations resolutions have remained a dead letter—these were the reasons for American intervention. Such intervention was only made possible by the ending of the Cold War, which also determined the perhaps temporary role that the United Nations played in this crisis. In that sense, we are already in a new international order.

The era of the gunboat is over—outside sub-Saharan Africa. Everywhere else, for the West, intervention now requires a considerable capacity to project forces. That is largely because of the enormous build-up of the military capacities of a number of Third World states equipped with modern and effective weapons, large armies, medium- or even long-range missiles, and chemical weapons.

The Middle East is particularly threatening in terms of the proliferation of missiles and chemical weapons: Egypt, Iraq, Israel, Saudi Arabia[1], Iran, Libya, and Syria all have fearsome weapons that have serious implications for the unfolding of future conflicts.

This proliferation of course goes beyond the framework of the Middle East and also constitutes a threat in other regions; South Asia (possible conflict between Pakistan and India), the Far East, and Latin America (Brazil, Argentina).

The six-week Gulf War calls for some essential comments:
- The growing importance of psychological warfare in the age of the masses, public opinion, and the media, especially the visual ones. After a prolonged period of relative prosperity, security, and aging of the population, the rear in the West seems particularly vulnerable, and now more fragile than the fighting forces. The human cost of hegemony seems more and more difficult to take on.
- No troublemaker that is simply a regional power can hope to take on the military capacities of an industrial superpower. Tomorrow's potential troublemaker will look twice before challenging a superpower. Technological advance remains the guarantor of victory in a conventional confrontation. As for the human cost, it falls mostly on the weakest, as is clearly and starkly shown by the disproportion between the losses of the coalition partners and the Iraqis, of the order of 1:1,000. In this the monopoly of air power played a key role. The United States strikingly reasserted its preeminence as a global power. However, the "new international order" called for by President Bush will have to take account, in both the Middle East and elsewhere, of a complex balancing game in which the role of local allies and their political autonomy will be infinitely greater than they were two or three decades ago. For the United States, Africa south of the Sahara, except for South Africa, is not a subject of political concern. What is important is to maintain a favorable balance within the Euro-Asian continental landmass insofar as the United States plays an insular role

---

[1] Which has the most effective missiles (sold by China) with a range of over 2,000 km.

comparable to that of the regulator of the powers that was once held by Britain vis-à-vis Europe.

But the adventure of the annexation of Kuwait and its terrible consequences (for Iraq) must not make us forget another series of challenges to which the West will have to find appropriate responses.

The Demographic Challenge

In a century world population rose from 1.6 billion to 6 billion. These figures are well known. But they do not bring out the demographic ratio between North and South that has markedly shifted, especially since the end of World War II. While in 1900 Europe and North America had 33% of the world population, in ten years' time they will account for only 18% (and 15% by 2025). The consequence of this is an aging of the populations of the industrial countries, including Russia.

Yet the importance of demography continues to be underestimated in the industrialized countries that will inevitably be faced with its most negative consequences. At the same time, the very high population growth rate in Third World countries is simply accentuating existing imbalances.

These imbalances reflect back on the developed countries notably through immigration.

The fact is that Europe, especially the twelve members of the EEC, and the United States are already experiencing significant pressure on their southern flank from immigration, mainly clandestine. This pressure is bound to increase in the near future and pose serious problems to society.

Yet the pressure cannot fail to outgrow the receiving capacity of the countries concerned, over the next fifteen or twenty years, if it is not stifled *at the source* by a more coherent and effective economic policy in the "countries of origin". The Maghreb, which had a population of about 10 million in 1900, when France had 38 million, will have 70 million by 1999 as against France's 57 million. Turkey had 10 million inhabitants in 1930 but will have 70 million in less than ten years' time. Today half those populations are under twenty years old.

Economic disparities between North and South and the rising unemployment and underemployment in the South will inevitably accentuate migratory flows that are becoming harder and harder to control. This is already the case with the southern border of the United States, where the illegal Mexican population is estimated at between 5 and 8 million.

Yet immigration can be a positive factor in restoring the demographic balance for the countries of the EEC on condition that the receiving countries take care to draw up policies to integrate migrants, designed to minimize the frictions inherent in such mass arrivals. This integration must be aimed at ensuring that immigrants and above all their children accept our democratic institutions and values. If this does not happen, if they are rejected or ghettoized, there are grave risks that these populations, subject to organization and control by representatives of their countries of origin, might make themselves their agents, voluntarily or otherwise, or bring their internal conflicts into Europe. In other words, failure to integrate immigrant populations, especially those from underdeveloped, generally undemocratic countries, may in the medium term engender more acute conflicts. Fundamentalist movements, through their militants and the social work they do in their communities, may attempt to introduce into Europe specific laws that are anti-secular and anti-democratic.

We are trying not to awaken a new psychosis or fuel an ever-recurrent racism but to deal with a very important phenomenon which is not simply a feature of this century but will also characterize the next one. The massive population movements from the 19th century to the First World War were virtually a monopoly of Europeans, but today's movements have already become and will increasingly become the monopoly of Third World populations, whose myriad consequences it is as yet difficult to perceive.

While, despite a permanent state of crisis due to accelerated change to which it is difficult to adapt, the North generally enjoys peace, the southern part of the planet is experiencing many conflicts.

Guerrilla Movements

There are many guerrilla movements:
- Marxist-Leninist-type guerrilla movements (declining): El Salvador (Farabundo Marti Front), Colombia, Peru (Shining Path), and in Asia the New People's Army in the Philippines and the Khmer Rouge in Cambodia.
- Guerrilla movements waged by ethnic or religious minorities against a central government that refuses to grant autonomy or allow secession: Kurds (Iraq, Iran, Turkey), southern Sudan, Tamils in Sri Lanka, Eritrea, Myanmar (Burma), etc.
- Guerrilla movements based on an ethnic conflict and seeking to take or share power: Angola (Savimbi), Somalia (inter-clan struggle), Liberia (ethnic conflict).

None of the causes that led to the appearance of these guerrilla movements appears to be weakening: tyranny, oppression of minorities, economic impasse, etc. On the contrary, population growth combined with economic stagnation, especially in sub-Saharan Africa, will accentuate the contradictions and lead to violence. The countries of the EEC, bound by the Lomé Agreements, will have partly to suffer the consequences of such disorders.

Urban Riots

But the newest phenomenon is undoubtedly the increase in the number of urban riots. Their origin lies in the combination of rapid population growth and the spread of urbanization.

While Third World countries doubled their population in 35 years, the capitals and large cities saw theirs rise fourfold, sixfold, or even more.

In 1945 fifteen of the twenty most populous cities in the world were in Europe or the United States. Today, they are in the Third World.

There are grounds for thinking that since the Iranian revolution (1979), which was strictly an urban affair, cities have become the seat of conflicts in the Third World; Algiers, Caracas, Beijing, Dakar, etc.

Without serious risk of error, it is possible to list a series of "sensitive" cities where very violent conflicts will surely occur: Lima, Karachi, Dhaka, Rio de Janeiro, Lagos. Africa is particularly vulnerable.

The conflict situations in the South must not make us forget the sometimes extremely sharp competition in the North among the United States, the twelve members of the EEC, and Japan.

Economic Competition

The United States is seeking to form a free trade area stretching from Canada to Mexico. The latter would supply cheap labor and also act as a shield that would contain the migratory movement from Latin America. The EEC, a front-rank economic power and a major market, remains politically and militarily very weak. The important changes under way are far from mastered: the role and vocation of reunited Germany, the monetary union that must come first if the future is to be more united, relations with Central Europe—especially with Czechoslovakia, Hungary, Poland, etc. Important minority questions still agitate the other Europe, which was long occupied by the Ottoman empire and neither Catholic nor Protestant: Yugoslavia, where centripetal forces are at work and have taken most of the member republics to secession; the Hungarian problem in Romanian Transylvania; other minority problems in Bulgaria and Greece.

The upheavals in central and southeastern Europe may suggest that migratory flows towards the EEC may well, in coming years, come not from the Mediterranean basin but from this previously satellite Europe. As for Japan, it is tranquilly pursuing its commercial policy to the furthest limit of dynamism and aggressiveness that its partners, led by the United States, can tolerate. Forty years ago who would have bet the dollar might be quoted in yen?

For some years to come competition will now above all be between industrial countries—or groups of industrial countries—in the economic, financial, and technological fields. However, in the next ten or fifteen years, during the first decade of the next century, it seems almost inevitable that a *military* multipolarity will emerge. A world made up of three or four major military powers is infinitely more complex than a bipolar world or one temporarily dominated by a single power. At that point, alliances themselves may well change and the stability of Cold War and post-Cold War alliances come to an end. No one can project the future role of the industrialized and militarized countries of East Asia and from which area threats might come.

The increasingly multipolar world is thus experiencing a permanent state of crisis, and it is important to be aware of the multiplicity of threats, which requires a variety of responses ranging from development aid to rapid intervention as well as an (unlikely) family planning policy in the North.

Gérard Chaliand
Jean-Pierre Rageau

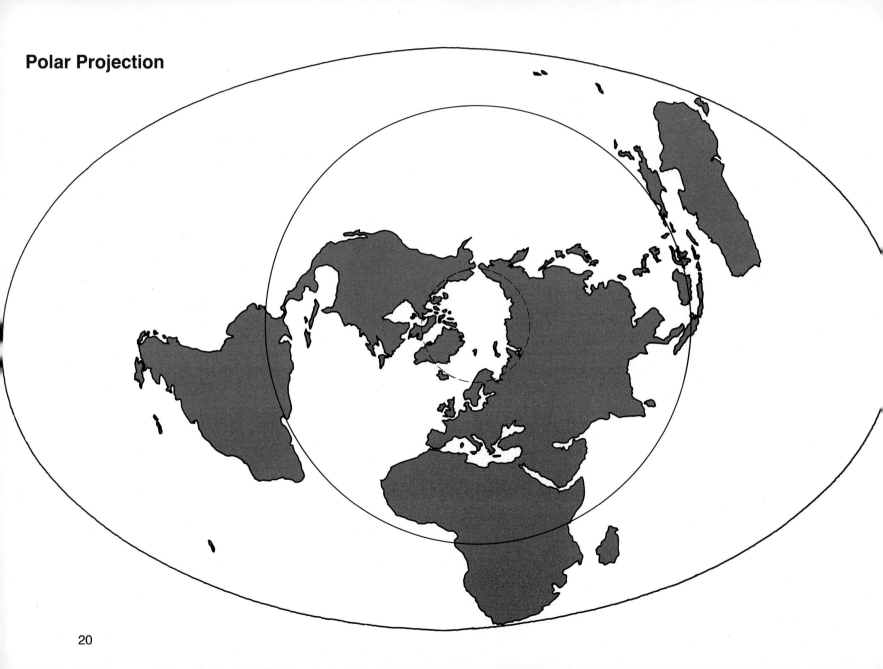

Polar Projection

Circular Projection

The earth is a sphere. Any representation of it on a two-dimensional plane is obtained by a projection. For example, the map on the left is a polar projection. For convenience, most maps and atlases use plane projections, which ignore the spherical nature of the globe. But this convention falsifies strategic perception as soon as it goes beyond the regional level. The circular projection on the right is modified, and hence misleading, but serves to illustrate our point.

VIEWS OF THE WORLD

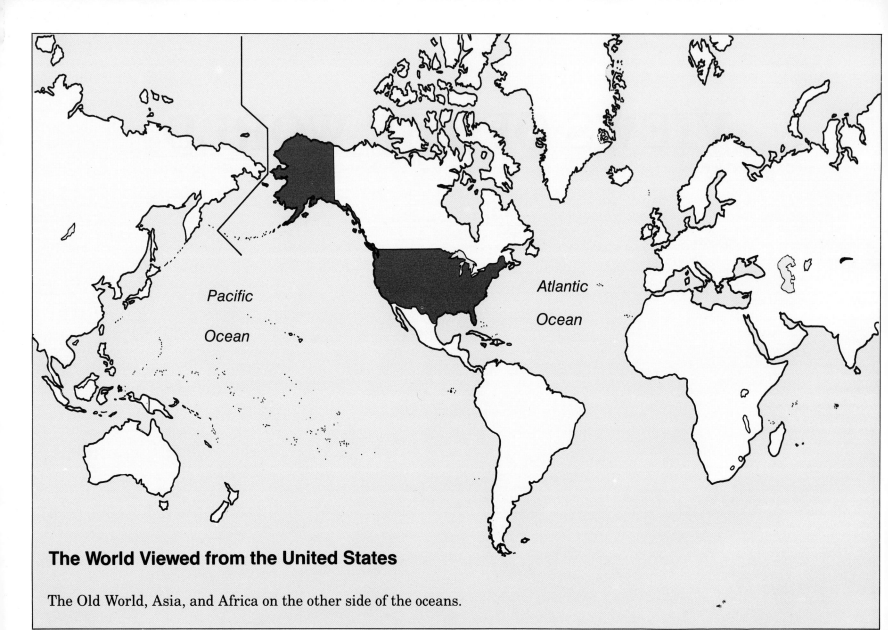

Pacific

Ocean

Atlantic

Ocean

The World Viewed from the United States

The Old World, Asia, and Africa on the other side of the oceans.

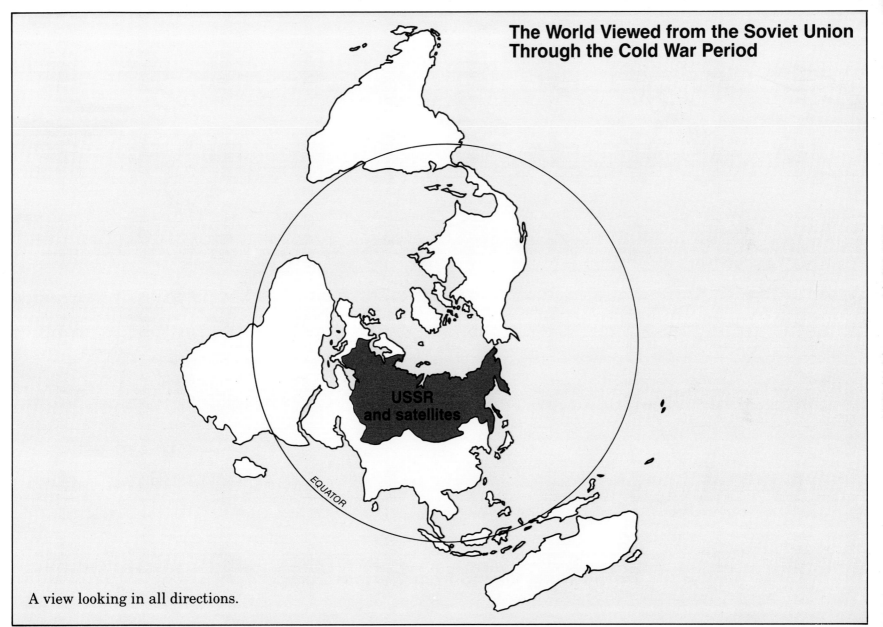

A view looking in all directions.

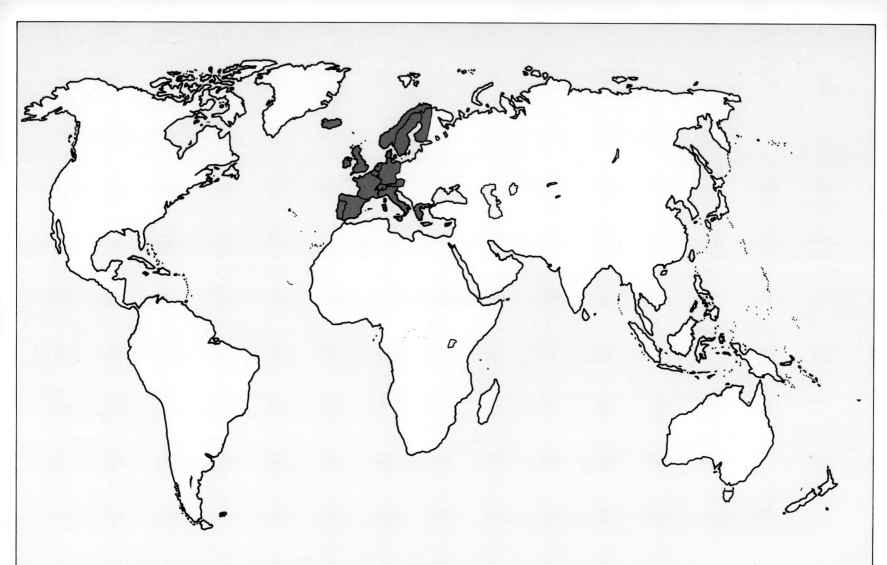

The World Viewed from Western Europe

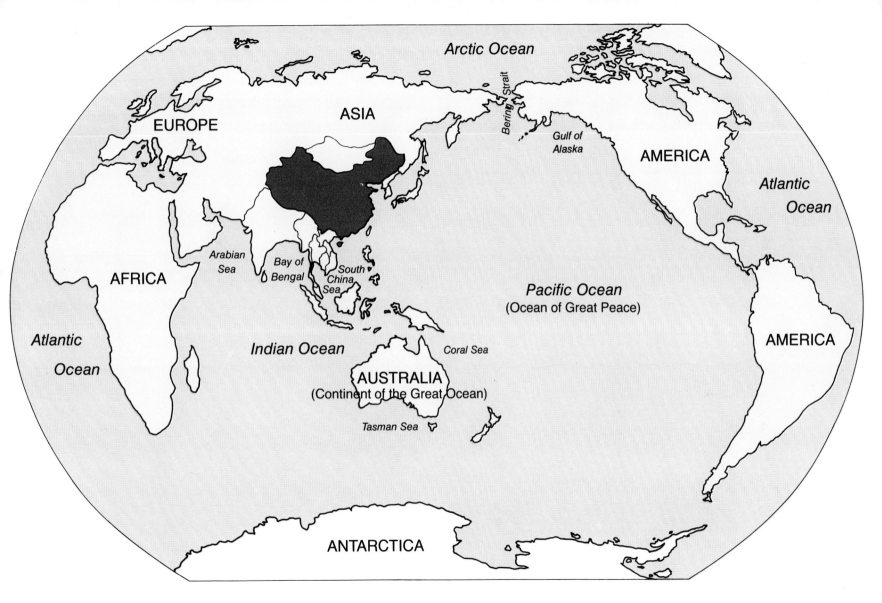

Arctic Ocean

EUROPE

ASIA

Bering Strait

Gulf of
Alaska

AMERICA

Atlantic
Ocean

AFRICA

Arabian
Sea

Bay of
Bengal

South
China
Sea

Pacific Ocean
(Ocean of Great Peace)

Atlantic

Ocean

Indian Ocean

Coral Sea

AMERICA

AUSTRALIA
(Continent of the Great Ocean)

Tasman Sea

ANTARCTICA

The World Viewed from China

From the *Contemporary Atlas of the People's Republic of China.*

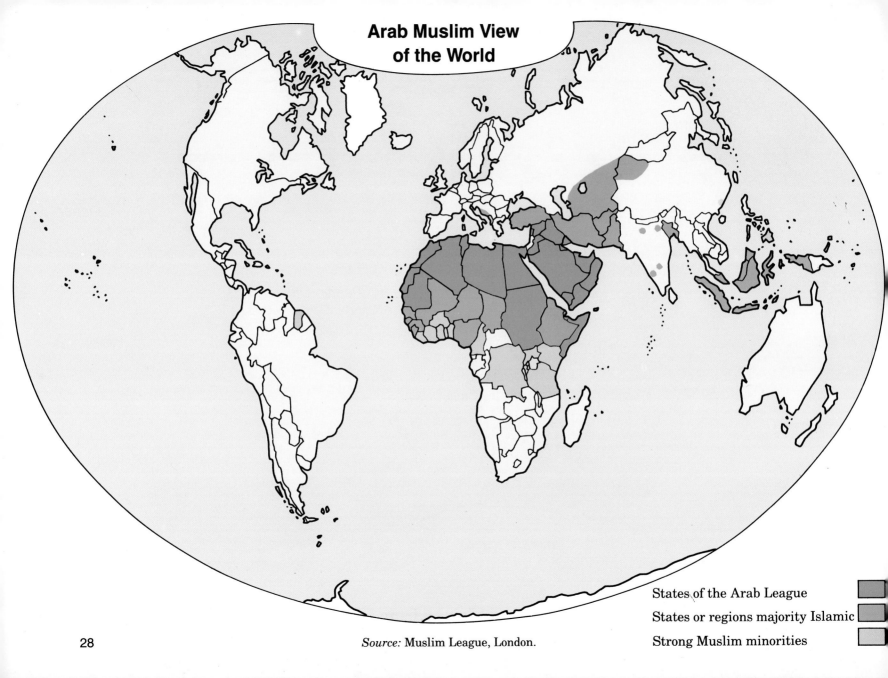

Arab Muslim View
of the World

States of the Arab League

States or regions majority Islamic

Strong Muslim minorities

28   *Source:* Muslim League, London.

THE GEOPOLITICIANS

The Geopoliticians

The German geographer Friedrich Ratzel, author of *Politische Geographie* (1897), developed a number of basic concepts, particularly concerning *space*, that have inspired geopoliticians. It was the British writer H. Mackinder who in 1904 proposed the notion that the continental part of Eurasia, by virtue of its land mass, forms the world Heartland. According to Mackinder (maps pp. 31 and 32), who several times revised his geographical delimitation of the heartland (in 1919 and 1943), the power that controls this land mass—once potentially Germany, now Russia—threatens the sea powers—once Great Britain, now the United States—that control the World Island—that is, our planet.

The factors that Mackinder came to include as his thinking developed were communications (including aviation), population, and industrialization. In 1943, he repudiated his 1919 theory (the state that controls the Heartland will dominate the World Island).

The American Mahan, a geopolitician before the word was invented, put forward as early as 1900 (in *The Problem of Asia and Its Effect upon International Politics*) the idea that the world hegemony of sea powers can be maintained by control of a series of bases around the Eurasian continent. This view foreshadowed Mackinder's concept of the World Island, but it led to the opposite strategic conclusions: Sea powers dominate land powers by hemming them in. Therein lies the seed of the theory of containment born of the Cold War.

Geopolitical concepts were systematized by the Swede Rudolf Kjellen and then adopted by the German geopoliticians, especially Karl Haushofer (1869–1946). German geopolitics developed in three directions: the concept of space (*Raum*) advanced by Ratzel, meaning the need for a great power to have space available to it; the concept of a World Island enunciated by Mackinder, implying sea power; and the North-South combination of continents put forward by Haushofer (map p. 34). This last concept is to be found today, for example, in the Eurafrican policy of Western Europe.

The American N. J. Spykman (map p. 33) followed Mackinder and adapted his concepts to the circumstances of the 1930s. He argued that only an Anglo-American (sea power) and Russian (land power) alliance could prevent Germany from controlling the Eurasian coastal regions and thus achieving world domination. But he rejected some of Mackinder's strategic conclusions concerning the importance of controlling the Heartland by giving greater importance to control of the Rimland.

Although it is sometimes excessively systematic, the geopolitical approach is stimulating; but it is so only if there is no lapse into geographical determinism and if all factors in the balance are taken into account. In the map on p. 35 we sketch our own approach along these lines, one more in conformity with present-day realities.

The World According to Mackinder (1904)

Control of the Heartland, the
Eurasian continental land mass,
constitutes a potential threat for
sea powers.

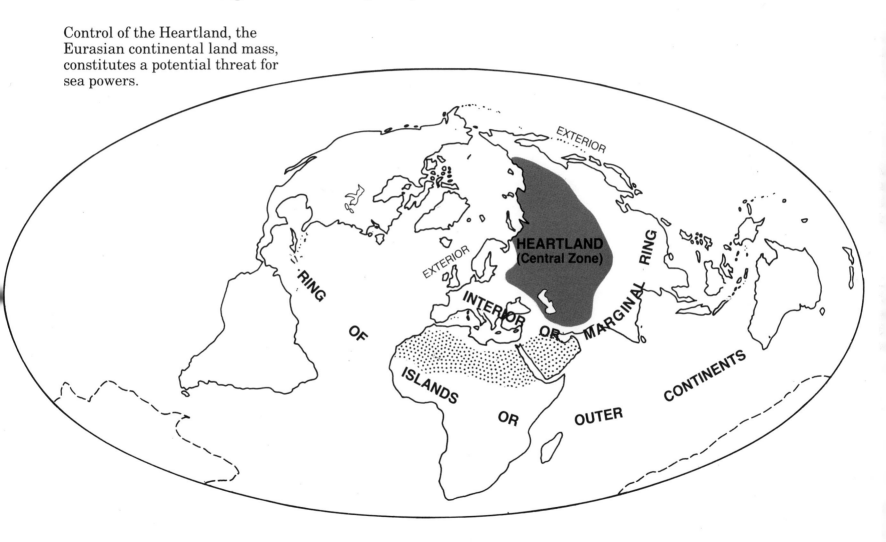

The World According to Mackinder (1943)

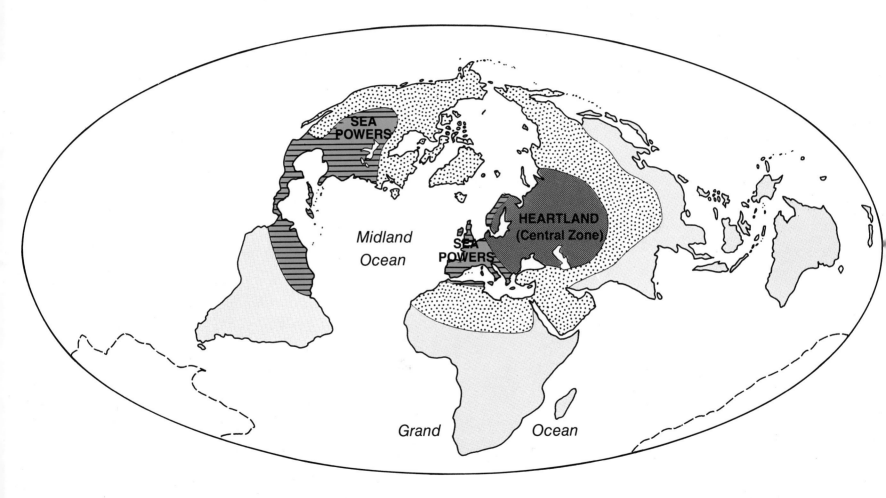

Spykman and the Importance of the Rimland

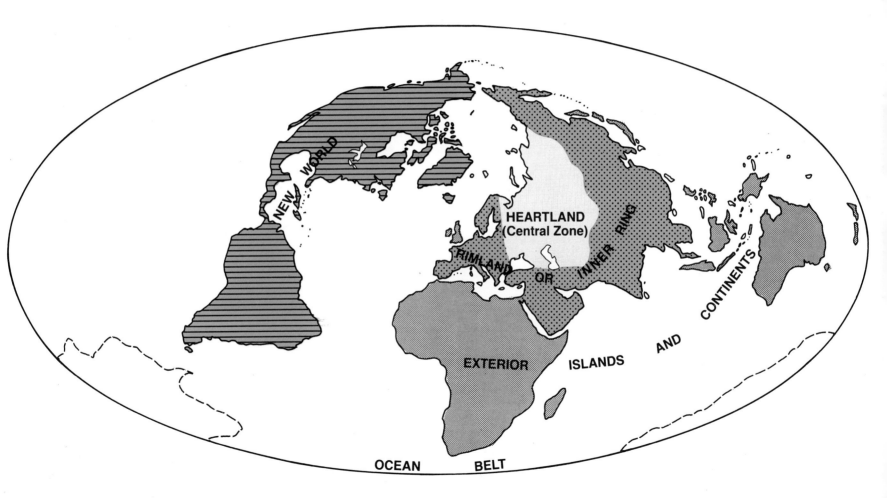

Haushofer and the North–South Combination

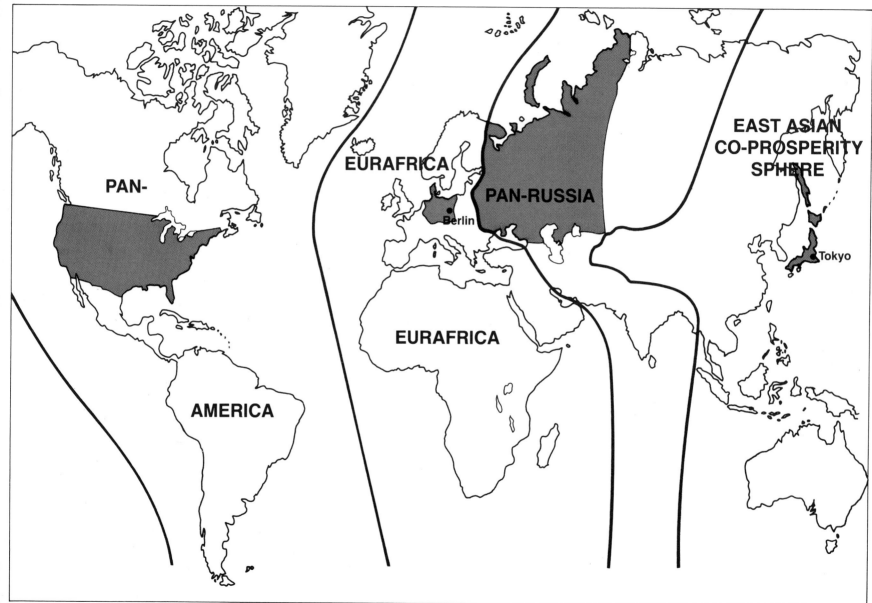

PAN-

PAN-RUSSIA

Berlin

EURAFRICA

EURAFRICA

AMERICA

EAST ASIAN CO-PROSPERITY SPHERE

Tokyo

Sketch of a Geopolitics in the 1980's

Taking into account inevitable developments and changes, we see that geopoliticians before World War II accurately assessed these basic factors:
- *Heartland*
- *Sea power*
- *Rimland*

We also see the appearance since 1945, with the independence of new states in Asia and Africa, of a fragile and unstable intertropical ring:
- *Ring of underdevelopment and poverty*

Gradual emergence of a *developed southern ring* is linked to sea power.

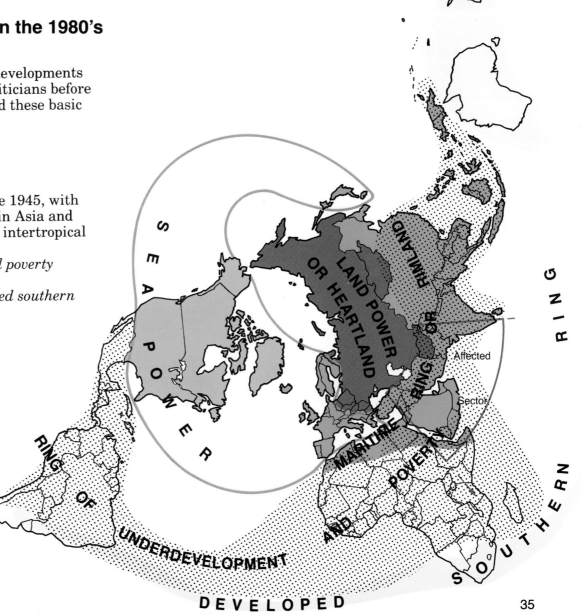

CULTURAL FACTORS

The Great Cultural Domains

The cultural area of which Europe is the center has undergone considerable expansion. So has that of Islam, which in Southeast Asia covers regions that were formerly Hindu while at the same time continuing its expansion in Africa.*

* Madagascar is attached to Africa for the sake of convenience, but ethnically does not belong to the African world. Bangladesh, Malaysia, and Indonesia have been Islamized. Until the 1970s Ethiopia was an officially Christian state.

European domain

Chinese domain

Russian domain

Islamic domain

Black African domain

Hindu domain

Latin American domain

South Africa (mixed)

The Great Religions

Religions were formerly the major source of identity, and since nationalism, rather than superseding religion, is often superimposed on it, religions continue to play a leading role.

Notes:
- Oriental Christians: principally Orthodox
- China: superimposition and interdependence of Confucianism, Buddhism, Taoism
- Japan: superimposition of Shintoism and Buddhism
- Gray areas: animism and others

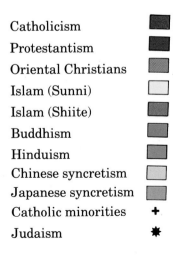

Catholicism

Protestantism

Oriental Christians

Islam (Sunni)

Islam (Shiite)

Buddhism

Hinduism

Chinese syncretism

Japanese syncretism

Catholic minorities ✛

Judaism ✶

Imperial Languages of the World

The criterion used to define an imperial language is the combination of its numerical importance *and* its geographic diffusion. In this respect Japanese is not imperial, and German since 1945 has lost its preponderance in Eastern Europe. Chinese (Peking Mandarin), although only partly meeting the criteria above, is still the most widely spoken language in the world.

English	
French	
Spanish	
Portuguese	
Arabic	
Russian	
Chinese	

Enduring Traditional Enmities

The traditional enmities noted here are those that still persist. Franco-German or Anglo-French rivalry, for example, no longer has a place here. Conversely, other enmities based on ancient geohistorical rivalries continue to revive latent tensions and, often hidden behind ideological arguments, fuel more or less open antagonisms.

↔ Interstate hostility

▨ Serious intrastate hostility

▨ Interethnic rivalry

▨ Indian-white hostility

◣ Black/white dividing line

40

Traditional Enmities*

ASIA:

China—Russia
China—Vietnam
Vietnam—Khmers
Thailand—Burma
China—Mongols
India—Pakistan
Korea—Japan
Thailand—Cambodia

MIDDLE EAST:

Although of recent origin, the enmity between the Arab countries and Israel has all the characteristics of a lasting rivalry.
Syria—Turkey (fueled by the claim to the *sanjak* of Alexandretta).

AFRICA:

A north–south line through the Sahel divides the black African populations to the south and the Arab and Saharan populations to the north along an ancient cleavage based on slavery. See, for example, Chad, southern Sudan, and so on.

In the Horn of Africa: Ethiopia—Somalia (enmity formerly based on religious rivalry at the present time based on rival nationalisms).

In sub-Saharan Africa, ethnic rivalries are legion. Among those that have been particularly active: Tutsi—Hutu relations in Burundi and Rwanda, or the better-known case of the Ibo of Biafra.

In southern Africa, ethnic and tribal strategies play an important role. Angola: UNITA represents the Ovimbundu, who are opposed to the Luanda government, which rests on the alliance between the Kimbundu and the Bakongo. In Zimbabwe, there is the rivalry between the Shona and the Ndebele, a source of conflict that could lead to civil war.

In South Africa, Pretoria uses and fosters tribal rivalries, especially between the Zulu and other ethnic groups.

AMERICA:

Brazil—Argentina
Latin America—United States. (The resentment, arising from humiliation, of some groups in Latin America toward the United States is ambiguous to the extent that the interests of privileged strata, however nationalistic they may be, coincide with those of the United States.)
Indians—whites (Peru, Ecuador, Bolivia, Guatemala, and others).

EUROPE:

Bulgaria—Turkey, Bulgaria—Yugoslavia
Greece—Turkey, Yugoslavia—Albania
Russia—Turkey
Romania—Hungary (claims relating to the Hungarians in Transylvania)
Poland—Russia
Poland—Germany
Serbs—Croats

---

* Interstate enmities not including minority problems. This list is far from complete.

THE HISTORICAL CONTEXT OF THE CONTEMPORARY WORLD

Europeanization of the World at the Beginning of the Twentieth Century

In an uninterrupted process, the expansion of Europe from the sixteenth century onward resulted in the occupation by Europe of the whole of the American continent. During the nineteenth century and until after World War I, European imperialism extended its domination over the whole globe, with the partial exception of Japan. The global superiority of Europe in both technology and *ideas* was at the time total.

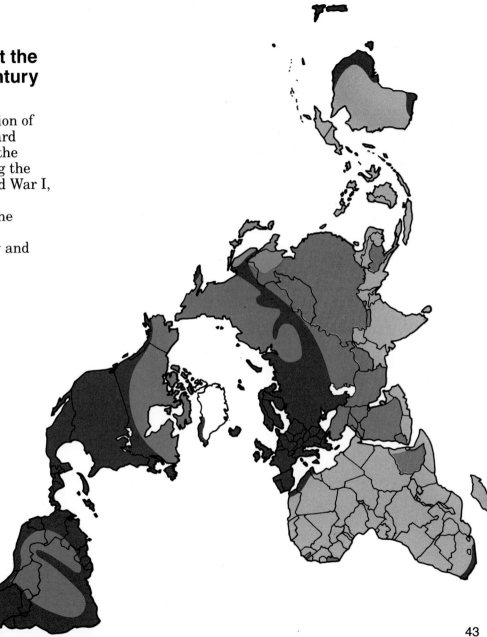

Europe

European population (dense)

European population (sparse)

European influence (semi-colonial)

European colonization

Japanese empire

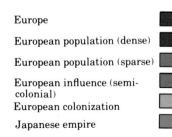

Territorial Changes in Europe Following World War I

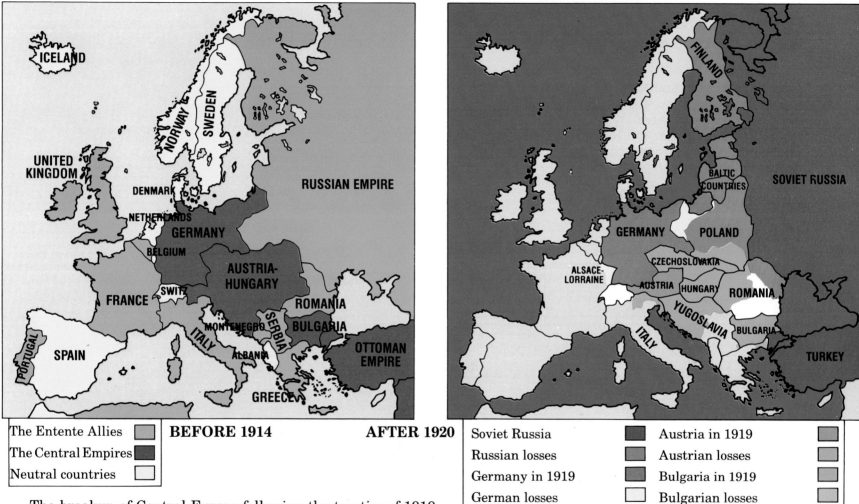

BEFORE 1914 **AFTER 1920**

The Entente Allies
The Central Empires
Neutral countries

Soviet Russia
Russian losses
Germany in 1919
German losses
Austria in 1919
Austrian losses
Bulgaria in 1919
Bulgarian losses
Turkey

The breakup of Central Europe following the treaties of 1919–1920 ended traditional German influence in this area and resulted, among other things, in the formation of nation-states based on the ideas of Woodrow Wilson. These states were formed mostly at the expense of the Austro-Hungarian Empire and Russia. By 1945, with few exceptions, all the new states had become part of the Soviet sphere.

The Colonial World Following World War I

Although the states of Latin America were formally fully sovereign, the United States enjoyed almost total economic domination there. Similarly, the few formally independent states in Asia and Africa were often more like semi-colonies, with variations that must not be allowed to obscure their political autonomy.*

*The Union of South Africa became independent in 1910 and obtained a mandate over South-West Africa (Namibia) after World War I.

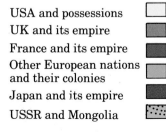

USA and possessions

UK and its empire

France and its empire

Other European nations and their colonies

Japan and its empire

USSR and Mongolia

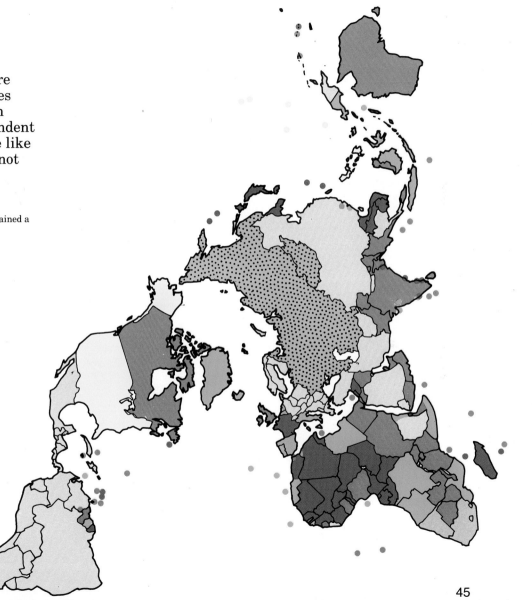

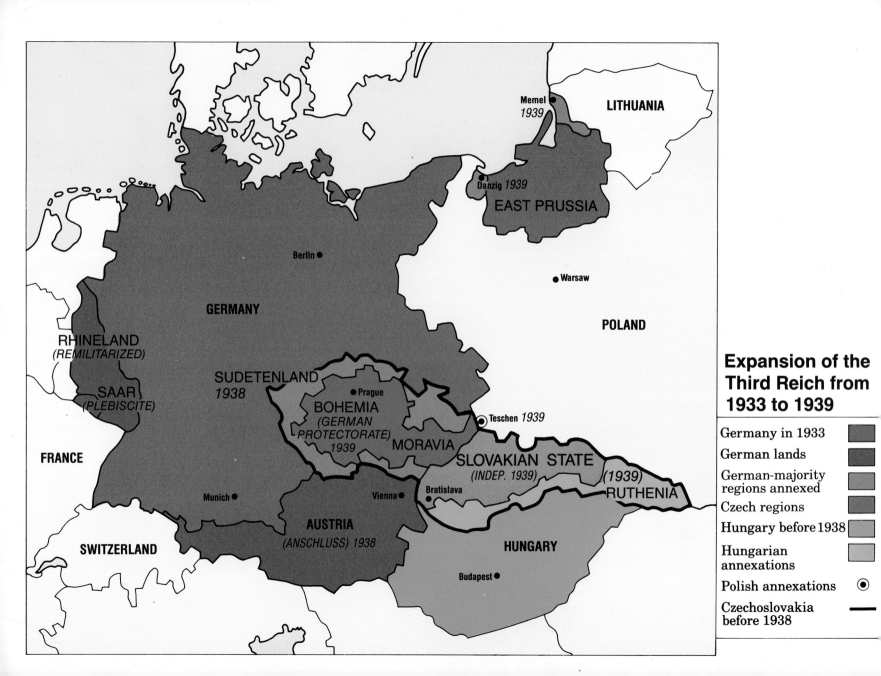

Expansion of the Third Reich from 1933 to 1939

MEMEL 1939
LITHUANIA
Danzig 1939
EAST PRUSSIA
Berlin ●
Warsaw ●
GERMANY
POLAND
RHINELAND
(REMILITARIZED)
SUDETENLAND
1938
SAAR
(PLEBISCITE)
Prague ●
BOHEMIA
(GERMAN
PROTECTORATE)
1939
Teschen 1939
MORAVIA
FRANCE
SLOVAKIAN STATE
(INDEP. 1939)
(1939)
RUTHENIA
Munich ●
Vienna ●
Bratislava ●
SWITZERLAND
AUSTRIA
(ANSCHLUSS) 1938
HUNGARY
Budapest ●

Expansion of the Third Reich from 1933 to 1939

Germany in 1933
German lands
German-majority regions annexed
Czech regions
Hungary before 1938
Hungarian annexations
Polish annexations ⊙
Czechoslovakia before 1938 ▬

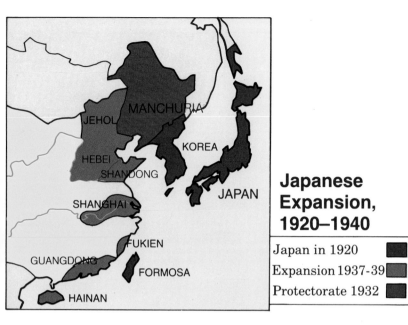

Japanese Expansion, 1920–1940

Japan in 1920	■
Expansion 1937-39	■
Protectorate 1932	■

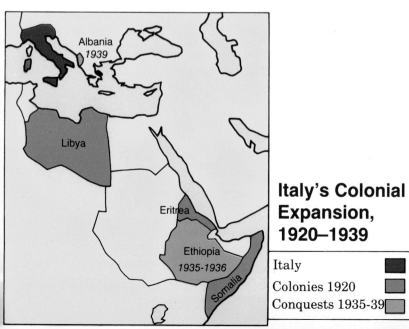

Italy's Colonial Expansion, 1920–1939

Italy	■
Colonies 1920	■
Conquests 1935-39	■

Expansion of the Axis Powers between the Two World Wars

GERMANY

- 1934—reunion of the Saar
- 1936—remilitarization of the Rhineland
- 1938 (March)—annexation of Austria
- 1938 (October)—annexation of the Sudetenland (Munich Conference)
- 1939 (March)—breakup of Czechoslovakia (annexation of Bohemia-Moravia)
- 1939 (March)—annexation of Memel (Lithuania)
- 1939 (September)—invasion of Poland

ITALY

- 1924—annexation of the city of Fiume (Istria)
- 1935–1938—colonization of Cyrenaica (Libya)
- 1935–1936—conquest of Ethiopia
- 1939 (April)—invasion of Albania

JAPAN

- 1931—occupation of Manchuria
- 1935—annexation of Chahar and Suiyuan (Chinese Mongolia)
- 1937–1939—occupation of northeast China, the lower Yangtse valley, and the southern coastal areas

The World at War—1942

This map shows the territorial imbalance between the Axis Powers at the time of their greatest expansion (late 1942) and the Allies, their possessions, and the states sympathetic to them.

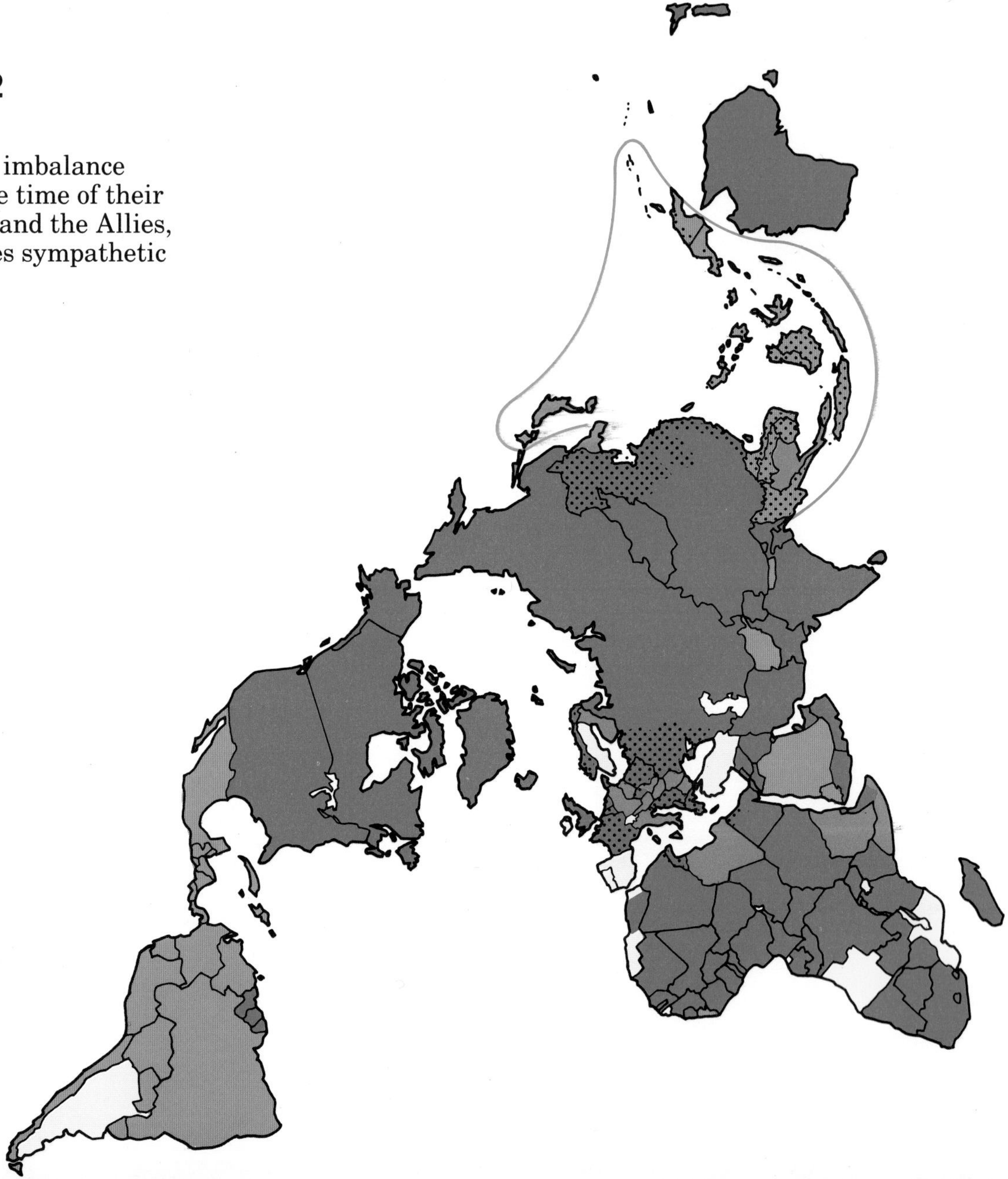

Allied nations

Favorable to Allies

Axis nations

Neutral

Maximum expansion
of Axis nations

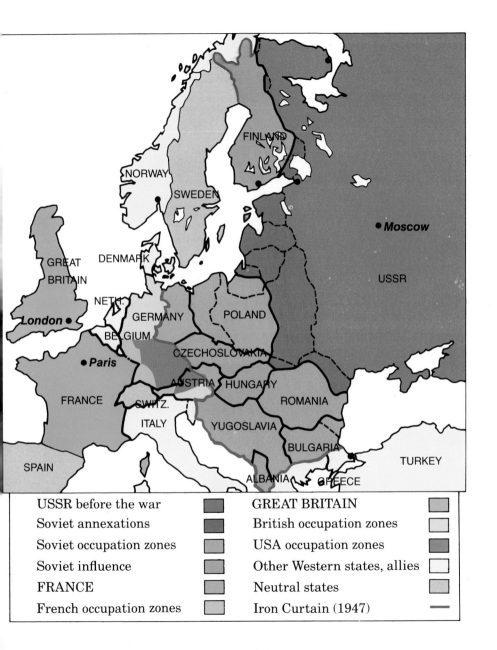

Europe at the End of World War II

The USSR gained some 600,000 square kilometers in the west at the expense of Poland, the Baltic countries, Romania, Czechoslovakia, and Finland. In terms of square kilometers, it recovered exactly what Russia had lost by the Treaty of Brest-Litovsk (1918).

The great loser was Germany, divided into occupied zones and then into two states. The beginning of the Cold War froze this division. The Helsinki Accords (1975) formally confirmed Soviet domination in Eastern Europe.

USSR before the war	■	GREAT BRITAIN	■
Soviet annexations	■	British occupation zones	■
Soviet occupation zones	■	USA occupation zones	■
Soviet influence	■	Other Western states, allies	■
FRANCE		Neutral states	■
French occupation zones	■	Iron Curtain (1947)	—

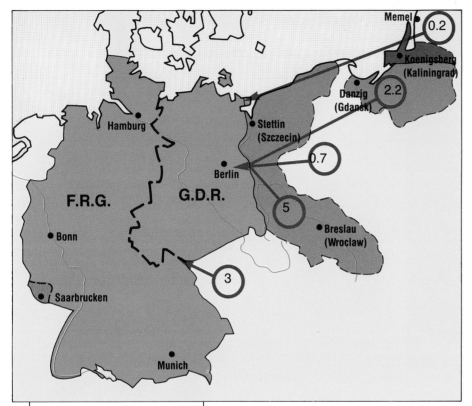

Germany 1945

Germany in 1945	
Regions ceded to Poland	
Regions ceded to USSR	
Saar ceded to France	
Limits of the two Germanys	– –
Displaced Germans (millions)	⊸○

Germany, which had an area of 540,000 sq. km. before 1914 and 474,000 sq. km. before 1938, was reduced to 248,000 sq. km. for the Federal German Republic and 108,000 sq. km. for the German Democratic Republic. Some 12 million Germans were expelled from various states in Central Europe and returned to occupied Germany. Between 1947 and 1961, some 4 million East Germans sought refuge in West Germany. For the next 28 years the *Ostpolitik*, which accepted the fact of the division, reflected the particular attitude of West Germany and of a large section of its public opinion toward problems of war and peace.

Gained from Germany	
Ceded to USSR	
Frontiers after 1945	– –
Displaced Poles (millions)	⊸○

Poland

Before 1939: 388,000 sq. km.
Today: 312,000 sq. km.
Six million Poles were deported and exterminated, including 3 million Jews. One million Poles were expelled from the eastern regions. The Soviet Union's territorial ambitions in the west led the Allies at Yalta (February 1945), and especially at Potsdam (July–August 1945), to compensate Poland for Soviet annexation of the eastern Polish provinces by granting Poland Silesia and part of Pomerania and East Prussia.

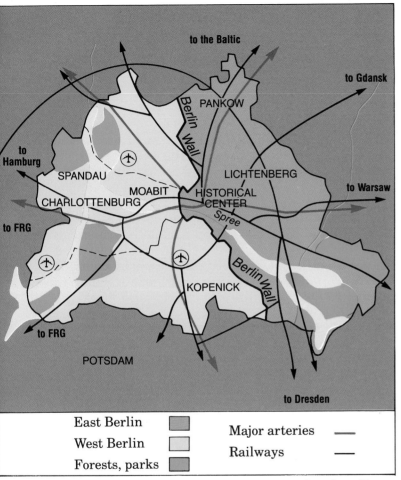

West Berlin, an Enclave in the East

East Berlin	▦	Major arteries	—	
West Berlin	▦	Railways	—	
Forests, parks	▦			

West Berlin: An Anomaly

West Berlin, situated in the middle of the German Democratic Republic, 110 km. from West Germany, was for a long time (1947–1961) an abscess in the body of the Cold War.

CHRONOLOGY:

1948–1949—blockade of Berlin by the USSR; American airlift
1961—construction of the wall cutting off West Berlin and preventing the exodus of East Germans
1989—dismantling of the wall, a symbol of the end of the Cold War and the division of Germany

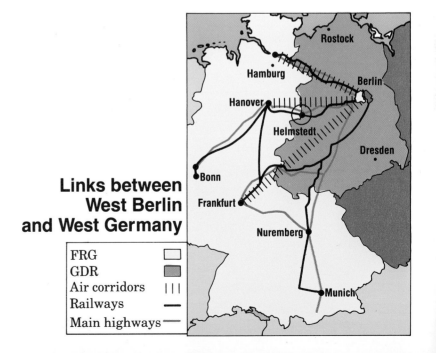

Links between West Berlin and West Germany

FRG	▢
GDR	▦
Air corridors	‖‖
Railways	—
Main highways	—

Defeated Japan in 1945

Japan after 1945 ⬜
Lost territories ⬜
Lost protectorates ⬜

Japan

The Japanese empire (630,000 sq. km., including 380,000 sq. km. for Japan proper) collapsed after the atomic bomb attacks on Hiroshima and Nagasaki in 1945. The USSR, which had declared war on Japan at the last moment, annexed strategic positions in the north of the archipelago, consisting of the Kuril Islands and the southern half of Sakhalin. China recovered its sovereignty over Manchuria and the island of Taiwan.

Japan was demilitarized and underwent a process of institutional democratization during the American occupation. In Micronesia, the United States secured trusteeship over the formerly Japanese island chains of the Marianas, the Carolines, and the Marshalls. In the late 1970s the United States handed back the Ryukyu archipelago (Okinawa). The Greater East Asia Co-Prosperity Sphere, envisaged militarily in the 1930s, appears to be becoming a reality today economically, although the impact of Japanese commercial penetration is worldwide.

The West's Perception, at the Beginning of the Cold War (1948–1952), of Soviet and Communist Expansionism Worldwide

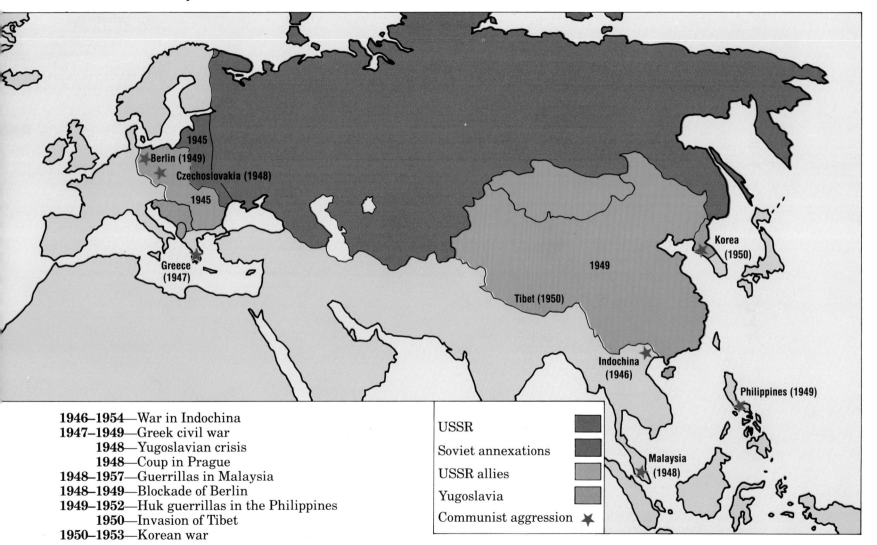

1945
Berlin (1949)
Czechoslovakia (1948)
1945
Greece (1947)
1949
Tibet (1950)
Korea (1950)
Indochina (1946)
Philippines (1949)
Malaysia (1948)

1946–1954—War in Indochina
1947–1949—Greek civil war
1948—Yugoslavian crisis
1948—Coup in Prague
1948–1957—Guerrillas in Malaysia
1948–1949—Blockade of Berlin
1949–1952—Huk guerrillas in the Philippines
1950—Invasion of Tibet
1950–1953—Korean war

USSR	
Soviet annexations	
USSR allies	
Yugoslavia	
Communist aggression	⭐

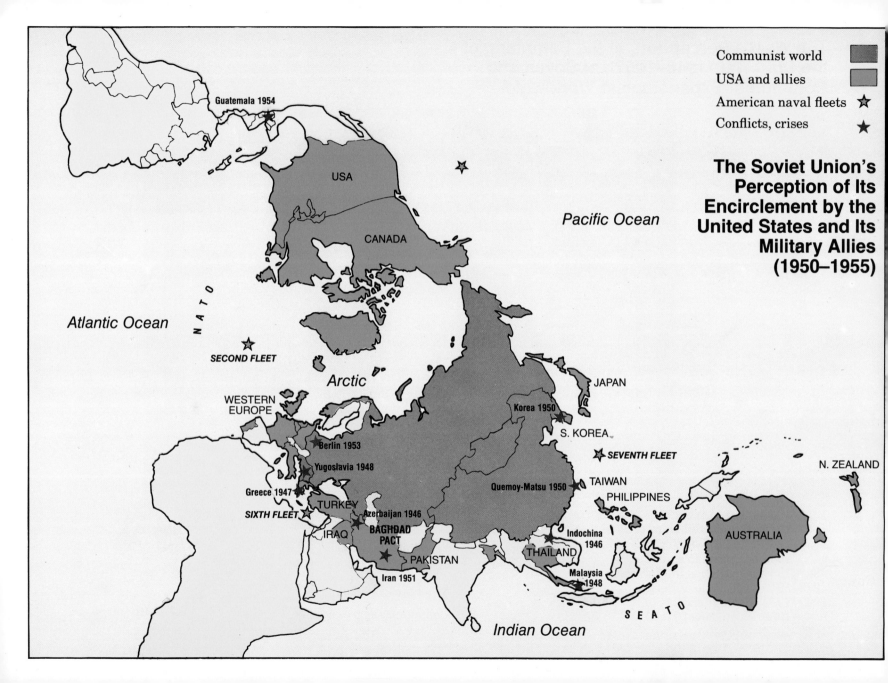

The Soviet Union's Perception of Its Encirclement by the United States and Its Military Allies (1950–1955)

Communist world
USA and allies
American naval fleets ☆
Conflicts, crises ★

Guatemala 1954

USA

CANADA

Pacific Ocean

Atlantic Ocean

NATO

SECOND FLEET

Arctic

WESTERN EUROPE

JAPAN

Korea 1950

Berlin 1953

S. KOREA

SEVENTH FLEET

Yugoslavia 1948

N. ZEALAND

Greece 1947

Quemoy-Matsu 1950

TAIWAN

TURKEY

PHILIPPINES

SIXTH FLEET

Azerbaijan 1946

BAGHDAD PACT

AUSTRALIA

IRAQ

Indochina 1946

PAKISTAN

THAILAND

Iran 1951

Malaysia 1948

SEATO

Indian Ocean

Decolonization and the New States, 1945–1990

From the end of World War II, first in Asia and then a decade later in Africa, in a process that was at times violent, national liberation movements brought about the independence of over a hundred new states.

Independent 1945

Independent since 1945

Guyana (in yellow) is a French department

Chronology of Decolonizations in the Eastern Hemisphere

THE NEAR EAST

	Date of Independence
Yemen	1918
Saudi Arabia	1926
Iraq	1932
Jordan (Trans-Jordan)	1946
Lebanon, Syria, Libya	1946
Israel (partition of Palestine)	1948

SOUTHEAST ASIA

Cyprus	1960
Kuwait	1961
South Yemen	1967
Oman, Bahrain, the Emirates	1971

Several archipelagos and islands in the Caribbean and the Pacific are not independent.

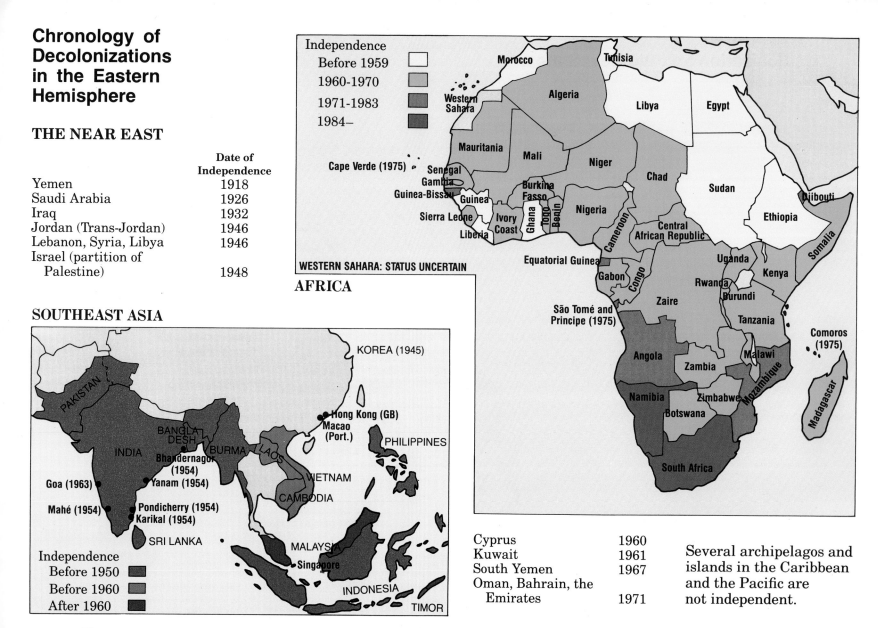

AFRICA

Independence
Before 1959
1960–1970
1971–1983
1984–

WESTERN SAHARA: STATUS UNCERTAIN

Morocco, Tunisia, Western Sahara, Algeria, Libya, Egypt, Mauritania, Mali, Niger, Chad, Sudan, Djibouti, Cape Verde (1975), Senegal, Gambia, Guinea-Bissau, Guinea, Burkina Fasso, Nigeria, Ethiopia, Sierra Leone, Ivory Coast, Ghana, Togo, Benin, Cameroon, Central African Republic, Somalia, Liberia, Equatorial Guinea, Uganda, Kenya, Gabon, Congo, Rwanda, Burundi, São Tomé and Principe (1975), Zaire, Tanzania, Comoros (1975), Angola, Malawi, Zambia, Mozambique, Madagascar, Namibia, Zimbabwe, Botswana, South Africa

Independence
Before 1950
Before 1960
After 1960

KOREA (1945)
PAKISTAN
BANGLA DESH
INDIA
BURMA
LAOS
Bhandernagor (1954)
Yanam (1954)
Goa (1963)
Mahé (1954)
Pondicherry (1954)
Karikal (1954)
SRI LANKA
VIETNAM
CAMBODIA
Hong Kong (GB)
Macao (Port.)
PHILIPPINES
MALAYSIA
Singapore
INDONESIA
TIMOR

Conflicts in the World since 1945

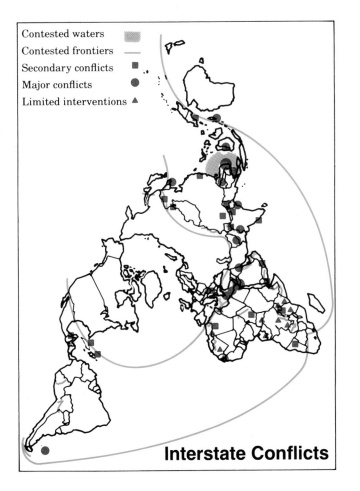

Contested waters
Contested frontiers
Secondary conflicts
Major conflicts
Limited interventions

Interstate Conflicts

There have been over a hundred significant conflicts during the period 1945–1992.

To classify them, the following typology may be proposed:
• Interstate conflicts (conventional wars)
• Liberation wars (in a colonial context or one of foreign occupation)
• Internal conflicts (civil wars arising out of class, ethnic, and/or religious conflicts)

It is estimated that these conflicts have generated, in the period 1945–1988, some 15.5 million victims, an annual rate of about 350,000. (We do not deal here with the wave of terrorist attacks, whether trans-state or not, which are often a substitute for guerrilla warfare but cause a very limited number of victims. When this form of conflict is used as the sole means, it is more than anything else a matter of psychological warfare.)

Ten of these wars, not necessarily those that have had most impact on public opinion, have alone involved over 10 million victims, three-quarters of the total. These are the two Indochina wars (1946–1975), the Indo-Pakistan wars (1947–1949 and 1971 Bangladesh), the Korean war, the Algerian war, the civil war in Sudan, the massacres in Indonesia (1965), and the Biafran war.*

Many conflicts have resulted in significant numbers of refugees: Palestinians, subcontinental Indians, Indochinese, Ethiopians, Afghanis, Central Americans, and so on.

---

* Apart from wars and guerrilla wars, other types of political conflict have resulted in large numbers of victims. For example in Cambodia (1975–1978), in China during the Cultural Revolution, in Equatorial Guinea under Macias or in Uganda under Idi Amin Dada, in Argentina, in Burundi (1972 and 1988), etc.

I. INTERSTATE CONFLICTS

A. MAJOR CONFLICTS:
India-Pakistan (1947–1949)
Arab-Israeli (1948–1949)
Korea (1950–1953)
Israel-Egypt (1956)
India-Pakistan (1965)
Vietnam (1965–1973)—massive U.S. intervention*
Arab-Israeli (1967)
India-Pakistan (1971)—Bangladesh
Arab-Israeli (1973)
Vietnam-China (1979)
Iran-Iraq (1980–1988)
Great Britain-Argentina (1982)—Falkland Islands
United States and Allies-Iraq (1991)—Kuwait

B. SECONDARY CONFLICTS:
China-Taiwan (1950)—Quemoy-Matsu
China-Tibet (1950–1951)
Guatemala-Honduras (1954)—Operation CIA
India-China (1959)—Ladakh
Netherlands-Indonesia (1960–1962)—New Guinea
India-China (1962)—Assam
Indonesia-Malaysia (1963)—Sarawak, Borneo
Algeria-Morocco (1963)
China-USSR (1969)—Ussuri
El Salvador-Honduras (1969)
Greece-Turkey (1974)—Cyprus
Syria-Lebanon (1976)—occupation
Indonesia-East Timor (1976)—annexation
Somalia-Ethiopia (1977–1978)
Vietnam-Cambodia (1978)

North Yemen-South Yemen (1979)
Israel-Lebanon (1982–1988)—PLO
Iraq-Kuwait (1990)—annexation

C. INTERVENTIONS:
Suez, French-British intervention (1956)
Budapest, Soviet intervention (1956)
Lebanon, U.S. intervention (1958)
Mauritania, French intervention (1961)
Cuba, U.S. intervention (1961)
Bizerte, French intervention (1961)
Goa (Portuguese), Indian intervention (1961)
Zaire, Belgian intervention (1961, 1964)
Gabon, French intervention (1964)
Uganda-Kenya-Tanzania, British intervention (1964)
Santo Domingo, U.S. intervention (1965)
Prague, Soviet intervention (1968)
Cambodia, U.S. intervention (1970)
Jordan, royal forces against the PLO (1970)
Angola, interventions by South Africa, Zaire, and especially Cuba (1975–1976)
Shaba (Zaire), French and Moroccan interventions (1977)
Djibouti, French intervention (1976–1977)
Ethiopia, Cuban intervention (1977)
Kolwezi (Zaire), French intervention (1978)
Chad, numerous interventions by French forces (1968–1980)
Uganda, Tanzanian intervention (1979)
Angola, South African interventions (1980, 1981, 1982)
Central African Republic, French intervention (1979)
Chad, Libyan intervention (1980)
Gambia, Senegalese intervention (1980)
Chad, French intervention (1983)

---

* Air strikes in North Vietnam; civil war in South Vietnam.

Grenada, U.S.-led intervention (1983)
Libya, U.S. air raid against (1985)
Persian Gulf, U.S. naval intervention (1986–1988)
Sri Lanka, Indian intervention (1987)
Panama, U.S. intervention (1989)

II. LIBERATION MOVEMENTS FOR INDEPENDENCE DIRECTED AGAINST FOREIGN DOMINATION OR OCCUPATION

Palestine (Zionist movement), against Great Britain (1945–1947)
Indochina (Vietnam), against France (1946–1954)
Laos (Pathet-Lao), against France (1946–1954)
Indonesia, against the Netherlands (1946–1949)
Malaysia, against Great Britain (1948–1957)
Kenya (Mau Mau insurrection), against Great Britain (1952–1954)
Tunisia, against France (1952–1956)
Morocco, against France (1953–1956)
Algeria, against France (1954–1962)
Cyprus, against Great Britain (1955–1959)
Cameroon, against France (1957–1960)
Belgian Congo (1958–1960)
Angola, against Portugal (1961–1974)
South Yemen, against Great Britain (1963–1967)
Guinea-Bissau, against Portugal (1963–1974)
Palestinians, against Israel (1965–)
Mozambique, against Portugal (1964–1974)
Namibia, against South Africa (1970–1989)
Rhodesia/Zimbabwe, against white rule (1972–1979)
East Timor, against Indonesia (1974–)
Western Sahara, against Morocco (1975–)
Cambodia, against a regime put in place by Vietnam (1979–)

Afghanistan, against the Soviet occupation (1979–1989)
Kuwait, against Iraqi annexation (1990–1991)

III. CONFLICTS OVER SECESSION* OR TO GAIN AUTONOMY WITHIN ESTABLISHED STATES

Azerbaijan and the Kurdish republic of Mahabad, Iran (1946)
Burma (Karens, etc.) (1948–)
Hyderabad, resistance to incorporation into India (1948)
South Moluccas (1950–1952)
Tibet, against China (1955–1959)
Katanga (Zaïre) (1960–1964)
Kurds in Iraq (1961–1970, 1974–1975, 1979–)
Eritrea, Ethiopia (1961–)
South Sudan (1966–1972, 1982–)
Biafra, Nigeria (1967–1970)
India (Nagas) (1967–1970)
Baluchistan (Pakistan) (1973–1977)
Ogaden (Ethiopia) (1974–1986)
Basques in Spain (1975–1981)
Philippine Muslims (1977–)
Kurds in Iran (1978–)
Tamils in Sri Lanka (1984–)
Kurds in Turkey (1984–)
Palestinians in territories occupied by Israel (1987–)
Nagorno-Karabakh, Azerbaijan (1988–)
Yugoslavia (1991–)

---

* As in civil wars (IV), the date of the beginning of the operations is often uncertain.

IV. CIVIL WARS FOUGHT TO CHANGE REGIMES

China (1945–1949)
Greece (1947–1949)
Huks (Philippines) (1949–1952)
Colombia, chronic upheaval (1953)
Cuba (1956–1959)
South Vietnam (1957–1964, 1973–1975)
Sumatra, insurrection against Jakarta (1957–1958)
Zaire (1960–1965)
Malaysia (sporadic)
Laos (1960–1975)
Thailand (sporadic)
Cameroon (1960–1966)
Guatemala (1961–1968, 1980–   )
Venezuela (1962–1967)
Yemen, with Egyptian intervention (1962–1967)
Rwanda (1963–1964, 1990–   )
Cyprus, intervention by the U.N. (1963–1964)
Cambodia (1965–1975)
Indonesia (1965)
Uruguay (1965–1973)
Peru (1965, 1982–   )
Bolivia (1967)
Brazil (1967–1970)
Northern Ireland (Catholics) (1968–   )
Chad (1968–1982, 1989–   )
Dhofar, in Oman, with intervention by Great Britain, Iran, and Jordan (1968–1976)
Nicaragua, (1972–1979)
Burundi (1972) (1988)
Chile, military repression (1973)
Argentina (1973–1977)
Lebanon, chronic upheaval (1975–1977)
Angola (UNITA), with South African aid (1976–1991)
Somalia (1985–   )
Liberia (1990–   )
Georgia (1991–   )
El Salvador (1976–   )
Iran (1978–1979)
Afghanistan (1978–1979) (1989–   )
Mozambique (FMN), with South African aid (1980–   )
Philippines (1980–   )
South Sudan (1982–   )

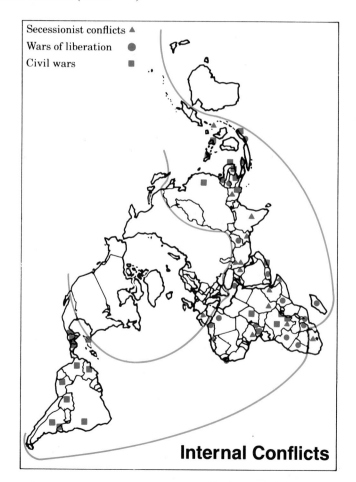

Secessionist conflicts ▲
Wars of liberation ●
Civil wars ■

Internal Conflicts

A WORLD OF OCEANS

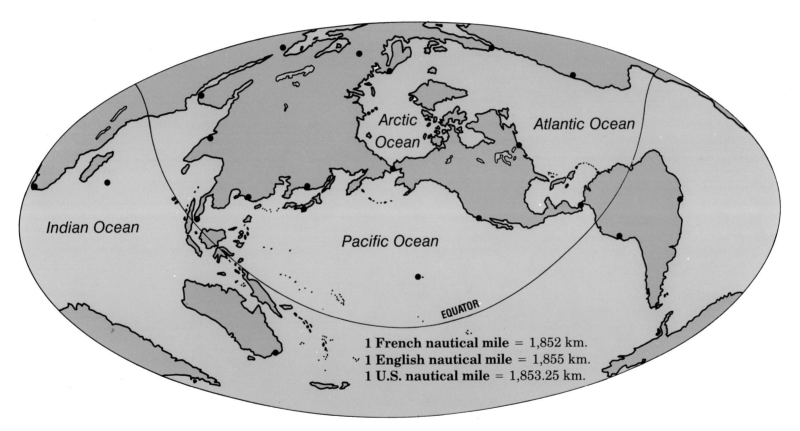

Arctic Ocean

Atlantic Ocean

Indian Ocean

Pacific Ocean

EQUATOR

1 **French nautical mile** = 1,852 km.
1 **English nautical mile** = 1,855 km.
1 **U.S. nautical mile** = 1,853.25 km.

Total surface of the world—510 million sq. km.
Land surface—149 million sq. km. (29%)
Covered by water—361 million sq. km. (71%)

Ocean surfaces
Pacific Ocean—161.7 million sq. km.
Atlantic Ocean—81.6 million sq. km.
Indian Ocean—73.4 million sq. km.
Arctic Ocean—14.3 million sq. km.

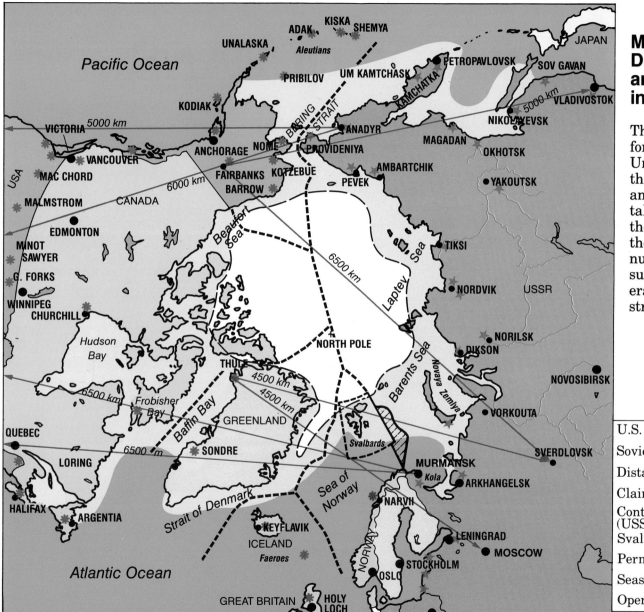

Military Dispositions around the Arctic in the 1980's

The Arctic separates the former USSR and the United States. Control of the surface of this ocean and its air space is of vital importance. Beneath the frozen stretches of sea there has developed, with nuclear submarines, a subglacial theater of operations of equally vital strategic importance.

Legend:

- U.S. and NATO bases ✳
- Soviet bases ★
- Distances ←
- Claims of sovereignty – – –
- Contested area (USSR-Norway) ▨
- Svalbard area ⌐–⌐
- Permanent ice cap ☐
- Seasonal ice ☐
- Open waters ☐

Map labels:

Pacific Ocean · Atlantic Ocean

ADAK · KISKA · SHEMYA · UNALASKA · Aleutians · PETROPAVLOVSK · SOV GAVAN · JAPAN · PRIBILOV · UM KAMTCHASK · KAMCHATKA · KODIAK · NIKOLAYEVSK · VLADIVOSTOK · VICTORIA · ANCHORAGE · NOME · ANADYR · MAGADAN · OKHOTSK · VANCOUVER · PROVIDENIYA · MAC CHORD · FAIRBANKS · KOTZEBUE · AMBARTCHIK · YAKOUTSK · MALMSTROM · BARROW · PEVEK · CANADA · EDMONTON · Beaufort Sea · MINOT SAWYER · G. FORKS · Laptev Sea · TIKSI · WINNIPEG · CHURCHILL · Hudson Bay · NORDVIK · USSR · NORTH POLE · NORILSK · DIKSON · THULE · Barents Sea · Novaya Zemlya · NOVOSIBIRSK · QUEBEC · Frobisher Bay · GREENLAND · Baffin Bay · Svalbards · VORKOUTA · SONDRE · MURMANSK · Kola · SVERDLOVSK · LORING · ARKHANGELSK · HALIFAX · ARGENTIA · Strait of Denmark · Sea of Norway · NARVIK · KEYFLAVIK · ICELAND · Faeroes · LENINGRAD · MOSCOW · NORWAY · STOCKHOLM · OSLO · GREAT BRITAIN · HOLY LOCH · BERING STRAIT

Distances: 5000 km · 6000 km · 6500 km · 4500 km

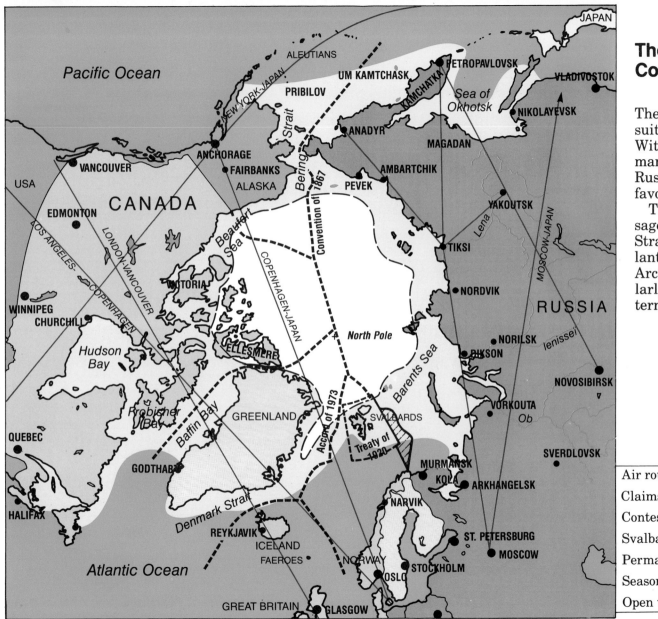

The Arctic: Communications

The Arctic is not well-suited to navigation. With the ports of Murmansk and Arkhangelsk, Russia has a relatively favorable position there.

The Faeroe Islands passages and the Denmark Strait, outlets to the Atlantic, are easy to watch. Arctic air space is regularly used by several international airlines.

Pacific Ocean

JAPAN

ALEUTIANS

UM KAMTCHASK

PRIBILOV

PETROPAVLOVSK

VLADIVOSTOK

Sea of Okhotsk

KAMCHATKA

NIKOLAYEVSK

ANADYR

MAGADAN

ANCHORAGE

VANCOUVER

FAIRBANKS

ALASKA

AMBARTCHIK

PEVEK

Bering Strait

Convention of 1867

YAKOUTSK

USA

CANADA

EDMONTON

Beaufort Sea

Lena

TIKSI

LOS ANGELES-COPENHAGEN

LONDON-VANCOUVER

COPENHAGEN-JAPAN

VICTORIA

NORDVIK

RUSSIA

WINNIPEG

CHURCHILL

NORTH POLE

North Pole

NORILSK

DIKSON

Ienissei

Hudson Bay

Barents Sea

NOVOSIBIRSK

VORKOUTA

Ob

Accord of 1973

SVALBARDS

QUEBEC

Frobisher Bay

Baffin Bay

GREENLAND

ELLESMERE

Treaty of 1920

SVERDLOVSK

HALIFAX

Denmark Strait

GODTHAB

MURMANSK

KOLA

ARKHANGELSK

NARVIK

REYKJAVIK

ICELAND

FAEROES

NORWAY

ST. PETERSBURG

MOSCOW

Atlantic Ocean

OSLO

STOCKHOLM

GREAT BRITAIN

GLASGOW

Air routes	——
Claims of sovereignty	- - -
Contested area	▨
Svalbard Is. area	⬚
Permanent ice cap	◻
Seasonal ice	◻
Open waters	◼

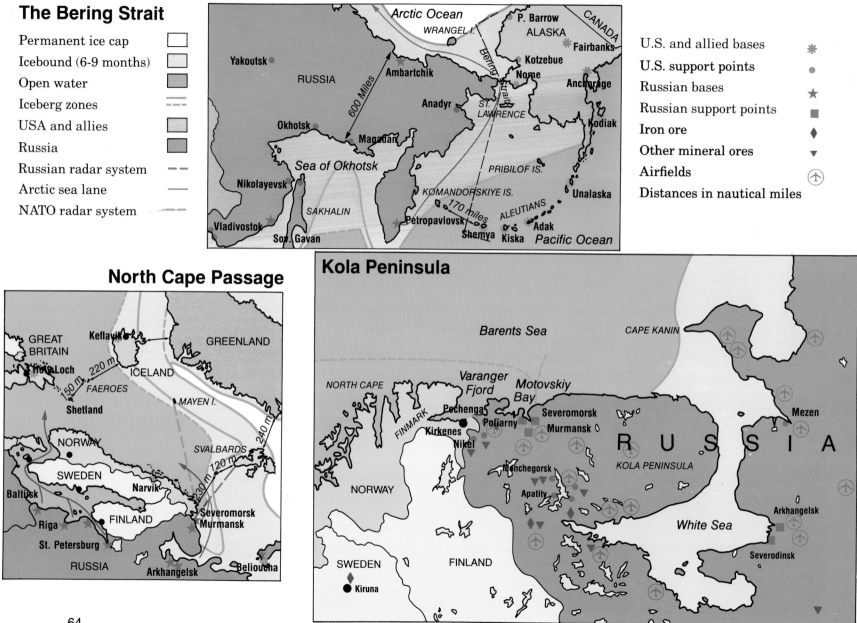

The Bering Strait

Permanent ice cap

Icebound (6-9 months)

Open water

Iceberg zones

USA and allies

Russia

Russian radar system

Arctic sea lane

NATO radar system

U.S. and allied bases

U.S. support points

Russian bases

Russian support points

Iron ore

Other mineral ores

Airfields

Distances in nautical miles

Arctic Ocean

WRANGEL I.

P. Barrow

ALASKA

CANADA

Fairbanks

Yakoutsk

RUSSIA

Kotzebue

Nome

Ambartchik

600 Miles

Bering Strait

Anchorage

Anadyr

ST. LAWRENCE

Okhotsk

Magadan

Kodiak

Sea of Okhotsk

PRIBILOF IS.

Nikolayevsk

KOMANDORSKIYE IS.

SAKHALIN

Unalaska

Vladivostok

170 miles

ALEUTIANS

Petropavlovsk

Adak

Sov. Gavan

Shemya

Kiska

Pacific Ocean

North Cape Passage

GREAT BRITAIN

Keflavik

GREENLAND

Holy Loch

220 m

150 m

ICELAND

FAEROES

MAYEN I.

Shetland

NORWAY

SVALBARDS

240 m

SWEDEN

Narvik

120 m

Baltisk

230 m

Severomorsk

Riga

FINLAND

Murmansk

St. Petersburg

RUSSIA

Arkhangelsk

Belioucha

Kola Peninsula

Barents Sea

CAPE KANIN

Varanger Fjord

Motovskiy Bay

NORTH CAPE

FINMARK

Pechenga

Severomorsk

Mezen

Poliarny

Murmansk

Kirkenes

Nikel

R U S S I A

NORWAY

Menchegorsk

KOLA PENINSULA

Apatity

White Sea

Arkhangelsk

SWEDEN

FINLAND

Severodinsk

Kiruna

Outlets from the Arctic

Since the early 1920s, the coastal states have pushed the limits of their territorial waters well beyond those then accepted. There was a dispute between the former USSR and Norway about this issue, covering an area of 15,000 sq. km. near the Svalbard Islands. By the Treaty of Paris (1920), 41 signatory states (including the USSR) share equal rights to mine coal in the Svalbard Islands—which, however, remain under Norwegian authority.

TOWARD THE ATLANTIC

This access route is essential to the northern Russian fleet based in the region of Murmansk and the White Sea. The polar basin between Greenland and the Svalbard Islands (Spitsbergen) is icebound most of the time and is difficult to navigate. The Barents Sea between North Cape and the Svalbard Islands is the only passage in open waters. Norway's position at North Cape is strategically vital, but highly vulnerable.

TOWARD THE PACIFIC

The Bering Strait (40 miles) is also icebound for more than six months a year. Its narrowness and shallowness (about 40 m.) make it easy to watch and blockade. Farther south, the string of the Aleutian (USA) and the Komandorskiye (Russia) islands complete control of this outlet from the Arctic toward the Pacific.

THE NORTHERN SEA ROUTE

This route, open two or three months a year, has made it easier for the USSR to develop northern Siberia and provides a shorter sea route between Murmansk and Vladivostok. There is no similar route open along the northern coasts of Canada. Only seasonal navigation is possible in Hudson Bay and the Baffin Sea.

Alaska

Alaska, the poleward extension of the United States, (1.5 million sq. km. and 400,000 inhabitants) is of major strategic significance and contains large reserves of oil and natural gas. Anchorage is heavily used by transpolar airlines.

Outlets

Barents Channel:
  North Cape → 280 NM ← Ours I. → 120 NM → Svalbard Is.

Denmark Strait: 150 NM
  Greenland → Svalbard: 240 NM
  Iceland → Faeroe Is.: 200 NM
  Faeroe Is. → Shetland Is.: 150 NM

Distances
  Bering Strait ↔ Denmark Strait: 3,000 NM
  Bering ↔ Murmansk (northern sea route): 3,800 NM

NM: Nautical miles.

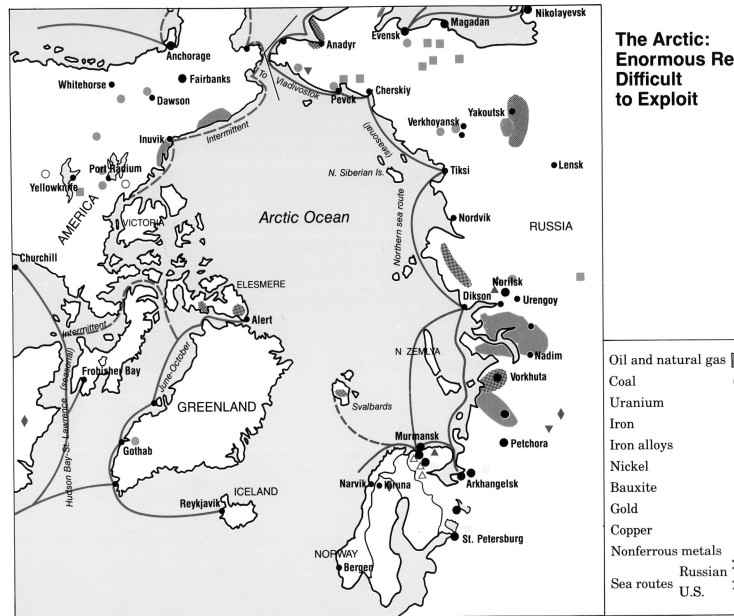

The Arctic: Enormous Resources, Difficult to Exploit

Nikolayevsk
Magadan
Evensk
Anadyr
To Vladivostok
Whitehorse
Anchorage
Fairbanks
Cherskiy
Dawson
Pevek
Yakoutsk
Verkhoyansk
Inuvik
Intermittent
Northern sea route (seasonal)
N. Siberian Is.
Lensk
Port Radium
Tiksi
Yellowknife
AMERICA
VICTORIA
Nordvik
RUSSIA
Arctic Ocean
Churchill
ELESMERE
Norilsk
Dikson
Urengoy
Intermittent
Alert
N ZEMLYA
Nadim
Frobisher Bay
Hudson Bay-St. Lawrence (seasonal)
June-October
Vorkhuta
GREENLAND
Svalbards
Petchora
Gothab
Murmansk
ICELAND
Narvik
Kiruna
Arkhangelsk
Reykjavik
NORWAY
St. Petersburg
Bergen

Legend	
Oil and natural gas	▬
Coal	●
Uranium	○
Iron	◆
Iron alloys	▼
Nickel	▲
Bauxite	▪
Gold	■
Copper	△
Nonferrous metals	●
Sea routes	Russian — —
	U.S. — —

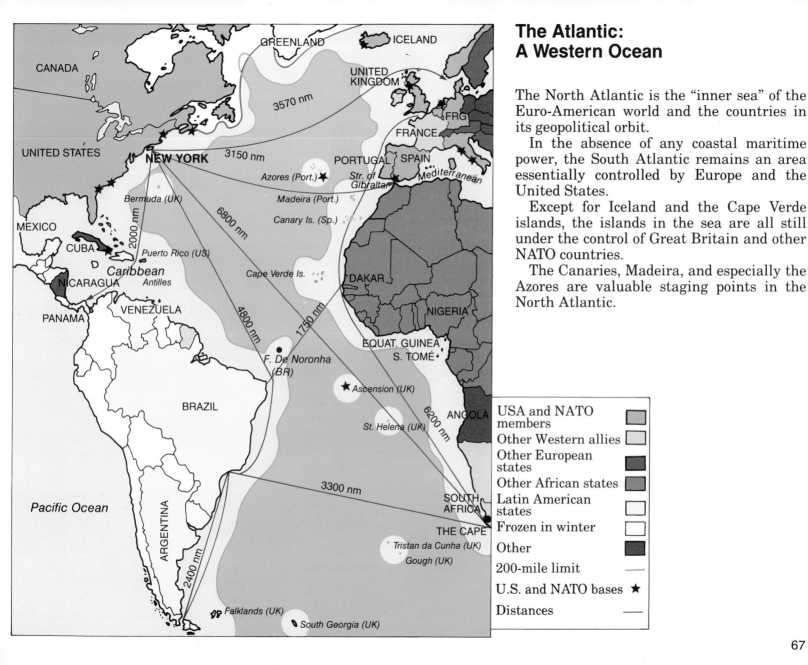

The Atlantic: A Western Ocean

The North Atlantic is the "inner sea" of the Euro-American world and the countries in its geopolitical orbit.

In the absence of any coastal maritime power, the South Atlantic remains an area essentially controlled by Europe and the United States.

Except for Iceland and the Cape Verde islands, the islands in the sea are all still under the control of Great Britain and other NATO countries.

The Canaries, Madeira, and especially the Azores are valuable staging points in the North Atlantic.

Map labels:

GREENLAND, ICELAND, CANADA, UNITED KINGDOM, FRG, FRANCE, UNITED STATES, NEW YORK, PORTUGAL, SPAIN, Mediterranean, Azores (Port.), Str. of Gibraltar, Bermuda (UK), Madeira (Port.), Canary Is. (Sp.), MEXICO, CUBA, Puerto Rico (US), Caribbean, Antilles, Cape Verde Is., DAKAR, NICARAGUA, VENEZUELA, NIGERIA, PANAMA, EQUAT. GUINEA, S. TOMÉ, F. De Noronha (BR), BRAZIL, Ascension (UK), ANGOLA, St. Helena (UK), Pacific Ocean, ARGENTINA, SOUTH AFRICA, THE CAPE, Tristan da Cunha (UK), Gough (UK), Falklands (UK), South Georgia (UK)

Distances: 3570 nm, 3150 nm, 2000 nm, 6800 nm, 4800 nm, 1750 nm, 6200 nm, 3300 nm, 2400 nm

Legend:
- USA and NATO members
- Other Western allies
- Other European states
- Other African states
- Latin American states
- Frozen in winter
- Other
- 200-mile limit
- U.S. and NATO bases ★
- Distances

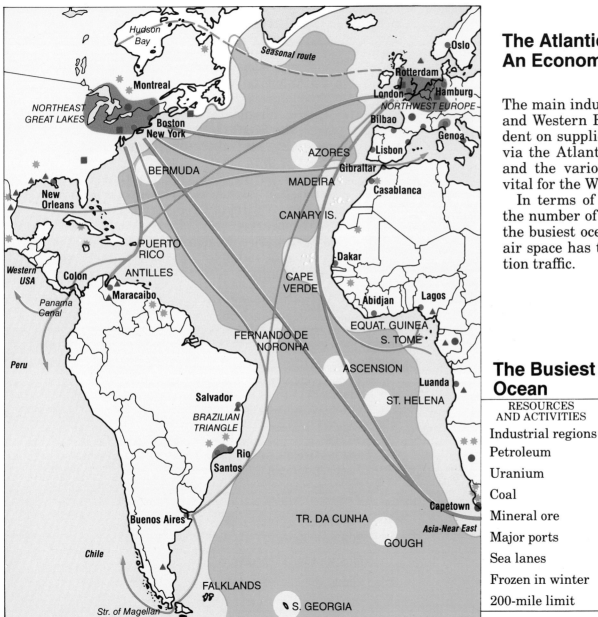

The Atlantic Ocean: An Economic Crossroads

The main industrial areas of North America and Western Europe remain heavily dependent on supplies of raw materials that come via the Atlantic. The security of sea routes and the various key access points is thus vital for the Western powers.

In terms of the tonnage transported and the number of ships using it, the Atlantic is the busiest ocean. Similarly, North Atlantic air space has the heaviest commercial aviation traffic.

The Busiest Ocean

RESOURCES AND ACTIVITIES

Industrial regions	▬
Petroleum	▲
Uranium	●
Coal	■
Mineral ore	✳
Major ports	●
Sea lanes	▬▬▬
Frozen in winter	☐
200-mile limit	──

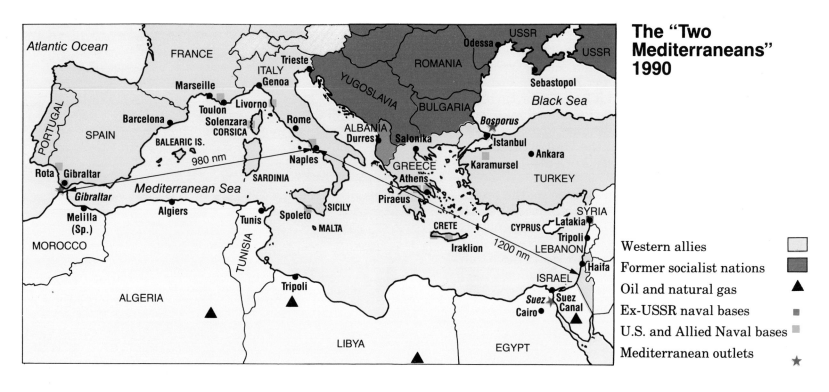

The "Two Mediterraneans" 1990

Western allies ▢
Former socialist nations ▆
Oil and natural gas ▲
Ex-USSR naval bases ▪
U.S. and Allied Naval bases ▫
Mediterranean outlets ★

THE MEDITERRANEAN

Since 1945, the strategic importance the Mediterranean had during the period of European hegemony has rapidly declined. Decolonization and the Arab–Israeli conflicts, which led on several occasions to the closure of the Suez Canal, have considerably reduced the level of its commercial activity. The main route for petroleum products today is around South Africa. Militarily, long-range strategic weapons have transformed this easily blockaded sea into a trap for fleets.

The role of the Mediterranean has become regional, even though at present the conflict in the Middle East and the upkeep of NATO's military forces in Italy, Greece, and Turkey require the presence of naval forces. After its disengagement from Egypt, the USSR retained only one staging area—in Syria.

Since 1990, threats have been perceived from the proliferation of missiles in the eastern Mediterranean and the South–North population imbalance.

THE CARIBBEAN BASIN

The Caribbean forms an "American Mediterranean." Traditionally, the United States has perceived this area as strategically vital, and it has numerous bases there, the main ones being in the Panama Canal Zone, in Puerto Rico, and at Guantanamo (Cuba). In the past, including the recent past, the United States has frequently intervened militarily in Central America and the Caribbean.*

Compared to North and South America, the proliferation of ministates and the large number of small islands (a minority of which are not independent) make this area particularly vulnerable. In the last twenty years, more than a dozen new states have won independence. Since it was built, the Panama Canal has been primarily a passageway between the east and west coasts of the United States.

The Caribbean basin, dominated by the United States (except for Cuba, which appears as a trouble-maker), is important for its oil and as a communications nexus. It has recently seen the emergence of two regional powers, Venezuela and Mexico. The states in this basin have been benefiting from favorable economic conditions assured by the United States, as well as from the low oil prices granted them by Venezuela and Mexico. Miami has become the real center of the Caribbean basin.

Free elections defeated the pro-Soviet Sandinistas of Nicaragua in 1989. Though a cease-fire has held, the essential conflict in El Salvador grinds on.

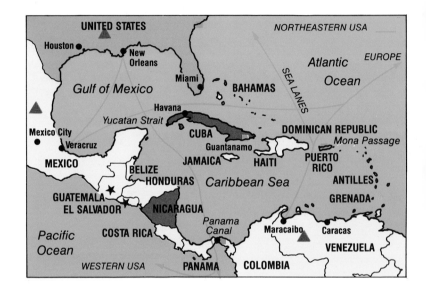

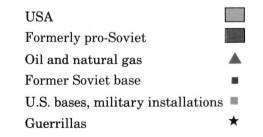

USA	■
Formerly pro-Soviet	■
Oil and natural gas	▲
Former Soviet base	▪
U.S. bases, military installations	▪
Guerrillas	★

---

* For example, in Grenada (1983) and Panama (1989).

The Indian Ocean

A MAJOR AREA OF CONFLICT

Because of the flow of petroleum from the Persian Gulf and the instability or fragility of many of the coastal states, the Indian Ocean—and particularly the Gulf—is a major area of conflict.

From its important base on Diego Garcia, the United States can launch an operational strike force (with Berbera and Al Masirah as support points). Naval intervention by the United States and its allies (Britain, France, etc.) played a not insignificant role in the Iran–Iraq conflict in 1986–1988.

During the years 1975–1988 the deployment of Soviet naval forces around the Gulf was stepped up considerably (Socotra, Aden, Ethiopia). The Gulf continues to be of vital importance, as witness the American reaction to Iraq's intervention in and annexation of Kuwait (1990). The United States remains—with the support notably of Britain and France—the guarantor of the status quo in this region.

No coastal state, neither India nor Australia, yet has the naval capacity to make a decisive impact. Oil usually goes around the Cape to Europe and through the two traditional routes of the straits of Malacca and Sunda* to eastern Asia, although increasingly the Strait of Lombok is used because of the depth of its waters.

* The distance from the Persian Gulf to Japan is 6,500 miles by the first route and 7,500 miles by the second.

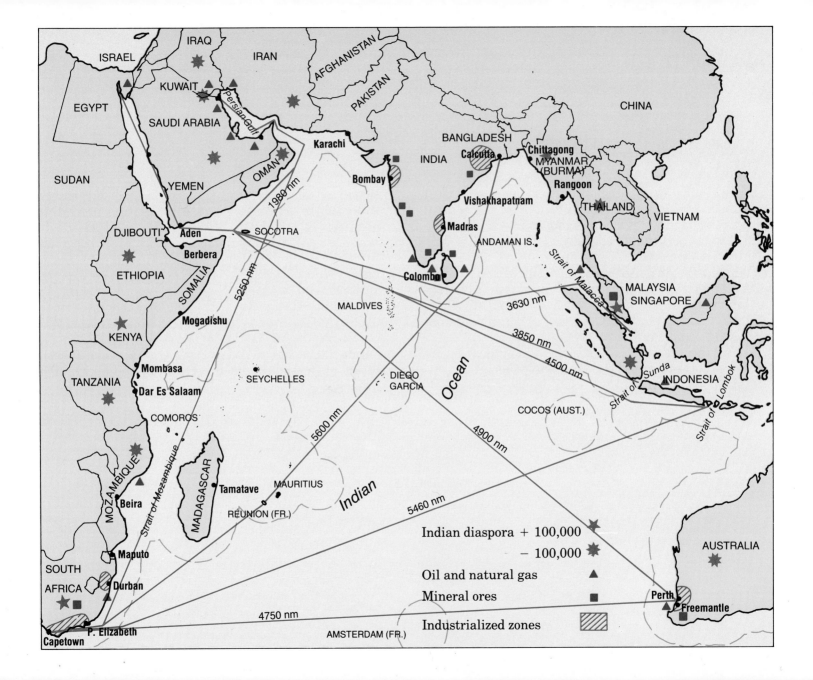

ISRAEL
IRAQ
IRAN
AFGHANISTAN
EGYPT
KUWAIT
SAUDI ARABIA
PAKISTAN
CHINA
Persian Gulf
SUDAN
YEMEN
OMAN
Karachi
BANGLADESH
Calcutta
Chittagong
MYANMAR (BURMA)
DJIBOUTI
Aden
SOCOTRA
INDIA
Bombay
Rangoon
Berbera
Vishakhapatnam
THAILAND
VIETNAM
ETHIOPIA
SOMALIA
Madras
ANDAMAN IS.
Strait of Malacca
MALAYSIA
SINGAPORE
Mogadishu
MALDIVES
Colombo
3630 nm
3850 nm
KENYA
4500 nm
Strait of Sunda
INDONESIA
Mombasa
SEYCHELLES
DIEGO GARCIA
Ocean
Strait of Lombok
TANZANIA
Dar Es Salaam
COCOS (AUST.)
COMOROS
5600 nm
4900 nm
MADAGASCAR
Tamatave
MAURITIUS
MOZAMBIQUE
Indian
5460 nm
Beira
REUNION (FR.)
Strait of Mozambique
1980 nm
5250 nm
AUSTRALIA
Maputo
SOUTH
Indian diaspora + 100,000
AFRICA
Durban
− 100,000
Oil and natural gas
Perth
Mineral ores
Freemantle
P. Elizabeth
AMSTERDAM (FR.)
4750 nm
Industrialized zones
Capetown

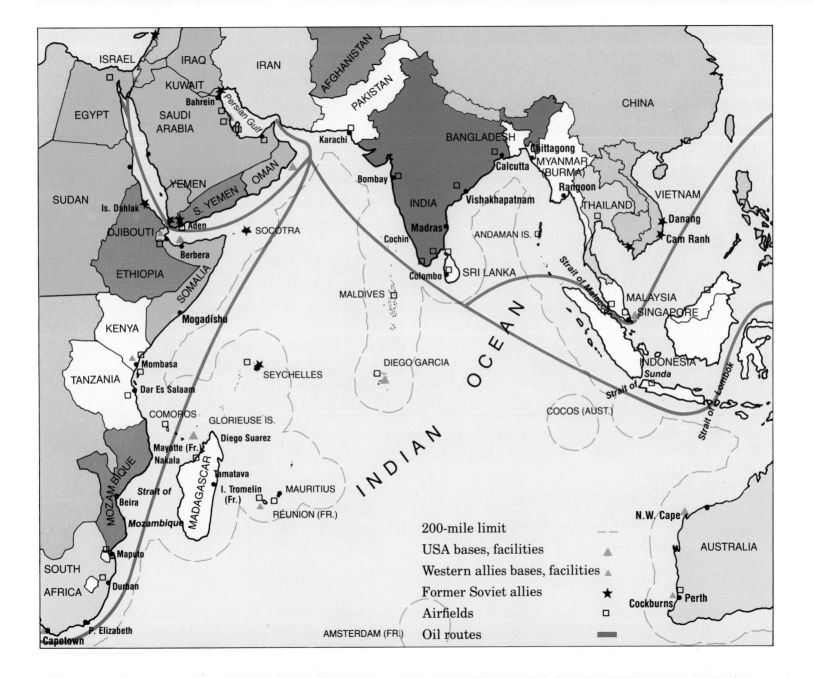

ISRAEL
IRAQ
IRAN
EGYPT
KUWAIT
Bahrein
SAUDI ARABIA
Persian Gulf
AFGHANISTAN
PAKISTAN
Karachi
CHINA
SUDAN
YEMEN
OMAN
S. YEMEN
Aden
Is. Dahlak
DJIBOUTI
Berbera
ETHIOPIA
SOMALIA
SOCOTRA
Bombay
INDIA
BANGLADESH
Calcutta
Chittagong
MYANMAR (BURMA)
Rangoon
VIETNAM
Danang
Cam Ranh
Madras
Vishakhapatnam
ANDAMAN IS.
THAILAND
Cochin
Colombo
SRI LANKA
MALDIVES
KENYA
Mogadishu
DIEGO GARCIA
Strait of Malacca
MALAYSIA
SINGAPORE
TANZANIA
Mombasa
Dar Es Salaam
SEYCHELLES
INDIAN OCEAN
INDONESIA
Sunda
COCOS (AUST.)
Strait of
Strait of Lombok
COMOROS
GLORIEUSE IS.
Mayotte (Fr.)
Diego Suarez
Nakala
MADAGASCAR
Tamatava
I. Tromelin (Fr.)
MAURITIUS
RÉUNION (FR.)
MOZAMBIQUE
Strait of
Beira
Mozambique
N.W. Cape
AUSTRALIA
SOUTH AFRICA
Maputo
Durban
P. Elizabeth
Capetown
Cockburns
Perth

200-mile limit
USA bases, facilities
Western allies bases, facilities
Former Soviet allies
Airfields
Oil routes

AMSTERDAM (FR.)

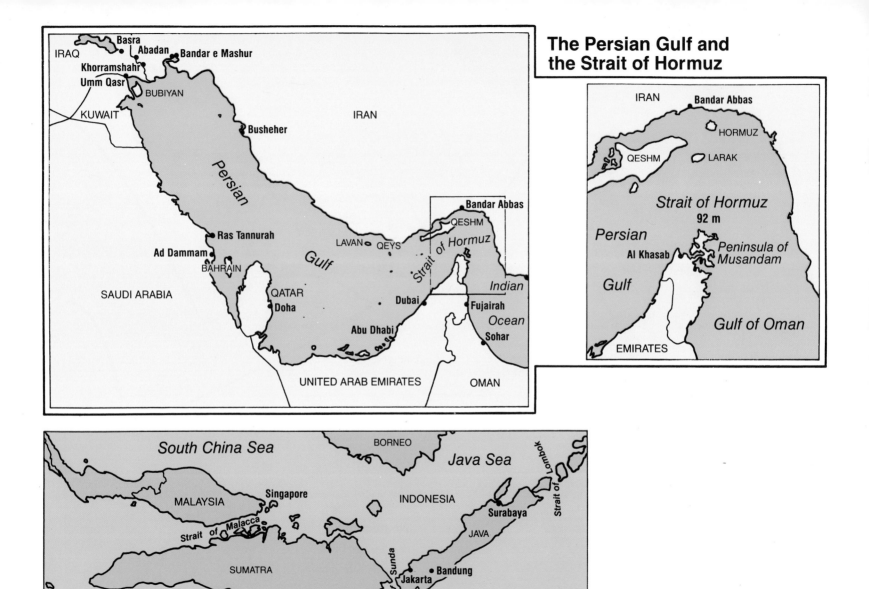

The Persian Gulf and the Strait of Hormuz

Map 1 (top left):

IRAQ
Basra
Abadan
Bandar e Mashur
Khorramshahr
Umm Qasr
BUBIYAN
KUWAIT
Busheher
IRAN
Persian
Ras Tannurah
Gulf
LAVAN
QEYS
Strait of Hormuz
Bandar Abbas
QESHM
Ad Dammam
BAHRAIN
SAUDI ARABIA
QATAR
Doha
Dubai
Abu Dhabi
UNITED ARAB EMIRATES
Fujairah
Indian
Ocean
Sohar
OMAN

Map 2 (top right):

IRAN
Bandar Abbas
HORMUZ
QESHM
LARAK
Strait of Hormuz
92 m
Persian
Gulf
Al Khasab
Peninsula of Musandam
Gulf of Oman
EMIRATES

Map 3 (bottom):

South China Sea
BORNEO
Java Sea
MALAYSIA
Singapore
INDONESIA
Strait of Lombok
Strait of Malacca
Surabaya
JAVA
SUMATRA
Strait of Sunda
Jakarta
Bandung
Indian Ocean
N

The Straits of Indonesia

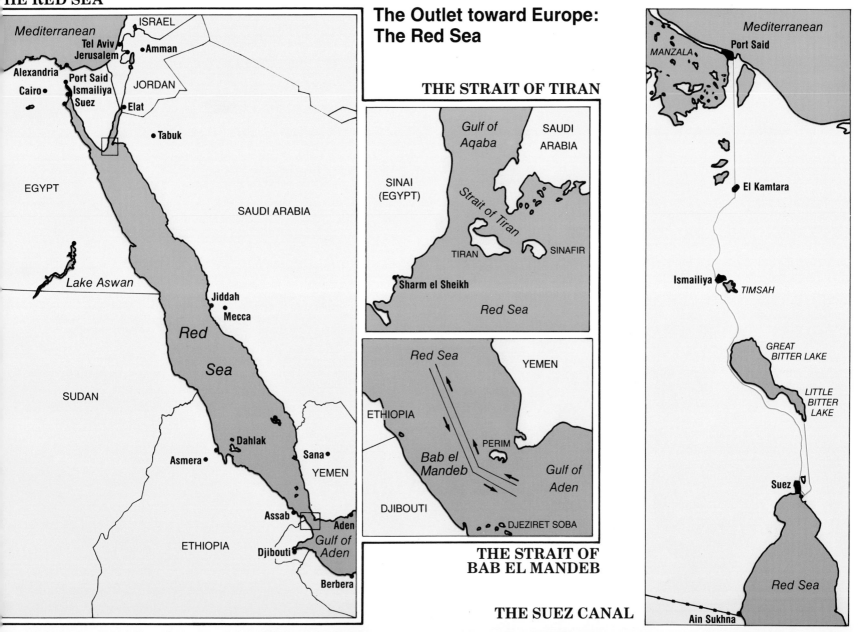

THE RED SEA

Mediterranean

ISRAEL

Tel Aviv
Jerusalem
Amman

Alexandria
Cairo
Port Said
Ismailiya
Suez
Elat

JORDAN

EGYPT

Tabuk

SAUDI ARABIA

Lake Aswan

Jiddah
Mecca

Red
Sea

SUDAN

Dahlak

Asmera
Sana

YEMEN

Assab
Aden

ETHIOPIA

Djibouti
Gulf of
Aden

Berbera

The Outlet toward Europe:
The Red Sea

THE STRAIT OF TIRAN

Gulf of
Aqaba

SAUDI
ARABIA

SINAI
(EGYPT)

Strait of Tiran

TIRAN
SINAFIR

Sharm el Sheikh

Red Sea

Red Sea

YEMEN

ETHIOPIA

Bab el
Mandeb

PERIM

Gulf of
Aden

DJIBOUTI

DJEZIRET SOBA

THE STRAIT OF
BAB EL MANDEB

THE SUEZ CANAL

Mediterranean

MANZALA
Port Said

El Kamtara

Ismailiya
TIMSAH

GREAT
BITTER LAKE

LITTLE
BITTER
LAKE

Suez

Red Sea

Ain Sukhna

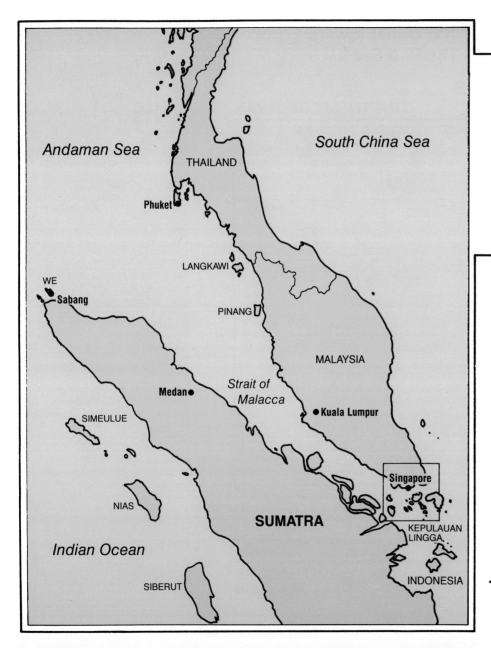

Andaman Sea

South China Sea

THAILAND

Phuket

LANGKAWI

WE

Sabang

PINANG

MALAYSIA

Strait of
Malacca

Medan

Kuala Lumpur

SIMEULUE

NIAS

SUMATRA

Singapore

Indian Ocean

KEPULAUAN
LINGGA

SIBERUT

INDONESIA

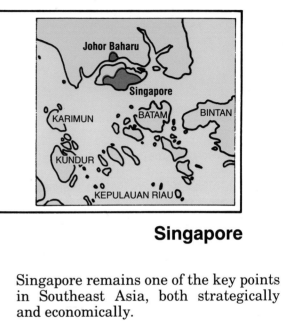

Johor Baharu

Singapore

KARIMUN

BATAM

BINTAN

KUNDUR

KEPULAUAN RIAU

Singapore

Singapore remains one of the key points in Southeast Asia, both strategically and economically.

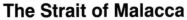

The Strait of Malacca

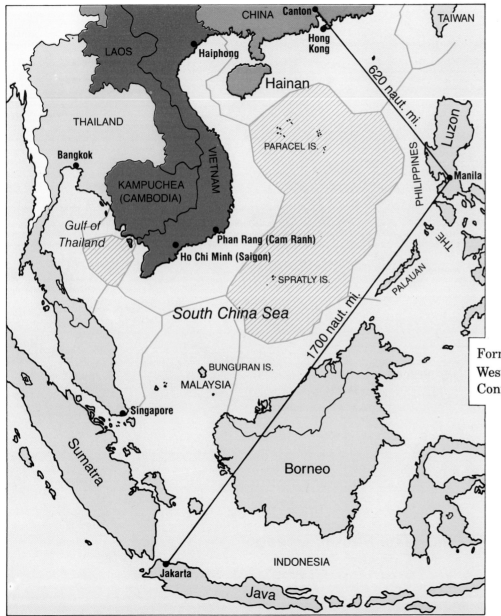

Disputed Areas in the South China Sea

In this region, there remain unresolved problems of sovereignty over parts of the continental shelf. In the northeast, the Chinese and Vietnamese are in dispute over the Paracel Islands, which have been occupied by the Chinese since the mid-1970s. In the south, Indonesia, the Philippines, Taiwan, and Vietnam all seek to assert their sovereignty over the Spratly Islands. Vietnam and Indonesia are in dispute over the continental shelf. In the Gulf of Thailand, Vietnam, Kampuchea, and Thailand are in dispute.*

Former Soviet allies	■
Western allies	□
Contested waters	▨

---

* Throughout the region, a principal source of dispute is the oil found in the South China Sea.

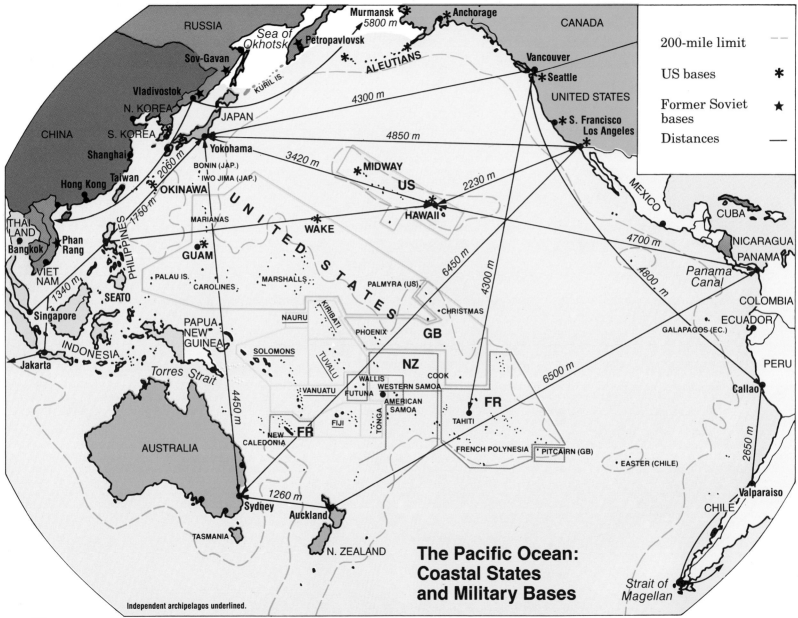

**The Pacific Ocean:
Coastal States
and Military Bases**

Independent archipelagos underlined.

Legend:
- 200-mile limit
- US bases ✳
- Former Soviet bases ★
- Distances ——

Labels on map:
RUSSIA, Sea of Okhotsk, Murmansk 5800 m, Anchorage, CANADA, Petropavlovsk, ALEUTIANS, Sov-Gavan, Vancouver, Vladivostok, Seattle, N. KOREA, JAPAN, UNITED STATES, S. KOREA, 4300 m, S. Francisco, Los Angeles, Shanghai, Yokohama, 4850 m, Taiwan, Hong Kong, BONIN (JAP.), 3420 m, MIDWAY, IWO JIMA (JAP.), US, OKINAWA, 2060 m, UNITED STATES, 2230 m, MEXICO, CHINA, THAILAND, Bangkok, Phan Rang, MARIANAS, WAKE, HAWAII, CUBA, 1750 m, VIET NAM, PHILIPPINES, GUAM, PALAU IS., MARSHALLS, PALMYRA (US), 4700 m, NICARAGUA, PANAMA, SEATO, CAROLINES, 6450 m, 4300 m, Panama Canal, 1340 m, CHRISTMAS, COLOMBIA, Singapore, PAPUA NEW GUINEA, NAURU, KIRIBATI, PHOENIX, GB, GALAPAGOS (EC.), ECUADOR, INDONESIA, SOLOMONS, TUVALU, NZ, COOK, 6500 m, PERU, Jakarta, Torres Strait, 4450 m, WALLIS, VANUATU, FUTUNA, WESTERN SAMOA, AMERICAN SAMOA, Callao, FIJI, TONGA, TAHITI, FR, NEW CALEDONIA, FR, FRENCH POLYNESIA, PITCAIRN (GB), EASTER (CHILE), 2650 m, AUSTRALIA, Valparaiso, Sydney, 1260 m, Auckland, CHILE, TASMANIA, N. ZEALAND, Strait of Magellan

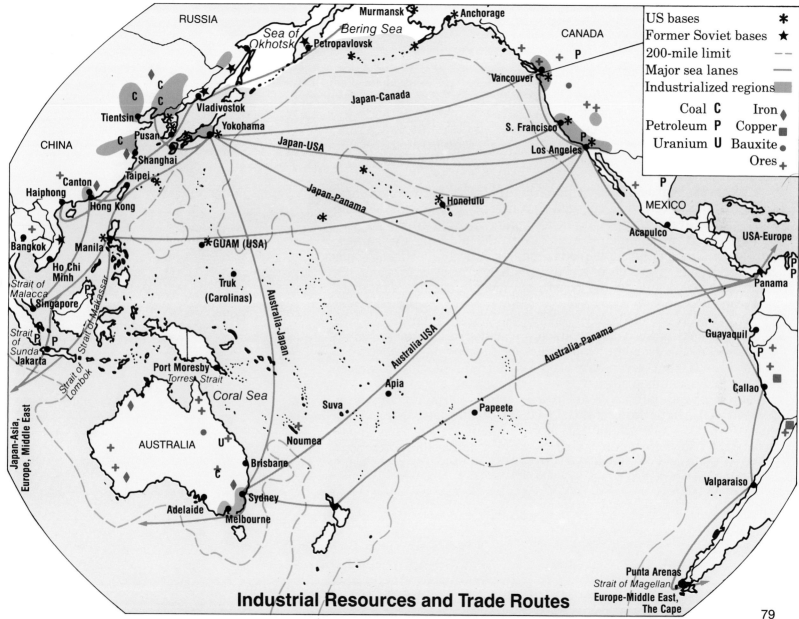

Industrial Resources and Trade Routes

US bases ✳
Former Soviet bases ★
200-mile limit – –
Major sea lanes —
Industrialized regions ▩

Coal **C** Iron ◆
Petroleum **P** Copper ■
Uranium **U** Bauxite ●
Ores ✚

RUSSIA
Murmansk
Bering Sea
Anchorage
CANADA
Sea of Okhotsk
Petropavlovsk
C   C
C
C
Vladivostok
Japan-Canada
Vancouver
P
Tientsin
Yokohama
S. Francisco
Pusan
Japan-USA
Los Angeles
CHINA
C
Shanghai
P
Taipei
Canton
Japan-Panama
Haiphong
Honolulu
Hong Kong
MEXICO
Acapulco
USA-Europe
Bangkok
Manila
GUAM (USA)
P
Ho Chi Minh
Strait of Malacca
Truk (Carolinas)
P
Singapore
Australia-Japan
P
Strait of Sunda
Jakarta
Strait of Makassar
Strait of Lombok
Australia-USA
Panama
P
P
Port Moresby
Torres Strait
Australia-Panama
Guayaquil
Coral Sea
Apia
P
Suva
Callao
Noumea
Papeete
AUSTRALIA
U
C
Brisbane
Adelaide
Sydney
Valparaiso
Melbourne
Japan-Asia, Europe, Middle East
Punta Arenas
Strait of Magellan
Europe-Middle East, The Cape

79

The Pacific Ocean

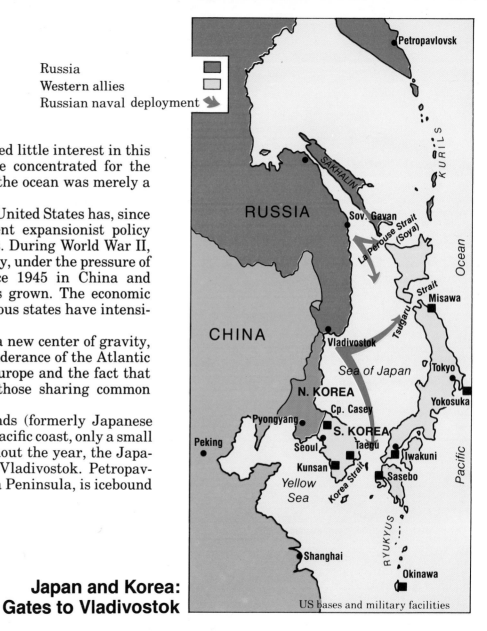

Russia
Western allies
Russian naval deployment

Before World War II, the great powers showed little interest in this vast ocean. Their maritime activities were concentrated for the most part in the southwestern Pacific, and the ocean was merely a secondary highway.

With its seaboard on the Pacific, only the United States has, since the nineteenth century, pursued a coherent expansionist policy through the archipelagos to the Philippines. During World War II, Japan saw its imperial plans thwarted. Today, under the pressure of political changes that have occurred since 1945 in China and Southeast Asia, the role of the Pacific has grown. The economic importance of Japan and the growth of various states have intensified trade flows.

However, the Pacific has not yet become a new center of gravity, equal to the Atlantic. The continued preponderance of the Atlantic derives from the economic importance of Europe and the fact that both sides of that ocean are peopled by those sharing common origins and a common culture.

Control of Sakhalin and the Kuril Islands (formerly Japanese possessions) is important for Russia. On its Pacific coast, only a small part of which is open to navigation throughout the year, the Japanese straits form so many gates opposite Vladivostok. Petropavlovsk, at the southern end of the Kamchatka Peninsula, is icebound three or four months of the year.

Japan and Korea: Gates to Vladivostok

US bases and military facilities

Hawaii: Key Position in the Pacific

Most of the islands in the Pacific are under the trusteeship of the West and its allies (USA, Great Britain, France, New Zealand, Australia, Japan). U.S. hegemony is almost total in the northern Pacific. The central position of Hawaii, as base and as staging area, is vital in this arrangement.

The archipelago contains the major base of Pearl Harbor, which acts as support base for the Pacific fleet, and Camp Nimitz, the seat of the Armed Forces Pacific Command, and it is also a major air traffic center.

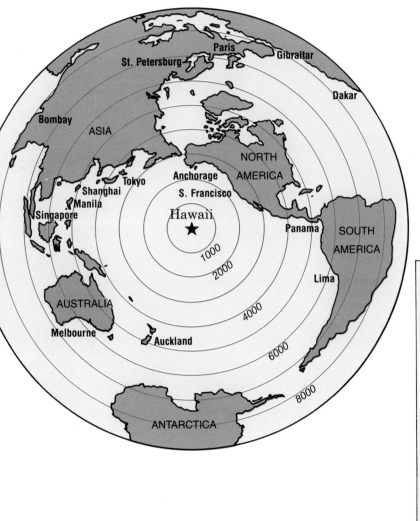

Hawaii: The Fiftieth American State

The Antarctic

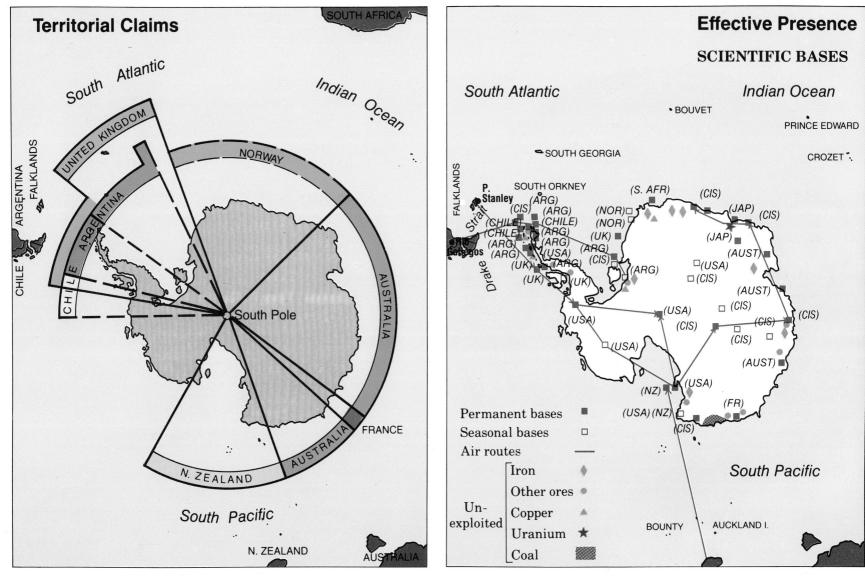

Territorial Claims

South Atlantic

Indian Ocean

South Africa

Falklands

ARGENTINA
FALKLANDS

CHILE

UNITED KINGDOM

NORWAY

ARGENTINA

CHILE ARGENTINA

South Pole

AUSTRALIA

FRANCE

N. ZEALAND

AUSTRALIA

South Pacific

N. ZEALAND

AUSTRALIA

Effective Presence

SCIENTIFIC BASES

South Atlantic

Indian Ocean

BOUVET

PRINCE EDWARD

SOUTH GEORGIA

CROZET

FALKLANDS

P. Stanley

SOUTH ORKNEY

(S. AFR)

(CIS)

(CIS)

(ARG)

(NOR)

(JAP)

(CIS)

Drake Strait

(CIS)

(ARG)

(CHILE)

(NOR)

(CHILE)

(ARG)

(CHILE)

(ARG)

(UK)

(JAP)

Rio Gallegos

(ARG)

(ARG)

(USA)

(ARG)

(AUST)

(UK)

(ARG)

(CIS)

(ARG)

(USA)

(UK)

(UK)

(CIS)

(USA)

(CIS)

(CIS)

(USA)

(CIS)

(AUST)

(CIS)

(CIS)

(USA)

(CIS)

(AUST)

(NZ)

(USA)

(USA) (NZ)

(FR)

(CIS)

BOUNTY

AUCKLAND I.

South Pacific

Permanent bases ■

Seasonal bases □

Air routes ——

Un-exploited

Iron ◆

Other ores ●

Copper ▲

Uranium ★

Coal

Antarctica

Since 1900, seven states have claimed territorial rights over portions of the Antarctic continent:

United Kingdom (1908)
New Zealand (1923)
France (1924 and 1938)
Australia (1933)
Norway (1939)
Chile (1940)
Argentina (1943)

More recently, Brazil has added itself to this list.

This partition is largely formal, since the United States, the USSR, and other states have always reserved their claims.

Brazil, Chile, and Argentina base their claims on geographic proximity, the latter two disputing rights asserted by the British. The British, by maintaining their sovereignty over the Falkland Islands in 1982, continue to exercise de facto authority over the sector they laid claim to in 1908.

On Antarctica itself, several countries have an effective presence, permanent or seasonal, in the form of meteorological or scientific stations: in quantitative order, the Commonwealth of Independent States (12), the USA (9), Argentina (8), United Kingdom (4), New Zealand (3), Australia (3), Japan (2), France (1).

The Falkland Islands and Antarctica

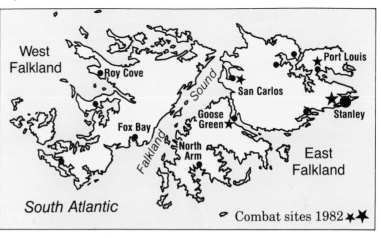

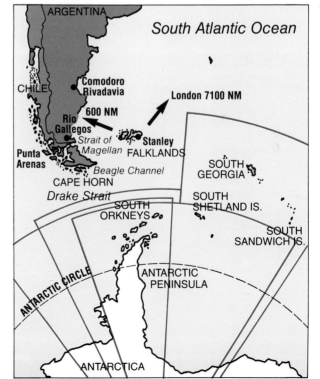

83

The World Seen from Antarctica

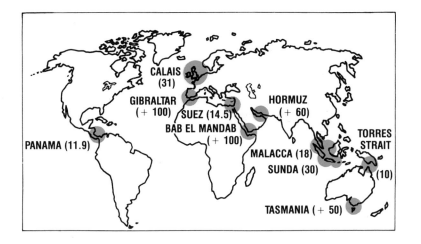

Depth of Main Transit Routes (meters)

CALAIS (31)
GIBRALTAR (+ 100)
SUEZ (14.5)
BAB EL MANDAB (+ 100)
HORMUZ (+ 60)
PANAMA (11.9)
MALACCA (18)
SUNDA (30)
TORRES STRAIT (10)
TASMANIA (+ 50)

SECURITY PERCEPTIONS OF WORLD AND REGIONAL POWERS

How the United States Was Settled

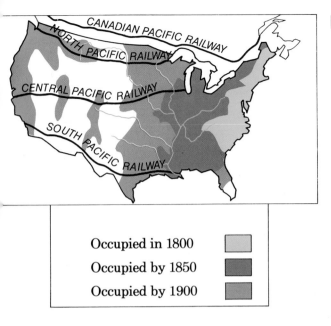

Occupied in 1800	
Occupied by 1850	
Occupied by 1900	

1. Delaware
2. New Jersey
3. Rhode Island
4. Massachusetts
5. New Hampshire
6. Connecticut
7. Vermont
8. Maryland
9. West Virginia

The United States

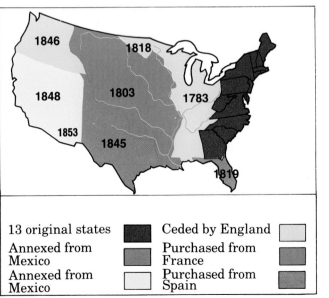

13 original states	Ceded by England	
Annexed from Mexico	Purchased from France	
Annexed from Mexico	Purchased from Spain	

Territorial Growth

The United States:
Formation and Settlement

In the first phase of its expansion, the United States was able, without fighting any major wars, rapidly to occupy its hinterland. It had no rivals on the continent. It was soon making its presence felt outside the continent (Liberia, 1820; Japan, 1854; China, 1859), and by the turn of the century had ensured its economic dominance over the American continent and occupied the Pacific as far as the Philippines. Until the Korean war, the USA had known only absolute victories, total successes: the conquest of the West, the purchase of land from foreign powers (Alaska in 1867), wars against Mexico and Spain. The interventions in 1917 and 1941 themselves were wars in which the United States was protected by its geographic isolation.

As a business society with an empirical philosophy, a Protestant ethic, and a liberal democracy with great social mobility, the United States, proud of having neither colonies nor rivals, had not throughout its history developed any real conception of interstate relations. Not having known the realities that spring from a constant struggle for national self-preservation, the United States became a world power with a historical experience very different from that of the European states.

After World War II, the United States, the dominant state on the planet, found itself faced with the task of containing Communist expansion (1947). Strong in its nuclear monopoly, then enjoying an undeniable superiority for two decades, the United States sought first and foremost to contain this expansion systematically.

The American withdrawal after the war in Vietnam (1973), which profoundly affected public opinion, and consequently American political will, is to be traced to a number of factors: conceptual weakness* and lack of knowledge of the outside world; frequent confusion of national aspirations with the expansion of communism; defense of notoriously corrupt and ineffective allies solely because they are pliable, combined with an inability to support allies that have been promised security. As for decisions, they are generally made in moments of crisis, while long-term planning is neglected.

However, by reintroducing human rights as a political point of reference, the United States launched the first Western ideological counteroffensive in four decades, not to mention, more recently, an ambitious rearmament program intended to reassert its superiority. The reduction of the arms race after 1987, the collapse of the Communist regimes in Central Europe (1989), and the collapse of the Communist party and of the Soviet empire (1991) have strengthened American hegemony.

Whatever its economic difficulties, the United States possesses the necessary technological advances, the resources, and the dynamism to continue to be the leading power in the world.

---

*The Nixon–Kissinger team is an exception.

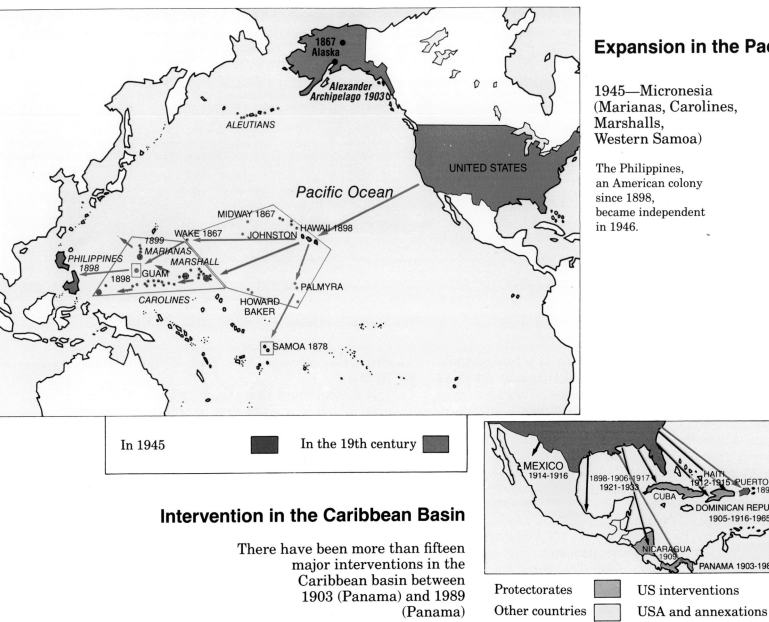

Expansion in the Pacific

1945—Micronesia
(Marianas, Carolines,
Marshalls,
Western Samoa)

The Philippines,
an American colony
since 1898,
became independent
in 1946.

1867
Alaska

Alexander
Archipelago 1903

ALEUTIANS

UNITED STATES

Pacific Ocean

MIDWAY 1867

WAKE 1867   HAWAII 1898
JOHNSTON

1899
MARIANAS
MARSHALL

PHILIPPINES
1898

1898   GUAM

CAROLINES   HOWARD
BAKER

PALMYRA

SAMOA 1878

| In 1945 | ■ | In the 19th century | ■ |

Intervention in the Caribbean Basin

There have been more than fifteen
major interventions in the
Caribbean basin between
1903 (Panama) and 1989
(Panama)

MEXICO
1914-1916

1898-1906-1917
1921-1933

HAITI
1912-1915   PUERTO RICO
1898

CUBA

DOMINICAN REPUBLIC
1905-1916-1965

NICARAGUA
1909

PANAMA 1903-1989

Protectorates   US interventions

Other countries   USA and annexations

Minorities in the United States

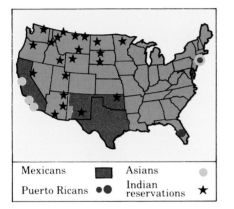

Mexicans · Asians

Puerto Ricans ●● · Indian reservations ★

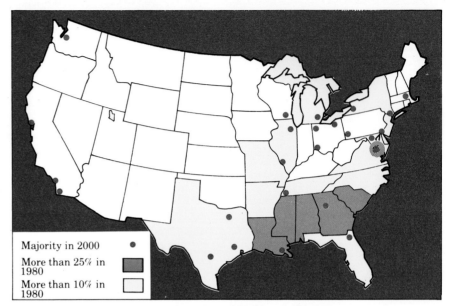

Majority in 2000 ●

More than 25% in 1980

More than 10% in 1980

Blacks in the United States

While the Indian minority forms only a tiny percentage of the population, blacks and Hispanics (such as the Chicanos or the Puerto Ricans) number some 50 million individuals: blacks, 26.5 million; Hispanics, 14.5 million (1980). In addition there are 8 million illegal aliens.

With Asians* and other minorities, the United States population is 20 to 22 percent "nonwhite." Blacks, increasingly numerous in the metropolitan areas of the Northeast and the West (New York, Philadelphia, Washington, Detroit, Chicago, Los Angeles, San Diego, Seattle), are also concentrated in several cities in the South (Houston, Dallas, Memphis, Atlanta). Hispanics are mainly settled in California, New Mexico, and Texas, and in the following cities: Los Angeles, New York, El Paso, Miami, San Antonio.

It is estimated that, since 1975, legally or otherwise, about 1 million immigrants have entered the United States each year, 82 percent of them from Latin America or Asia. Over the last decade, Los Angeles has come to play the role formerly held by New York as the mecca for immigrants from all over the world. The combination of poverty and racial tensions, particularly among blacks, intensifies the feeling of insecurity in the big cities.

---

*The Asian communities (Japanese, Chinese, Koreans, and so on) are often well-to-do.

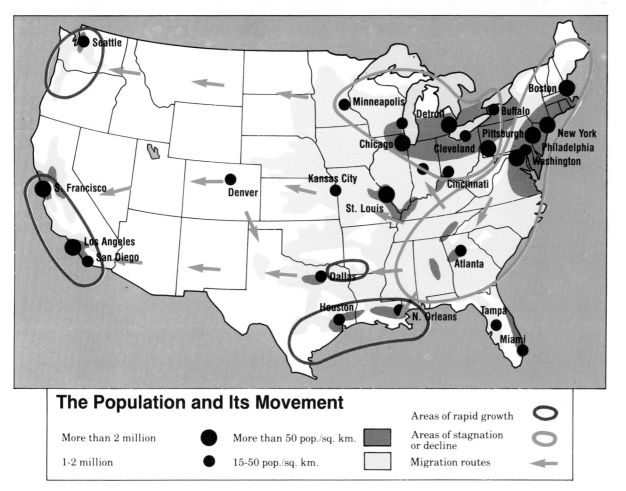

The Population and Its Movement

More than 2 million ●

1-2 million ●

More than 50 pop./sq. km. ●

15-50 pop./sq. km. ●

Areas of rapid growth ⬭

Areas of stagnation or decline ▨

Migration routes ⬅

United States: Internal Migrations

The old industrial East, bordered by the Great Lakes–Washington–Boston triangle, is increasingly being replaced, in terms of resources and soon in terms of population, by the West, especially California and Texas.

Migration movements, both internal and external (coming mainly from Mexico and the Caribbean), are toward the southern and western parts of the country. A gradual movement of the country's center of gravity is thus under way.

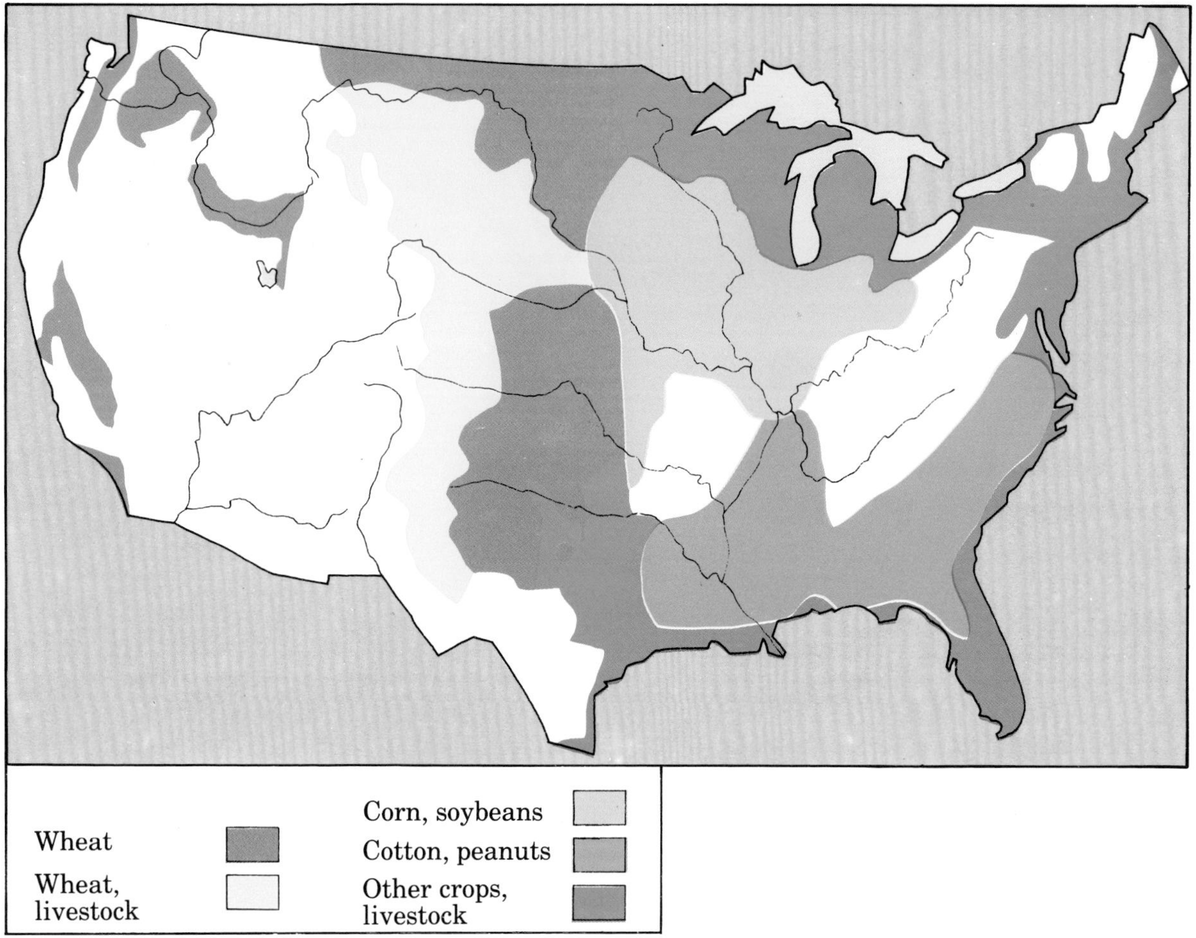

Wheat	▨	Corn, soybeans	▢
Wheat, livestock	▢	Cotton, peanuts	▨
		Other crops, livestock	▨

Main Agricultural Regions

Thanks to a remarkable productivity, the United States is the leading agricultural producer in the world. It is far and away the leading exporter of grains and soybean products.

Soybeans	First in world	53%
Corn (maize)	First in world	41%
Millet-sorghum	First in world	18%
Cotton lint	Second in world	16%
Sunflower	Second in world	11%
Wheat	Third in world	11%
Barley	Third in world	—
Pigs	Third in world	—

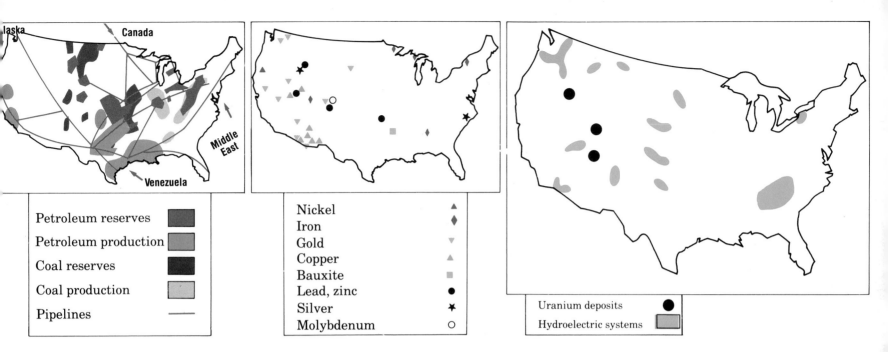

Petroleum reserves
Petroleum production
Coal reserves
Coal production
Pipelines

Nickel ▲
Iron ◆
Gold ▼
Copper ▲
Bauxite ■
Lead, zinc ●
Silver ★
Molybdenum ○

Uranium deposits ●
Hydroelectric systems ■

United States: Resources

With substantial energy and mineral resources, the United States remains the world's leading industrial power.

In leading sectors such as aerospace, aeronautics, and computers, the United States effectively demonstrates its determination to maintain or increase its lead.

Energy Resources

Electricity	First in world	26%
Petroleum	First in world	13.5%
Natural gas	Second in world	24%
Uranium	Second in world	13%
Coal	Third in world	19%

Minerals

Molybdenum	First in world	54%
Phosphates	First in world	—
Silver	Second in world	13%
Copper	Second in world	16%
Gold	Third in world	12%

Industrial Centers

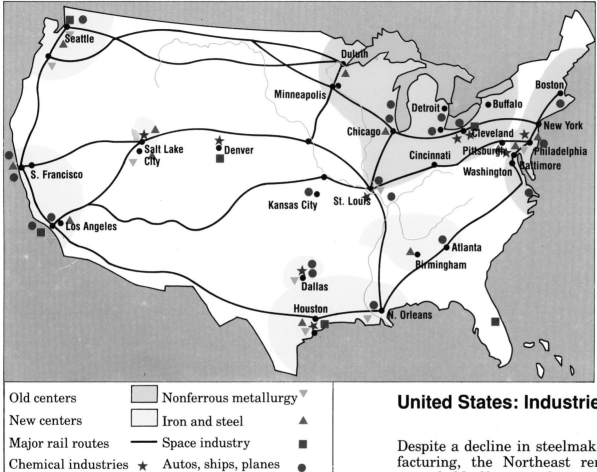

Legend:
- Old centers
- New centers
- Major rail routes
- Chemical industries ★
- Nonferrous metallurgy ▼
- Iron and steel ▲
- Space industry ■
- Autos, ships, planes ●

Information industry: the Northeast, Texas

Map labels: Seattle, Duluth, Minneapolis, Boston, Detroit, Buffalo, Chicago, Cleveland, New York, Cincinnati, Pittsburgh, Philadelphia, Washington, Baltimore, Salt Lake City, Denver, S. Francisco, Kansas City, St. Louis, Los Angeles, Atlanta, Birmingham, Dallas, Houston, N. Orleans

United States: Industries

Despite a decline in steelmaking and vehicle manufacturing, the Northeast remains the traditional stronghold of heavy industry.

The South (particularly Texas), the Pacific coast, and more recently the Rockies (around Salt Lake City and Denver) are undergoing rapid development thanks to new industrial sectors (such as aeronautics and chemicals).

Agricultural Regions

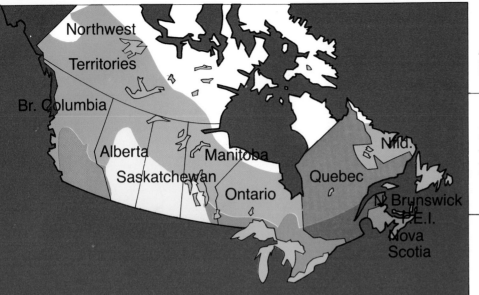

Legend	
Forests	
Various crops, livestock	
Grain regions	

A Rich Subsoil

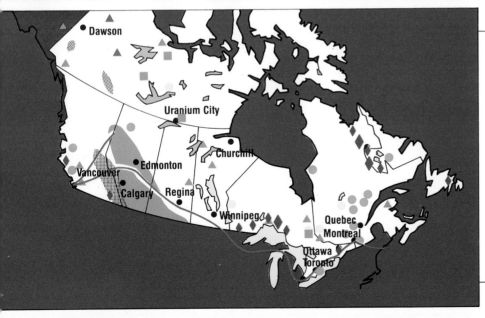

Legend	
Petroleum	
Pipelines	—
Coal	
Iron	♦ ♦
Uranium	■
Copper	▲
Silver	▲
Gold	●
Hydroelectricity	●

Canada: A Federal State

A RESERVOIR OF RESOURCES

Situated between the United States and Alaska, Canada is marked by its vast size, its continental climate with an exceptionally harsh winter, and its very small population. Settlement quite closely follows the line of the border with the United States, although the country also has an Arctic inclination. The economy is largely integrated into the United States market.

Does such a situation encourage the building of a nation? Paradoxically, the particularism of French-speaking Quebec, involving a degree of linguistic and cultural opposition to the United States and Anglo-American hegemony, may contribute to nationhood.

To remain a viable state Canada needs the province of Quebec, even if Quebec has to be granted more sovereignty to achieve that.

Zinc	First in world	17%
Nickel	Second in world	22%
Molybdenum	Second in world	12%
Titanium	Second in world	14%
Uranium	First in world	30%
Natural gas	Third in world	5%

Russia and Its Successors: Historical Expansion

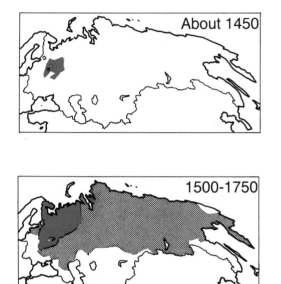

About 1450

1500-1750

1790-1914

Long occupied by the Mongols (thirteenth through fifteenth centuries), Russia underwent two processes: The first, uninterrupted since the sixteenth century, was the conquest of its hinterland, followed by imperial conquests at the expense particularly of the Ottoman and Chinese empires; the other was the pursuit of Europeanization to overcome its backwardness.

If we ignore Leninism and socialist ideology, we see that the Soviet Union retained and increased the imperial heritage in new forms. With the beginning of the five-year plans, it attempted to make up for its industrial backwardness and to develop its military capacities.

In 1948 Finland and Yugoslavia left the Soviet sphere of influence, followed by Albania in 1960.

Expansion from 1938 to 1950

USSR in 1938	
Annexations	
Sphere of Influence	

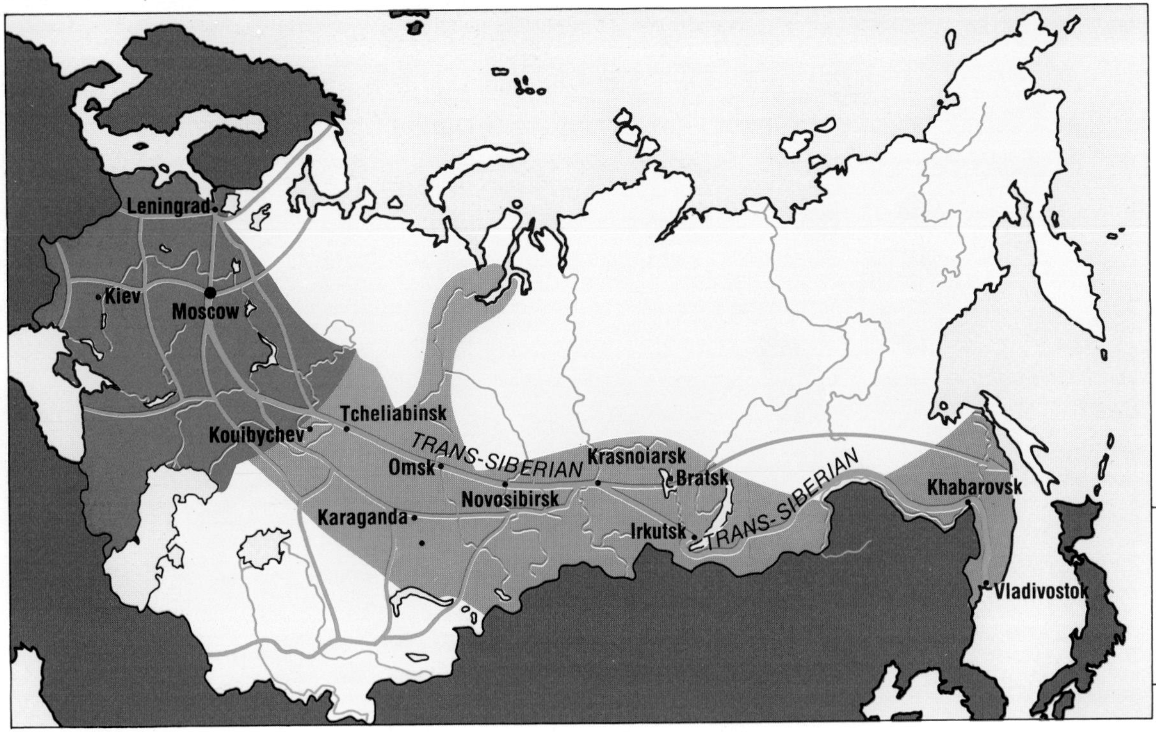

The Conquest of the East

Stages in the occupation of the land

Before 1920
1920-1955
1955-1991
Railways

Expansion of the Slavs in the USSR

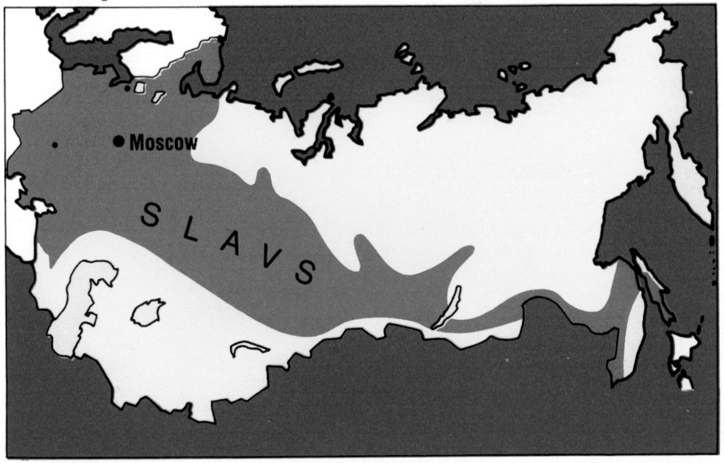

Although tsarist Russia conquered Siberia over the last few centuries and built the first Trans-Siberian railway, significant settlement, the development of communications, and industrialization date from the last five decades. Southern Siberia was settled mostly by Slavs. In this way, despite ideological rivalries, Europe has reached the Pacific. American conquest of its Far West corresponds, making all due allowances, to the Russian conquest of the East.

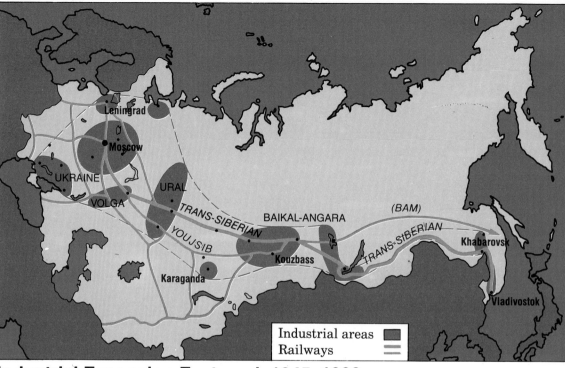

Industrial Expansion Eastward, 1945–1990

Industrial areas ▮
Railways ▬

Soviet Strategic Bases, 1990

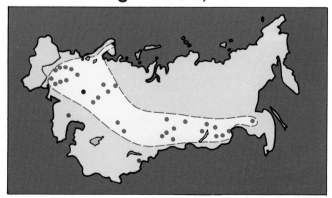

Nuclear sites stretched through Soviet territory along a line that closely followed the area of Slavic settlement.

Kazakhstan, which is the only Muslim republic of the former USSR to have major nuclear and aerospace sites, has a population that is 43 percent Slavic.

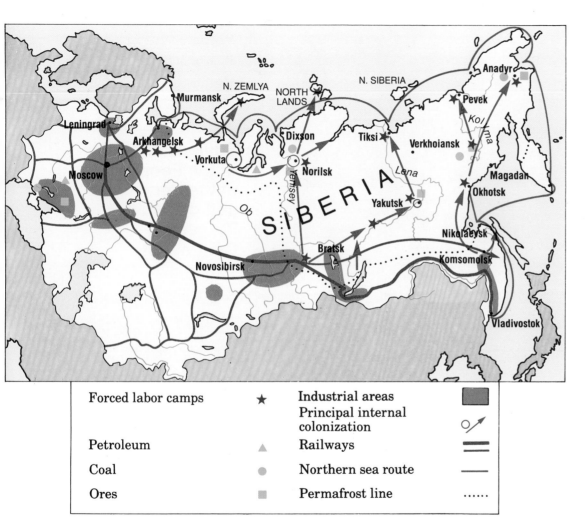

Expansion to the Far North

Moving out from the Trans-Siberian railway, the gradual and arduous conquest of northern Siberia has been carried out along the great rivers (Ob, Yenisey, Lena, Kolyma) and along the main sea route linking the White Sea and Vladivostok through the Arctic Ocean. It is likely that the Siberian camps have played a not insignificant part in the process of opening up the area.

Forced labor camps	★	Industrial areas	▓
		Principal internal colonization	⟋
Petroleum	▲	Railways	══
Coal	●	Northern sea route	—
Ores	■	Permafrost line	......

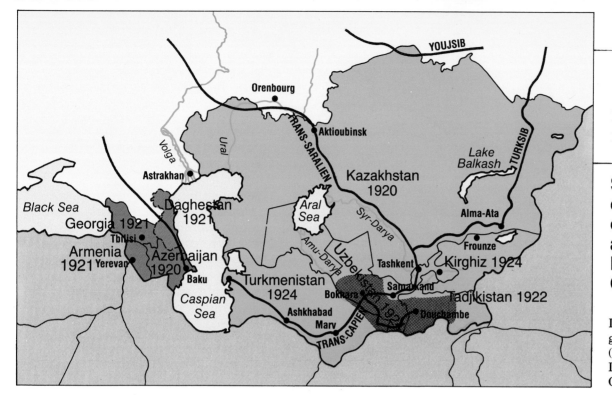

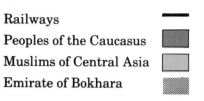

Railways ———
Peoples of the Caucasus ▓
Muslims of Central Asia ▒
Emirate of Bokhara ▒

Sovietization of the Peoples of the Caucasus and the Muslim Peoples of Central Asia

In these regions, some groups were given autonomous status: Cherkesses (1922), Abkhazes (1921), Ossetes (1924), Ingouches (1934), Kara Kalpaks (1925), Ouigours, Adjars, and so on.

From USSR to CIS

Muslim Central Asia and the Islamic part of the Caucasus were conquered during the nineteenth century, often in the face of fierce resistance.

These regions were divided into six republics. This division was established by the Bolshevik government at Stalin's instigation. The Emirate of Bokhara was annexed and divided among several republics in 1920 and was the scene of a prolonged uprising (1920–1928). The nationalities policy sought to differentiate rather than to unify ethnic groups that are relatively homogeneous (only the Tadjiks are not Turkish-speaking).

The alphabet adopted for the transcription of the languages of these republics is Cyrillic (1928). The population growth rate is distinctly higher than that of the Slav groups. The economic growth of these republics has been spectacular, and Uzbekistan has long been held up as a model for the countries of the Middle East.

Georgia and Armenia were sovietized in 1920, after a short-lived independence. These two republics are not Muslim.

The Commonwealth of Independent States (1992)

Latvia
Lithuania
Russia
Belarus
Karelian A.R
Estonia
Moldova
Ukraine
Russia
• Moscow
Chuvash A.R
Mari A.R
Mordvinian A.R
Adygei A.D
Caucasian A.D
Kalmyk A.R
Tatar A.R
Georgia
Armenia
Dagestan A.R
Bashkir A.R
Nakhichevan A.R. (Azer.)
Nagorno-Karabakh A.D.
Azerbaijan
Turkmenistan

Nenets A.D
Komi A.R
Yamalo-Nenets A.D
Khanty-Mansi A.D
Udmurt A.R
Taimyr A.D
Evenki A.D
Yakut A.R
Chukchi A.D
Buriat-Mongol A.R

Kazakhstan
Aral Sea
Uzbekistan
Lake Balkash
Gorno-Altaï A.D
Khakass A.D
Lake Baikal
Tuva A.R
Kyrgyzstan
Tajikistan

A.R.: Autonomous republics
A.D.: Autonomous districts

Republic of Russia, member of CIS

Autonomous republics and districts of the republic of Russia

European republics, members of CIS

Central Asian republics and Azerbaijan, members of CIS

Baltic republics and Georgia, non-members of CIS

In terms of area, the Soviet Union was the largest country in the world (22,000,000 sq. km), with 70% of its population living in the European part on 20% of its area. Today, the republic of Russia is still the largest country in the world despite the fact that the 14 other republics have chosen to be independent.

Along with Russia, ten of these republics are part of a "Commonwealth of Independent States." This group excludes the three Baltic states (Latvia, Lithuania, and Estonia), which are no longer a de facto part of the former USSR, and Georgia, whose future is not yet settled.

Six of the CIS republics are Muslim: Azerbaijan and the five Central Asian states (Uzbekistan, Turkmenistan, Tajikistan, Kyrgyzstan, and Kazakhstan). The Muslim population of the Commonwealth is about 50 million. Kazakhstan, by far the largest of the Central Asian states, is made up of 40% Russians and about 40% Kazakhs, the remaining 20% of the population comprising several minority groups.

Both Turkey and Iran—and to a lesser extent Pakistan—are trying to exert an influence in this area. In the Caucasus, Armenians and Azerbaijanis have been in conflict for more than three years over the question of Nagorny-Karabakh. This territory within Azerbaijan, whose population is about 80% Armenian, has been deprived of its former autonomy by the Azerbaijani government. Peace-keeping forces may be sent into the area as in the case of Yugoslavia.

Georgia has been in a state of unrest for some time, and order will have to be restored there as well. The three Baltic countries are heading toward total independence from the CIS and Russia. Moldova, although it adjoins Romania and has a predominantly Romanian population, may choose not to become part of Romania.

A crucial issue for Russia will be what kind of a relationship it can maintain with Ukraine, Belarus, and to a lesser extent, Kazakhstan, as these countries have Slavic populations and nuclear weapons.

Russia, by far the most populous and largest republic, has enormous potential and considerable problems. But these problems are not ethnic in nature. In fact, the largest territorial minority within Russia (the Tartars) represents only 4% of the total population. About 90% of Russia's population is Russian, making it as ethnically homogeneous as China.

The real problem of the CIS, and of Russia alone, is economic. Whether they will be able to avoid economic collapse and its consequences—social disorder and the rise of a strong ultranationalist or populist regime—will be the essential question in the coming years.

The Transcaucasian Republics and Their Minorities

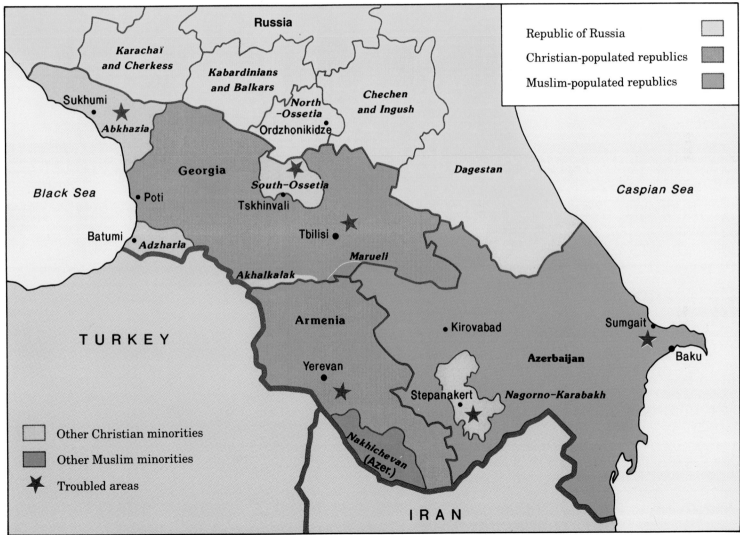

Republic of Russia

Christian-populated republics

Muslim-populated republics

Russia

Karachaï and Cherkess

Kabardinians and Balkars

North -Ossetia

Chechen and Ingush

Sukhumi

Abkhazia

Ordzhonikidze

Dagestan

Georgia

Black Sea

Poti

South-Ossetia

Tskhinvali

Caspian Sea

Batumi

Adzharia

Tbilisi

Marueli

Akhalkalak

TURKEY

Armenia

Kirovabad

Sumgait

Azerbaijan

Baku

Yerevan

Stepanakert

Nagorno-Karabakh

Other Christian minorities

Other Muslim minorities

Troubled areas

Nakhichevan (Azer.)

IRAN

Ukraine and Moldova

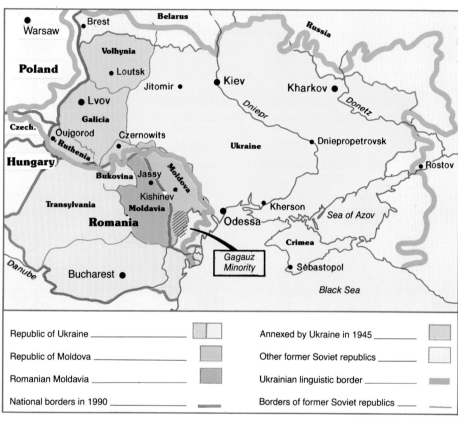

The Baltic States

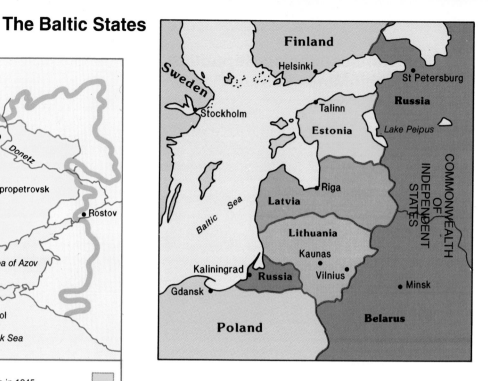

Republic of Ukraine _____

Republic of Moldova _____

Romanian Moldavia _____

National borders in 1990 _____

Annexed by Ukraine in 1945 _____

Other former Soviet republics _____

Ukrainian linguistic border _____

Borders of former Soviet republics _____

Populations of the Republics in the Late 1980's

70% in Europe on 20% of the land area
30% in Asia on 80% of the land area
126 nationalities on 15 republics*:

---

* 126 nationalities were officially recognized. The 15 with over one million inhabitants formed federated Soviet Socialist Republics. Depending on their size—population being the determining factor—the others formed Autonomous Republics (notably the nomadic peoples) or Autonomous Oblasts within the larger republics.

Republic	Population (1000's) (1987)	Holders of republic's official nationality (%) (1989)
Russia	145,311	82.6
Ukraine	51,201	73.6
Belarus	10,078	79.4
Estonia	1,556	64.7
Latvia	2,647	53.7
Lithuania	3,641	80.0
Moldova	4,185	63.9
Georgia	5,266	68.7
Armenia	3,412	96.0
Azerbaijan	6,811	82.2
Kazakhstan	16,244	36.0
Uzbekistan	19,026	68.7
Kyrgyzstan	4,143	47.9
Tajikistan	4,807	58.8
Turkmenistan	3,361	68.4

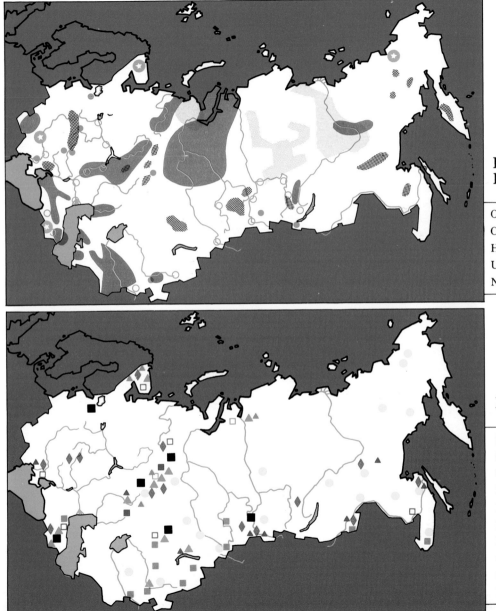

Subsoil of the Commonwealth, the Baltic States, and Georgia

ENERGY RESOURCES

Oil and natural gas	▬
Coal	▦
Hydroelectricity	○
Uranium	●
Nuclear energy	✪

METALS

Platinum	□
Silver	▲
Chrome	■
Manganese	□
Nickel	▲
Lead-Zinc-Tin	▣
Iron	◆
Copper	▲
Gold	●
Bauxite	■

105

Chronology of Main Events—1985–1992

1985 March — Election of Gorbachev to head the Communist Party of the Soviet Union (CPSU).

October — Launching of slogan of *perestroika*.

November — First Gorbachev-Reagan summit in Geneva.

1986 February–March — 27th congress of the CPSU in Moscow.
New USSR line in foreign policy and reassertion of the need for *perestroika*.

April — Nuclear disaster at Chernobyl.

October — Second Gorbachev-Reagan summit in Reykjavik.

December — Nationalist disturbances in Alma-Ata (Kazakhstan).
Return of Andrei Sakharov from Gorki.

1987 February — Freeing of most political prisoners.

July — Demonstration in Moscow by Crimean Tatars collectively exiled by Stalin.

December — Third Gorbachev-Reagan summit in Washington.

1988 January — Signing of INF treaty.
Demonstration in Estonia.

February — Anti-Armenian pogroms in Sumgaït (Azerbaijan) following the demand by the Armenians of Nagorno-Karabakh to join Armenia.

May — Beginning of withdrawal of Soviet troops from Afghanistan.

September — Replacement of Gromyko by Gorbachev as head of state.

October — Congress of Sajudis (nationalists) in Vilnius (Lithuania).

November — Anti-Armenian pogrom in Kirovabad (now Gyandzha) (Azerbaijan).

December — Earthquake in Armenia (55,000 casualties).

1989 March — First multiparty legislative elections in the USSR.

April — Bloody repression by the army in Tbilisi (Georgia).

May — Election of Gorbachev as head of state.

June — Anti-Meskh pogroms in Ferghana (Uzbekistan).

July — Miners' strike in Siberia.

August — Protest in the three Baltic republics to mark the 50th anniversary of the Nazi-Soviet pact.

November — Dismantling of Berlin Wall.

December — Meeting between Gorbachev and Pope John Paul II.
Gorbachev-Bush summit in Malta.
Lithuanian CP's declaration of independence from CPSU.

1990 January — Red Army intervention in Baku (Azerbaijan).

February — Abandonment of CPSU's monopoly by plenum of Central Committee.
Interethnic clashes in Dushanbe (Tajikistan).

March — Lithuania's declaration of independence.
Election of Gorbachev as

	president of the USSR with extensive powers.	
	Estonia's declaration of its sovereignty.	
May	Latvia's declaration of its sovereignty.	
	Election of Boris Yeltsin to head the Russian Supreme Soviet.	
June	Russia's declaration of its sovereignty.	
July	28th congress of the CPSU.	
	Ukraine's declaration of its sovereignty.	
September	Gorbachev-Bush summit in Helsinki devoted to the Gulf crisis (annexation of Kuwait by Iraq).	
October	Adoption of 500-day plan intended to make economic *perestroika* a reality.	
November	Disturbances in Moldova.	
	Georgia's declaration of its sovereignty.	
December	Shipments of food aid from the West to deal with shortages in the USSR.	

1991 January — Repression by the army in Vilnius (Lithuania).

August — Failure of a coup to restore old order.

End of the CPSU and of the Bolshevik Revolution (1917–1991).

Declarations of independence by Estonia and Latvia.

Lithuania's reaffirmation of 1990 declaration of independence.

Recognition of the three Baltic republics by the EEC and the U.S.

Declarations of independence by Ukraine, Belarus, Moldova, Azerbaijan, Uzbekistan, Kyrgyzstan, and Tajikistan.

September/October — Beginning of civil war in Georgia growing out of opposition to President Zviad Gamsakhurdia.

November — Authorization by Russian Congress of People's Deputies for Yeltsin to lift most price controls.

December — Approval by Ukrainian voters of declaration of independence. Russian recognition of Ukrainian independence.

Official abolition of all central government structures of the Soviet Union and proclamation of a new Commonwealth of Independent States, with 11 of the former Soviet republics as members (all but the three Baltic states and Georgia).

Resignation of Gorbachev as president of the Soviet Union.

Agreement to give Russia the USSR's permanent UN Security Council seat.

Official transfer of control of the Soviet nuclear arsenal to Yeltsin.

1992 January — Agreement between Bush and Yeltsin on the limitation and control of nuclear weapons.

February/March — Beginning of Yeltsin's economic reform of most of Russia's light industry and more than 100,000 businesses.

USSR/Middle East

The map on the right shows Soviet aspirations in the region that they had hoped to control through the Nazi–Soviet Pact (1939).

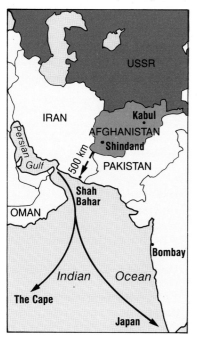

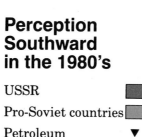

Perception Southward in the 1980's

USSR ■
Pro-Soviet countries ■
Petroleum ▼

Afghanistan, 1979–1987

The Soviet intervention in Afghanistan (December 1979) brought the Soviets to within 500 km. of the Indian Ocean and underlined the vulnerability of a Pakistan already weakened by its Indian rival.

Eight years later the Soviet troops, held in check by Afghan guerrillas, withdrew. This military failure was turned into a diplomatic victory by Mr. Gorbachev for a Soviet Union that was trying to offer a new, more moderate image of itself to the rest of the world.

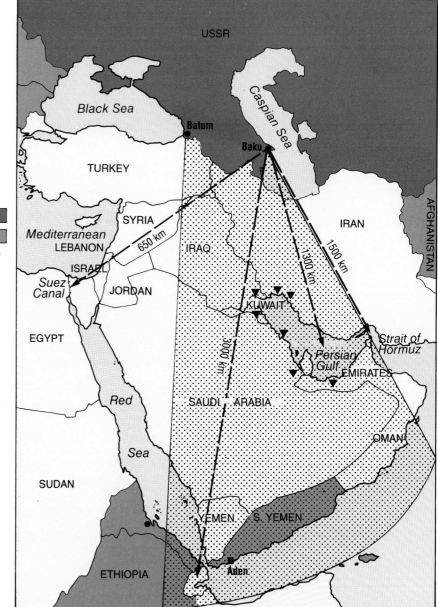

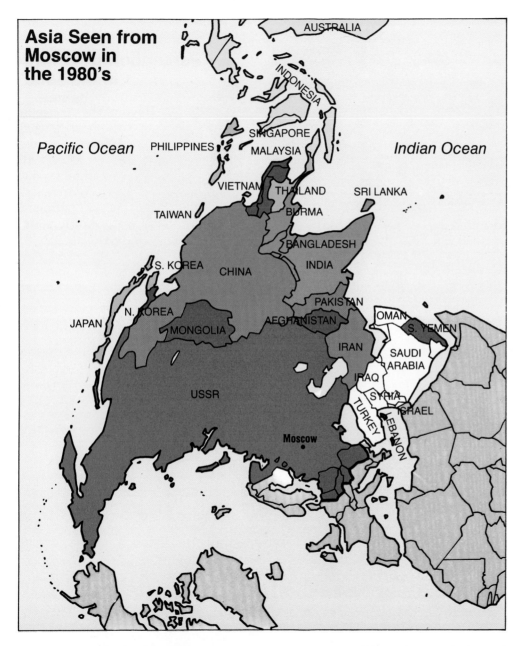

Asia Seen from Moscow in the 1980's

AUSTRALIA

INDONESIA

Pacific Ocean

SINGAPORE

PHILIPPINES

MALAYSIA

Indian Ocean

VIETNAM

THAILAND

SRI LANKA

TAIWAN

BURMA

BANGLADESH

S. KOREA

CHINA

INDIA

JAPAN

N. KOREA

PAKISTAN

MONGOLIA

AFGHANISTAN

OMAN

S. YEMEN

IRAN

SAUDI ARABIA

IRAQ

USSR

SYRIA

ISRAEL

TURKEY

LEBANON

Moscow

For the USSR, whose northern reaches were in the polar region and which had limited access to the open sea, it was vital to have maritime staging areas for its rapidly growing fleet along the peninsular and insular belt of Asia. Geopolitical logic required the Soviet Union to have control of the arc running from the Indian subcontinent to the Horn of Africa.

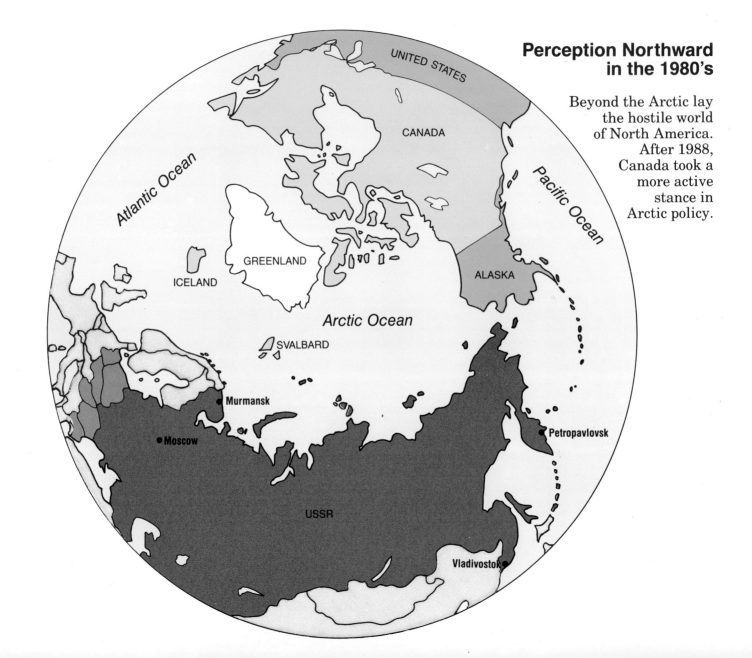

Perception Northward in the 1980's

Beyond the Arctic lay the hostile world of North America. After 1988, Canada took a more active stance in Arctic policy.

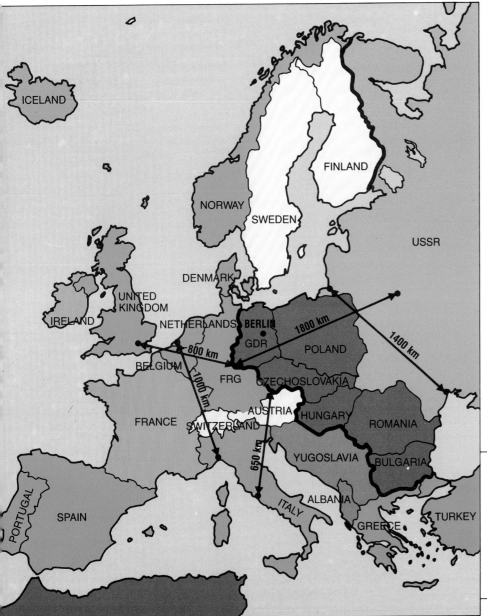

Europe 1966–1989: Two Hostile Blocs of States

Western Europe, the center of the planet until 1918 and the continent on which was played out the future of the world until 1945, is marked today by its political division, its economic power, and its relative military vulnerability.

Whereas the whole of Central Europe fell into the Soviet orbit in 1945, Western Europe, with American support, was able to maintain its overall position. Austria and Finland retained or regained their independence through their neutrality. The only setbacks in the Soviet camp, in Yugoslavia (1948) and Albania (1960), were due not to Western pressure, but to the contradictions engendered by Soviet hegemony, and were made possible by the nationalism and determination of the Yugoslav and Albanian leaders.

Cold War Europe, marked by the division of Germany and the Soviet grip on central and southeastern Europe, came to an end in 1989. Until then the USSR had retained control of its satellites despite some violent crises (Berlin, 1953; Budapest, 1956; Czechoslovakia, 1968; Poland, 1980–1982).

Begun by the Marshall Plan, the recovery of Western Eu-

Iron Curtain	
USSR	
Warsaw Pact	
Other Socialist countries	
Neutral states	
NATO nations	
Western allies	

rope, which between 1945 and 1973 benefited from very favorable world economic conditions, was consolidated around the European Economic Community (the EEC), to which 12 countries have gradually adhered. Despite various proposals, the EEC has led neither to political integration nor to the elaboration of a strictly European common defense within the Atlantic Alliance.

Western Europe, as it is defined in the framework of the EEC—and consequently the middle powers that belong to it—seems to have regional interests articulated around Eurafrica and the Mediterranean basin. Germany, the leading economic power in Western Europe, remains politically determined by its past, the new problems that came with its reunification, and its geographical situation to the east.

For Germany as for France, the Franco-German alliance represents the heart of Europe. For many years France was bogged down in Indochina and Algeria in rearguard wars. After leaving NATO, while remaining a member of the Atlantic Alliance, France acquired nuclear firepower and laid down a strategy of self-protection based on deterrence of the strong by the weak. It is France that, politically and diplomatically, has conceptualized and continues to guarantee the Eurafrican—and Mediterranean—strategy for Europe, guided by a foreign policy laid down by General de Gaulle.

In spite of a distinct decline, the only other nuclear power, the United Kingdom—a latecomer into the Common Market—continues to retain a not insignificant weight in a number of sectors (finance, nuclear power, shipping, oil).

Great Britain, the creator of the first worldwide colonial empire, which laid the basis of the contemporary preeminence of the English language, has also been responsible for a large share of postcolonial conflicts and crises: the Indian subcontinent, the Israeli–Arab conflict, Cyprus, and so on. Great Britain has gradually abandoned most of the strategic positions it held, including the Persian Gulf region, to the benefit of the United States (1971). The Falklands war (1982) demonstrated the political determination of an old European power, its logistical capability, and the high quality of its professional army.

Italy, the fourth great European power, has vigorously industrialized over the last three decades. The longstanding technological backwardness of its southern portion, the Mezzogiorno, is slowly being corrected.

In the north, bordering neutral Finland and Sweden, NATO member Norway has a vulnerable Arctic position opposite what was one of the key zones of the Soviet military system.

Portugal and Spain have been members of the EEC since 1986. The Spanish economy is extremely dynamic. Militarily, the Spaniards want to assume a strategic role from the Canary Islands to the Western Mediterranean. The North/South balance within the EEC has a better equilibrium now that Spain and Portugal have joined the community.

Gibraltar is the only interstate problem (United Kingdom–Spain) remaining in Western Europe.

Europe and the East

Since the end of World War II, Western Europe's security has been guaranteed by the Atlantic Alliance based on the power of the United States. Both the presence of American troops on the European continent and U.S. nuclear capacities have provided physical and psychological security for the Europeans.

In 1989 Mikhail Gorbachev embarked on a foreign policy that enabled the countries of Central Europe to express their political and economic aspirations without having to fear armed repression. The existing regimes collapsed one after the other, leading to the dissolution of the Warsaw Pact.

Reunited Germany alters the outlook in Europe in many ways.

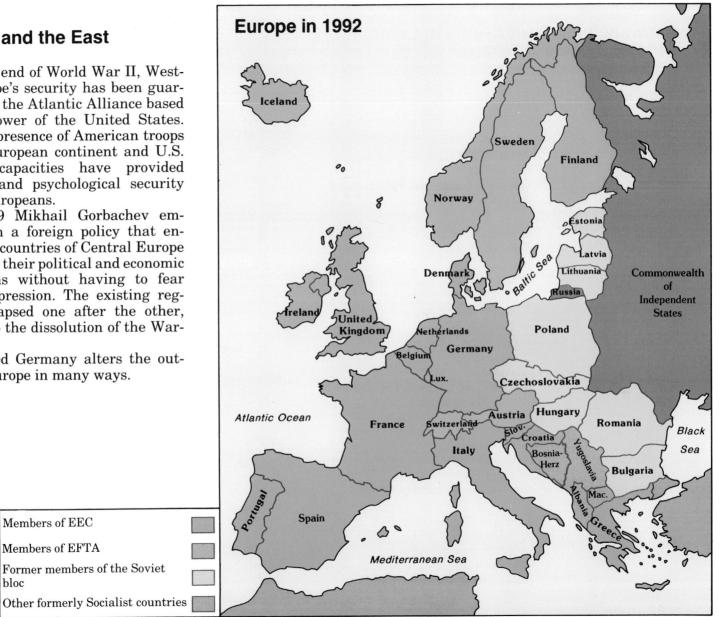

Europe in 1992

Members of EEC

Members of EFTA

Former members of the Soviet bloc

Other formerly Socialist countries

Chronology of Main Events in Central and Southeastern Europe 1985–1990

1985 March	Election of Gorbachev as head of the CPSU. General Jaruzelski Polish head of state.	
1986	Freeing of political prisoners in Poland.	
1987	Third visit of Pope John Paul II to Poland (previous visits in 1979 and 1983).	
1988 March	Opposition demonstration in Budapest.	
April	Wave of strikes in Poland.	
May	Removal of Kadar from leadership of Hungarian CP.	
August	Demonstration in Prague for the 20th anniversary of Soviet intervention.	
October	Demonstration in Prague for the 70th anniversary of Czechoslovakian independence.	
1989 January	Arrest of Vaclav Havel.	
February–April	Talks between government and opposition in Warsaw.	
May	Abolition of Iron Curtain between Hungary and Austria.	

June — Victory of Solidarity in elections in Poland. Rehabilitation and reburial of Imre Nagy in Budapest.

July — Beginning of mass emigration from GDR.

October — Declaration of the Republic of Hungary.

November — Demolition of Berlin Wall. Removal of Todor Zhivkov in Bulgaria. Election of Havel as president of Czechoslovakia.

December — Fall of Ceaucescu in Romania.

1990 March — Victory of Christian Democrats in elections in East Germany.

May — Victory of former Communist Party (led by Ion Iliescu) in elections in Romania.

June — Repression in Bucharest. Bulgarian elections in which CP retains its majority in parliament.

July — Agreement by Gorbachev that reunited Germany can remain in NATO.

October — Reunification of Germany.

December — Lech Walesa elected president of Poland.

Reunified Germany

Serbian republics	
Secessionist republics	
Autonomous and formerly autonomous areas in Serbia	
Serbian minorities	
Hungarian minority in Voivodina	

Yugoslavia

There is nothing surprising about the internal evolution of Yugoslavia. The unstable balance that had put Tito in power depended on both his character and recourse to the role of the Communist Party during the Second World War. But nothing could efface the fact that for centuries the two Catholic republics in the north (Slovenia and Croatia) had been an integral part of the Hapsburg empire whereas those in the south (including Serbia), either Orthodox or with a large Muslim minority in the case of Bosnia-Herzegovina, had been an integral part of the Ottoman empire.

The last four decades had only accentuated the economic gap between Slovenia, particularly, and Croatia and most of the southern republics. Finally, two further factors entered into the situation: the hate-ridden rivalry which had pitted the (right-wing) Croatian nationalists against the Serbs since the Second World War, and the ultranationalism used by the Communist Slobodan Milosevic and transformed into a Greater Serbia populist movement.

The exaltation of Greater Serbian feelings is not something new. This shift was already discernible as soon as the status of autonomy of the Albanians in Kossovo was suppressed and recourse to force was the sole means of managing the crisis in this region symbolically dear to the Serbs (Kossovo was the great lost battle against the Ottomans in the fourteenth century). Greater Serbia does indeed seem to be the goal sought if one follows the operations being conducted by the Serbian forces—the bulk of the federal army being made up of Serbs or Montenegrins—in Croatia: systematic occupation of the southern Dalmatian coast northward and the Croatian regions in the southeast.

As for the West, whether the United States or Europe, what stands out most, in both the Yugoslav crisis and the Baltic one, is less its pusillanimity—the status quo is always more comfortable for those used to it—than its complete absence of intellectual preparation for any event that goes outside the patterns established in the postwar period. It is not a matter of favoring the endless fragmentation of existing states. But that a historic upheaval should bring back to the surface a whole series of frozen but still existing conflicts is in no way surprising.

For a long time the West had believed that Serbia was trying to keep the federation together, while in fact Serbian ultranationalism was seen as a threat not only by the Albanians of Kossovo, the Slovenes, and the Croats, but also by the Hungarian minority of Voivodina and by almost all the non-Serbian elements of Yugoslavia except the Montenegrins.

In October 1991, the Yugoslav army (composed mostly of Serbs since other minorities, particularly Croats, defected), attacked the city of Dubrovnik. In November, Serbia rejected the EEC peace proposal that had been accepted by Yugoslavia's other republics. The EEC imposed economic sanctions on Yugoslavia; meanwhile, Croatian forces were defeated in Vukovar. The UN tried several times to impose an agreement, but it was repeatedly broken by Serbia. In January 1992, the EEC finally recognized Yugoslavia's two breakaway republics of Slovenia and Croatia as independent states.

A UN peace-keeping force is in place in Yugoslavia; however, Bosnia-Herzegovina and Macedonia also began to head toward independence through a process of violence.

Central Europe and Its Economic Perspectives

Western Europe (EEC)

Economic areas favored by their proximity to the EEC

Other areas of Central Europe

Sweden

Stockholm

St. Petersburg

Estonia

Russia

Latvia

Denmark

Copenhagen

Baltic Sea

Lithuania

Russia

Hamburg

Gdansk

Byelorussia

Netherlands

Germany

Berlin

Poland

Warsaw

Brussels

Dusseldorf

Lodz

Belgium

Leipzig

Dresden

Kiev

Lux.

Frankfurt

Wroclaw

Paris

Prague

Cracow

Ukraine

France

Munich

Ostrava

Czechoslovakia

Vienna

Moldova

Zurich

Austria

Switzerland

Budapest

Romania

Slovenia

Hungary

Galati

Milan

Zagreb

Ploesti

Croatia

Belgrade

Bucharest

Italy

Bosnia

Serbia

Adriatic Sea

Sarajevo

Black Sea

Yugoslavia

Sofia

Rome

Bulgaria

Istanbul

Macedonia

Albania

Greece

Turkey

COMMONWEALTH OF INDEPENDENT STATES

Major industrial areas

Major economic centers   Zagreb

117

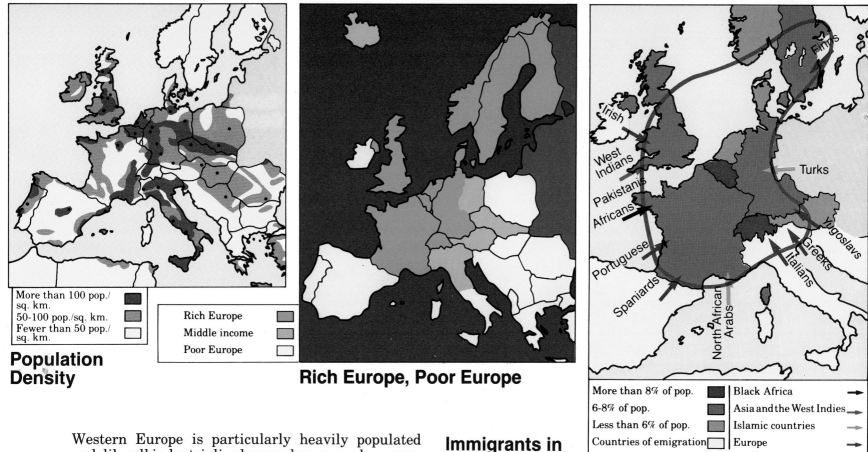

Population Density

More than 100 pop./sq. km.

50-100 pop./sq. km.

Fewer than 50 pop./sq. km.

Rich Europe, Poor Europe

Rich Europe

Middle income

Poor Europe

Immigrants in Western Europe

More than 8% of pop.

6-8% of pop.

Less than 6% of pop.

Countries of emigration

Black Africa

Asia and the West Indies

Islamic countries

Europe

Immigration zone

Finns

Irish

West Indians

Pakistanis

Africans

Portuguese

Spaniards

North African Arabs

Turks

Yugoslavs

Greeks

Italians

Western Europe is particularly heavily populated and, like all industrialized areas, has a very low population growth rate.

Europe, like the United States and the Persian Gulf countries, is a magnet for migrant workers (about 11 million). The percentage of migrants hovers around 7.5 for France, West Germany, the United Kingdom, and Belgium; 6 percent for Austria; 5 percent for Sweden; 4 percent for the Netherlands; 1.5 percent for Denmark; 17 percent for Switzerland; and over 30 percent for Luxembourg.

A source of hard currency for their home countries, the immigrant workers constitute a pool of cheap labor for the host countries; they pose a special political problem in times of economic crisis. Their integration corrects the relative demographic stagnation of the industrialized countries.

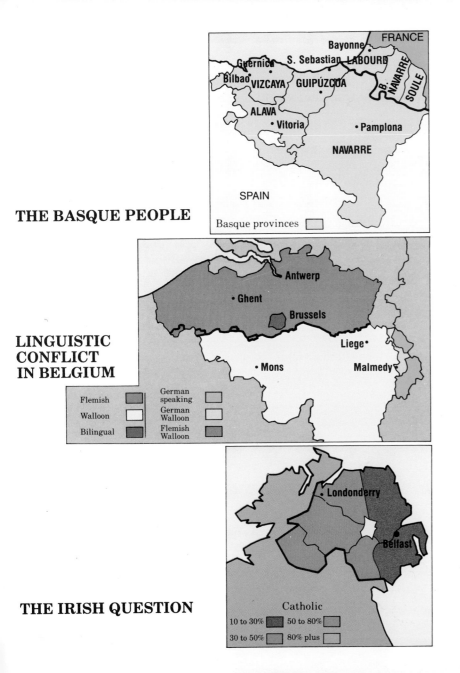

THE BASQUE PEOPLE

LINGUISTIC CONFLICT IN BELGIUM

Flemish		German speaking	
Walloon		German Walloon	
Bilingual		Flemish Walloon	

THE IRISH QUESTION

Catholic

10 to 30%		50 to 80%	
30 to 50%		80% plus	

Minority Problems

Caught between the idea of the nation-state and the idea of human rights, both born of the Enlightenment, and both of which mark the emergence of individual rights as well as modern nationalism, the rights of minorities (particularly ethnic ones) have been largely neglected. It is often a crucial problem in Third World countries, but minorities in Europe, including those in the liberal democratic countries, have suffered or still suffer more or less overt oppression or pressure for assimilation. In Central Europe: Hungarians in Transylvania (Romania); Albanians in Yugoslavia; Turks in Bulgaria. In Western Europe: Irish Catholics in Ulster; Catalans and Basques in Spain; and, in a more specific way, the Flemish-Walloon conflict (originating in Walloon predominance until recently) in Belgium.

These more or less conflict-laden situations, often the result of pressures toward centralism, are generally resolved by either autonomy or federalism.

Unlike ethnic difficulties elsewhere, in Western Europe minorities are internal problems that do not precipitate destabilizing interference from other states.

Importance of the EEC

GNP per capita	$9,700 in 1988
Share of gross world product	28%
Population per vehicle	3.5
Share of world output	
Wheat	12.3%
Sugar beets	32.5%
Wine	62%
Milk products	24.2%
Nuclear electricity	31.4%
Cars	38.6%
Steel	17%
Shipbuilding	12.9%
Synthetic textiles	17.1%
Container fleet	= 25% of traffic

Source: *Images économiques du Monde 88*, SEDES

External trade in 1986 (billion ECUs)

	EEC	USA	Japan
Imports	334	387	126
Exports	342	217	209

Unlike its European neighbors, France is one of the leading world exporters of grain. Europe's livestock is considerable. Agribusiness is developing rapidly, and, in a world context, agriculture remains one of Europe's best assets.

The EEC is the world's second largest industrial power—and the leading one in manufacturing—just behind the United States. West Germany alone produces almost half of most of the industrial goods manufactured by the 12 member states. Since the end of World War II, Europe's weakness in energy and mineral resources has continued to grow and constitutes—as it does for Japan, but to a lesser extent—a serious handicap.

European Economic Community

SWITZERLAND
AUSTRIA
YUGOSLAVIA

ICELAND

NORWAY SWEDEN FINLAND

TURKEY

MALTA
TUNISIA
MOROCCO

CYPRUS SYRIA
ISRAEL IRAQ AFGHANISTAN
JORDAN IRAN

ALGERIA LIBYA EGYPT

UNITED ARAB EMIRATES

SAUDI ARABIA OMAN

CAPE VERDE

MAURITANIA MALI NIGER CHAD SUDAN YEMEN

DJIBOUTI

SENEGAL
GAMBIA
GUINEA BISSAU
GUINEA
SIERRA LEONE
LIBERIA
BURKINA FASO
BENIN
IVORY COAST
GHANA
TOGO
NIGERIA
CAMEROON
CENTRAL AFRICAN REP.
ETHIOPIA

S. TOME
EQUAT. GUINEA
GABON
CONGO
ZAIRE
RWANDA
BURUNDI
UGANDA
KENYA
SOMALIA
TANZANIA

Atlantic Ocean

COMOROS

ANGOLA ZAMBIA MALAWI MOZAMBIQUE

MAURITIUS
RÉUNION

MADAGASCAR

Indian Ocean

NAMIBIA ZIMBABWE BOTSWANA

SWAZILAND
SOUTH AFRICA LESOTHO

European Economic Community
Other Western nations
Lomé Convention
Arab–Islamic World

Geopolitical and Geostrategic Aspects of Western Europe

The geopolitical and strategic area of western Europe includes the Mediterranean basin and the Gulf as well as subsaharan Africa. This situation determines policy towards Arab states and Iran. All states south of the Sahara, with the exception of South Africa, are members of the Lome Convention of 1979. With the aid of this convention, the EEC initiated a system of regulations stabilizing exports from its traditional base of activity in Africa, and accepted tariff-free market access for most products exported by its African associates. Several Caribbean and Pacific states also signed the convention.

The military buildup in several states over the last decade has caused a proliferation of missiles in the eastern Mediterranean and the Middle East as a response to perceived security threats. Equally threatening are problems of demographics and South-North migration, and the degradation of economic and social conditions in subsaharan Africa.

Africa

Sub-Saharan Africa had remained largely outside East-West confrontations until 1975, but after the withdrawal of Portugal and the radicalization of Ethiopia (1977), it ceased to be a Western preserve. Until that date, the major strategic issues in the Third World had been fought out along the peninsular belt that stretches from the eastern Mediterranean to the Far East. The USSR had made its presence felt in Egypt, Guinea, Zaire, Sudan, and Somalia, though generally without much success: withdrawal from Egypt, failure in Zaire, cool relations with Guinea, withdrawal from Sudan, expulsion from Somalia. The end of Portuguese colonialism created a vacuum that the USSR boldly exploited in concert with Cuba, and that created a new situation militarily, in both Angola and Ethiopia, in the 1970's and 1980's.

Southern Africa has an important role to play in terms of access to raw materials essential to the West and to Japan. South Africa is the only regional power there.

At the end of three decades of independence, the balance sheet in terms of development in sub-Saharan Africa is meager. The conditions typical of most African states are decline or stagnation of agriculture, and economic stagnation for the vast majority that lack a raw materials export base.

Contrary to the desires of the Organization of African Unity, all the inter-African associations launched over the last twenty years have collapsed. Even the principle of the inviolability of frontiers, which had been respected over quite a long period, has been broken over the last few years by sovereign states: the Somali-Ethiopian war over the Ogaden; annexation attempts by Libya in Chad.

With an average rate of population increase of over 2.5 percent, projections give the following growth: 220 million in 1950, 350 million in 1970, and over 800 million in 2000.

To handicaps of recent origin, such as Balkanization, monoculture, economies geared to serve outside needs, and heavy cultural dependence, must be added others with deeper roots: ethnic divisions and antagonisms; low levels of social stratification, and low levels of productive forces.

Africa south of the Sahara is marked by weak states and virtually nonexistent nations.

It seems unlikely that there will be any major changes in the short term in the continuation of Western, and particularly European, influence in Africa. Given the inability of the USSR to give any aid other than military aid, Soviet advances were countered in Southern Africa by the action of South Africa and the United States. Mozambique was the first to abandon Marxism-Leninism. The withdrawal of Cuban troops from Angola in 1990, linked to the independence of Namibia, considerably reduced tensions in the region while South Africa was speeding up its transition.

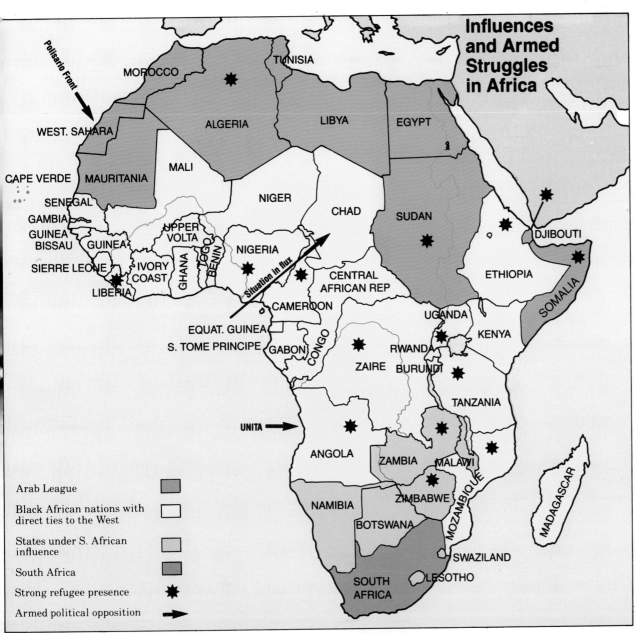

Influences and Armed Struggles in Africa

Polisario Front

MOROCCO
TUNISIA
WEST. SAHARA
ALGERIA
LIBYA
EGYPT
CAPE VERDE
MAURITANIA
MALI
NIGER
CHAD
SUDAN
SENEGAL
GAMBIA
GUINEA BISSAU
GUINEA
UPPER VOLTA
NIGERIA
DJIBOUTI
SIERRE LEONE
IVORY COAST
GHANA
TOGO
BENIN
Situation in flux
CENTRAL AFRICAN REP
ETHIOPIA
SOMALIA
LIBERIA
CAMEROON
EQUAT. GUINEA
S. TOME PRINCIPE
GABON
CONGO
ZAIRE
RWANDA
BURUNDI
UGANDA
KENYA
UNITA
ANGOLA
ZAMBIA
MALAWI
TANZANIA
NAMIBIA
ZIMBABWE
MOZAMBIQUE
BOTSWANA
MADAGASCAR
SWAZILAND
SOUTH AFRICA
LESOTHO

Arab League

Black African nations with direct ties to the West

States under S. African influence

South Africa

Strong refugee presence

Armed political opposition

Polisario: Popular Front for the Liberation of Saguia El-Hamra and Rio de Oro
UNITA: Union for the Total Independence of Angola
ANC: African National Congress (Pan African Congress—P.A.C.—and Azanian People's Organization—AZAPO—are also active)
SWAPO: South West African People's Organization
EPLF: Eritrean Popular Liberation Front
TPLF: Tigrean Popular Liberation Front
SPAL: Sudanese People's Army of Liberation

123

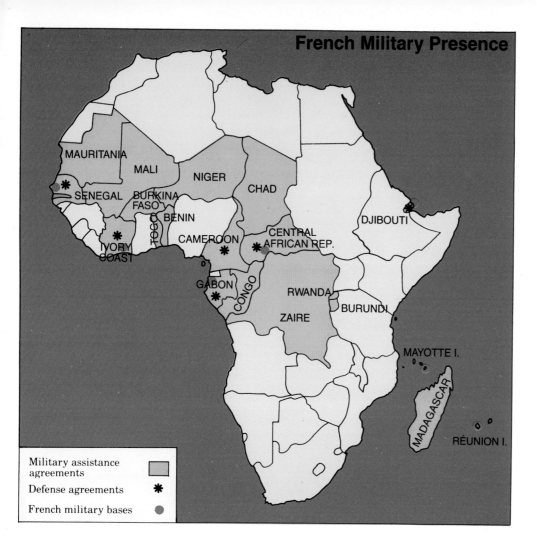

French Military Presence

MAURITANIA

MALI

NIGER

CHAD

SENEGAL

BURKINA FASO

BENIN

IVORY COAST

CAMEROON

CENTRAL AFRICAN REP.

DJIBOUTI

GABON

CONGO

RWANDA

ZAIRE

BURUNDI

MAYOTTE I.

MADAGASCAR

RÉUNION I.

Military assistance agreements

Defense agreements ✳

French military bases ●

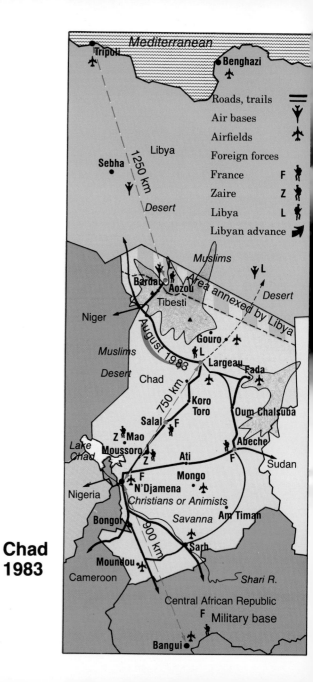

Mediterranean

Tripoli

Benghazi

Roads, trails

Air bases

Airfields

Foreign forces

France — F

Zaire — Z

Libya — L

Libyan advance

Libya

Sebha

1250 km

Muslims

Desert

Bardai

Aozou

Tibesti

Area annexed by Libya

Niger

Desert

L

Muslims

Gouro

L

Desert

Chad

Largeau

Fada

August 1983

750 km

Koro Toro

Oum Chalouba

Salal

F

Z Mao

Abeche

Moussoro

Z

Ati

F

Lake Chad

Mongo

Sudan

Nigeria

N'Djamena

Christians or Animists

F

Bongor

Savanna

Am Timan

900 km

Sarh

Moundou

Cameroon

Shari R.

Central African Republic

F Military base

Bangui

Chad 1983

The Vulnerability of Africa
The Military Dimensions of the French Presence in Africa

France has defense agreements with several African countries—Djibouti, Gabon, Ivory Coast, Senegal, Cameroon, Central African Republic, and Togo—and military technical assistance agreements with these same countries, plus Mauritania, Niger, Burkina Faso, Benin, Congo, Madagascar, Mali, Burundi, Rwanda, and Zaire.

Agreements on joint military maneuvers are in force with Djibouti, Gabon, Ivory Coast, Senegal, Togo, and Zaire. The total number of French military advisers in Africa is close to a thousand (the largest missions are in Djibouti, Gabon, Zaire, and the Ivory Coast). There are about 7,000 troops stationed on the continent, including 3,500 in Djibouti, 1,200 in Senegal, and 1,100 in the Central African Republic. French troops have intervened several times in Africa, notably: Gabon (1964), Chad (1968–1980), Mauritania (1977–1978, air support against the Polisario), Djibouti (1976–1977), Zaire (1977–1978), and Central African Republic (1979).

At the present time, the major strategic bases in Africa are Dakar, Gabon, Central African Republic, Djibouti, and Réunion Island.

France has a 47,000-man rapid intervention force stationed on its territory, with logistical support that has undergone continuous improvement since 1978 (the Shaba operation in Zaire). It may be that this force is currently able to intervene more rapidly than that of other powers, including the USA.

In twenty years, French positions in Africa have suffered little erosion. In various ways, France supplies annual aid totaling nearly a billion dollars. The policy of cooperation formulated by General de Gaulle has basically continued up to the present day. These alliances, based on political, economic, and cultural interests (most are with former colonies), have been shaped over several decades by the governing elites and France and seem likely to endure.

There are about 200,000 French technical assistants in "French-speaking" Africa. In these countries, as in other African countries, France is a major arms exporter.

As for religion, the importance of Islam in northern and central Africa is great and spreading. In the southern half, Christianity is widespread. There are also numerous animists.

The states of tropical Africa are marked by religious diversity, ethnic fragmentation, and weak political structures. Except for Nigeria and Ethiopia, the states are underpopulated. These special characteristics favor ethnically based strategies, attempts at destabilization, and interventions by troops from outside the continent. Tropical Africa remains highly vulnerable.

Southern Africa

Southern Africa is the richest part of the continent. After fifteen years of conflicts (proclamation of Marxist-Leninist regimes in Angola and Mozambique; Soviet support for these regimes and a massive Cuban military presence in Angola, precipitating active hostility from apartheid South Africa in support of UNITA [Angola] and RENAMO [Mozambique] so as to weaken the USSR's allies), the situation today in Southern Africa is undergoing marked improvement. The Cubans have withdrawn from Angola and the South Africans from Namibia, which became independent in 1990.

Relieved of their East-West dimension, regional conflicts are returning to their local one: the government in Luanda vs. Jonas Savimbi's UNITA, the government in Maputo vs. RENAMO. Talks with a view to eventual negotiated solutions are under way, while Angola and Mozambique have abandoned their previous political orientations.

South Africa's strength lies in its military and industrial power as well as in its de facto alliance with the West, given, inter alia, its strategic location and its mineral resources. Since 1973, thanks to NATO equipment, South Africa has possessed at Simonstown a Silvermine detection network capable of reaching Australia and South America. South Africa's power has also fed on the military and economic weakness of its opponents. The front-line states (Tanzania, Botswana, Zambia, Mozambique, and Angola) have hardly had the means to alter the status quo. Despite a declared hostility, South Africa's commercial ties with many African states (Kenya, Zaire, Malawi, etc.) have been significant all through the crisis.

Apartheid, an unjustifiable system, strengthened the hand of Pretoria's opponents and undermined its diplomatic position, especially after the disturbances of 1984–1986. The demographic weakness of the white minority (15 percent) remains the Achilles' heel of the system, as that minority becomes proportionally smaller each year. Pretoria's racial strategy consisted in trying to win over the nonblack minorities (Indians, Malays, Coloreds) while keeping the blacks out. But the disturbances of 1984–1986 altered the situation both domestically and internationally. Despite divisions and dissensions, blacks in the major urban centers (Johannesburg-Pretoria, Durban, Port Elizabeth, and Cape Town), especially the youth and trade unionists, altered the psychological situation in South Africa. International public opinion became increasingly aware of apartheid. In South Africa the basic problem is that of black political rights.

In 1989–1990, with the coming to power of de Klerk, the political situation gradually shifted: Nelson Mandela was freed, the African National Congress (ANC) was unbanned, and talks to speed up the transition got under way. Interethnic clashes, notably between Zulus belonging to the Inkatha movement and ANC militants, further complicated an already complicated situation in which white extremists are using violence to delay a process that is irreversible.

South Africa

Chromium	First in world	36%
Platinum	First in world	69%
Gold	First in world	33%
Vanadium	First in world	30%
Manganese	Second in world	15%
Titanium	Second in world	15%
Diamonds	Third in world	10%
Uranium	Fourth in world	8%

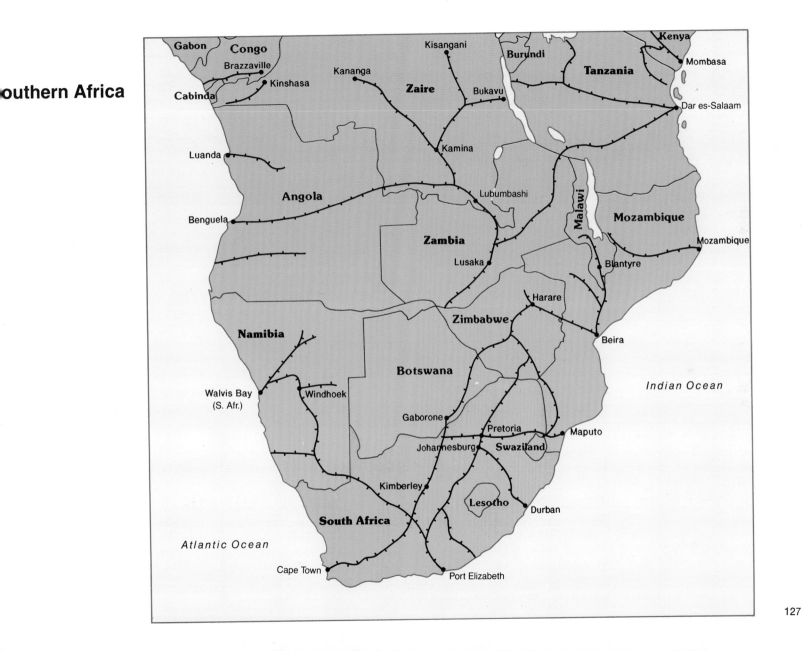

outhern Africa

Gabon

Congo

Brazzaville

Cabinda

Kinshasa

Kisangani

Kananga

Burundi

Zaire

Bukavu

Kenya

Mombasa

Tanzania

Dar es-Salaam

Luanda

Kamina

Angola

Lubumbashi

Malawi

Mozambique

Benguela

Zambia

Mozambique

Lusaka

Blantyre

Harare

Namibia

Zimbabwe

Beira

Botswana

Indian Ocean

Walvis Bay
(S. Afr.)

Windhoek

Gaborone

Pretoria

Maputo

Johannesburg

Swaziland

Kimberley

Lesotho

Durban

South Africa

Atlantic Ocean

Cape Town

Port Elizabeth

127

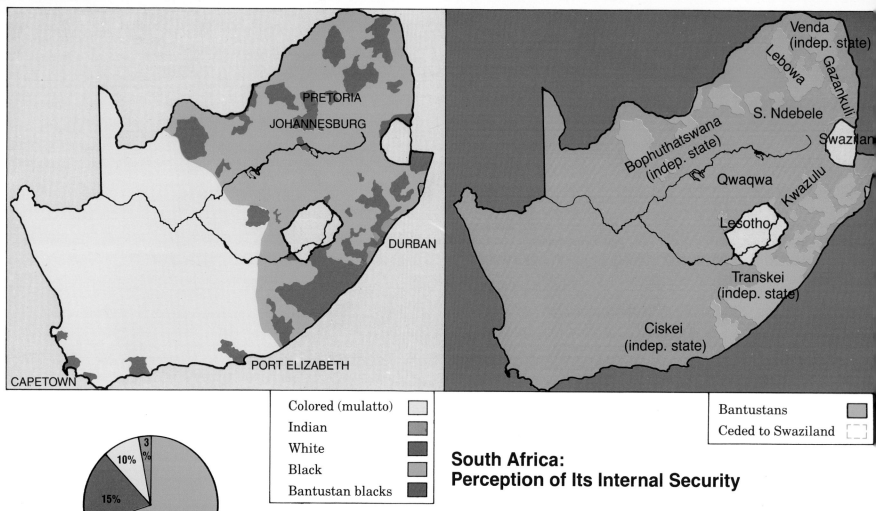

Colored (mulatto)
Indian
White
Black
Bantustan blacks

Bantustans
Ceded to Swaziland

3%
10%
15%
72%

PRETORIA
JOHANNESBURG
DURBAN
PORT ELIZABETH
CAPETOWN

Venda (indep. state)
Lebowa
Gazankuli
S. Ndebele
Swaziland
Bophuthatswana (indep. state)
Qwaqwa
Kwazulu
Lesotho
Transkei (indep. state)
Ciskei (indep. state)

South Africa:
Perception of Its Internal Security

The policy of Bantustans, gradually renamed independent states, consists in turning about half the black population into foreigners in their own country. In Cape Province (the western part), there are few blacks. Ciskei, Transkei, Bophuthatswana, and Venda are considered to be "independent states" by South Africa.

The area of the independent states and other black homelands is not even 15 percent of the country.

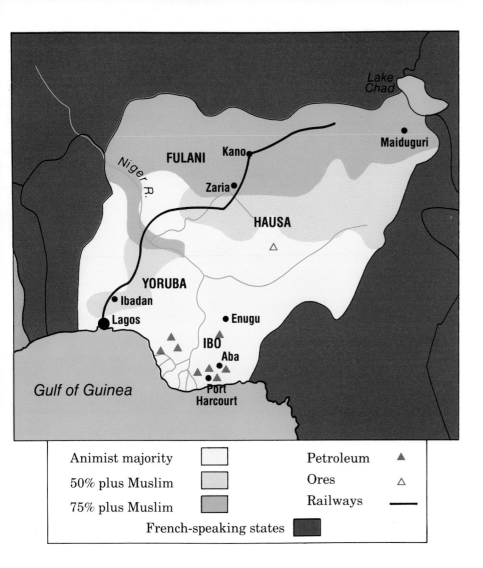

Animist majority
50% plus Muslim
75% plus Muslim
French-speaking states
Petroleum
Ores
Railways

Nigeria: A Regional Power in Tropical Africa

Nigeria is the only state that can aspire to be a regional power in tropical Africa, and it is also the most populous country in Africa (about 90 million inhabitants).

The republic's federal system seeks to resolve the ethnic and religious problems that were largely responsible for the attempted Biafran secession (1967–1970).

With its large oil resources, Nigeria saw real growth in the 1970s, which enabled it to play a continent-wide political role. The direct impact of Nigeria on its neighbors is partly hampered by the fact that they are French-speaking. The relatively rapid end of the oil boom has brought Nigeria, like all the populous oil states, back to its former difficulties, as was shown by the expulsion of 2 million foreign immigrant workers to neighboring countries in 1983.

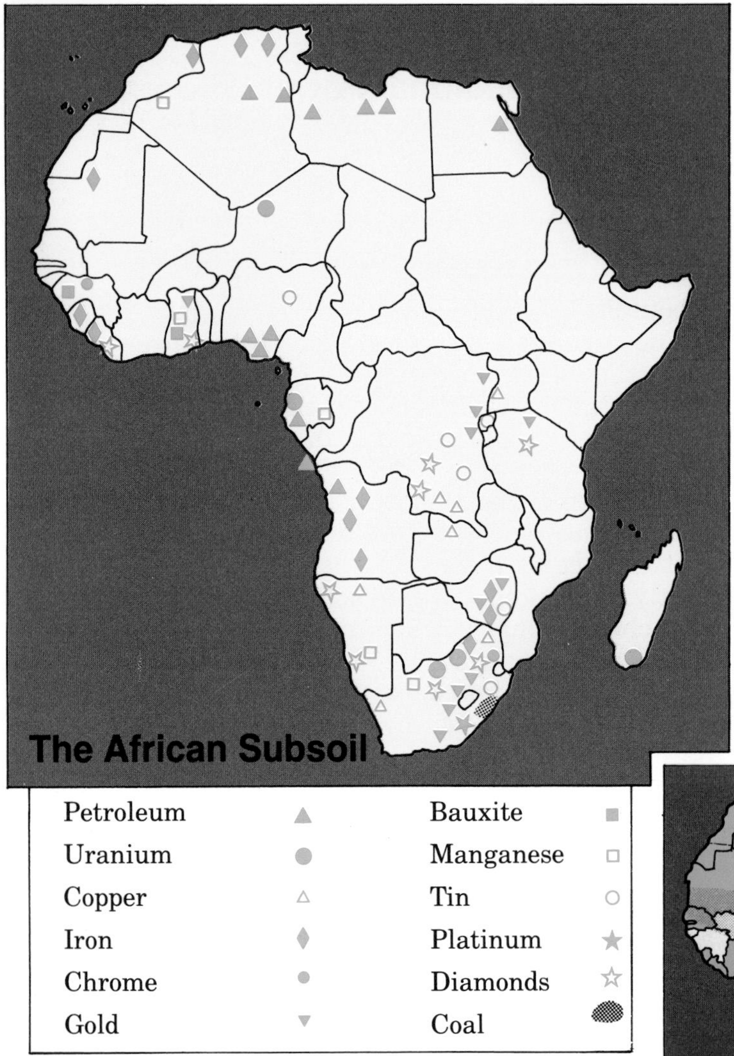

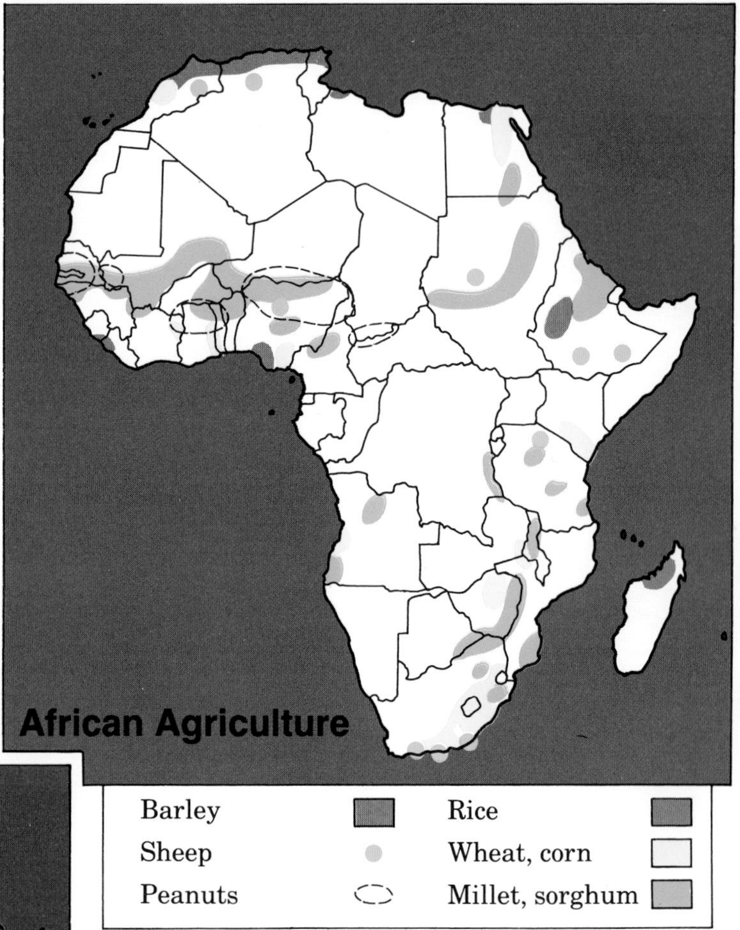

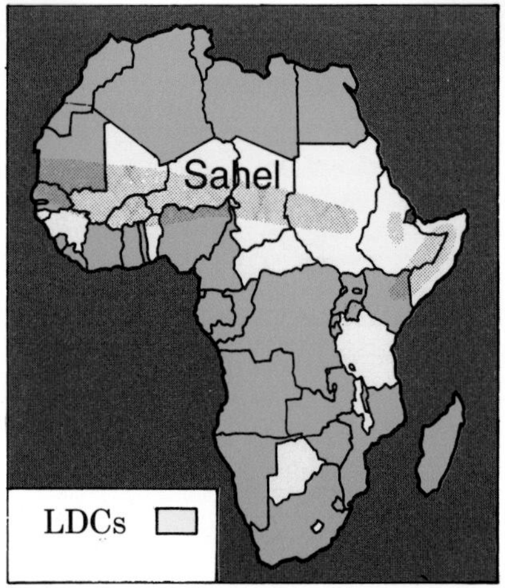

The African Subsoil

Petroleum	▲	Bauxite	■
Uranium	●	Manganese	□
Copper	△	Tin	○
Iron	◆	Platinum	★
Chrome	●	Diamonds	☆
Gold	▼	Coal	▨

African Agriculture

Barley	▨	Rice	▨
Sheep	●	Wheat, corn	▨
Peanuts	⬯	Millet, sorghum	▨

Sahel

LDCs ▢

The Least Developed Countries

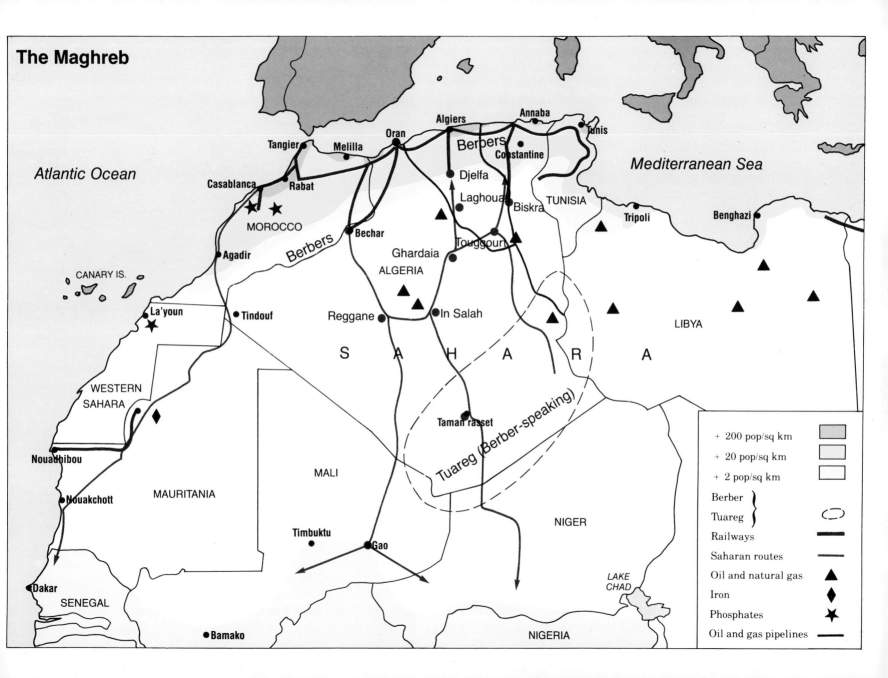

The Maghreb

Atlantic Ocean

Mediterranean Sea

Tangier
Melilla
Oran
Algiers
Annaba
Tunis
Berbers
Constantine
Casablanca
Rabat
Djelfa
MOROCCO
Laghouat
Biskra
TUNISIA
Tripoli
Benghazi
Agadir
Berbers
Bechar
Ghardaia
Touggourt
ALGERIA
CANARY IS.
La'youn
Tindouf
Reggane
In Salah
LIBYA
WESTERN
SAHARA
S A H A R A
Nouadhibou
Tamanrasset
Tuareg (Berber-speaking)
Nouakchott
MALI
MAURITANIA
NIGER
Timbuktu
Gao
LAKE
CHAD
Dakar
SENEGAL
Bamako
NIGERIA

+ 200 pop/sq km	▨
+ 20 pop/sq km	▨
+ 2 pop/sq km	☐

Berber }
Tuareg } ⬭

Railways ▬▬
Saharan routes ──
Oil and natural gas ▲
Iron ◆
Phosphates ★
Oil and gas pipelines ▬

The Maghreb extends, geographically, from Mauritania to Libya. It is peopled by Arab Berbers and has more than 50 million inhabitants, most of whom are concentrated in the coastal strip or on the slopes of the Atlas Mountains. After southern Africa, it is the richest region in Africa (oil and gas, phosphates, iron).

Maghreb unity, although an oft-proclaimed goal, remains in the realm of the hypothetical, and has been dominated for the last two decades by the rivalry between Morocco and Algeria, further fueled by the conflict in and over Western Sahara. One of the issues at stake in this conflict is dominance in the Maghreb. Morocco would win a virtual monopoly on the world supply of phosphates (outside the USA and the CIS); Algeria would obtain indirect access to the Atlantic and at the same time finally destroy Moroccan dreams of a "Greater Morocco."

Western Sahara (256,000 sq. km.) has the distinction of being the only decolonized African territory (in addition to Eritrea) not to have gained independence automatically. The Polisario Front, set up in 1973, first fought Spanish colonialism. In 1975, basing itself on what it asserted were its historical rights, Morocco occupied two-thirds of the then Spanish Sahara, from which Madrid had just withdrawn. Mauritania occupied a third of the country (1975–1979), and then gave it up. Heavily supported by Algeria, the Polisario carried on an effective guerrilla war (1976–1982), and won recognition, thanks to Algeria, from a large number of members of the OAU as the representative of the Saharan Arab Democratic Republic. (Neither the USA nor the USSR recognized the SADR.)

In 1988 Morocco and Algeria renewed their diplomatic relationship, while the Polisario declared that it wanted to go on with its fight—one which is becoming

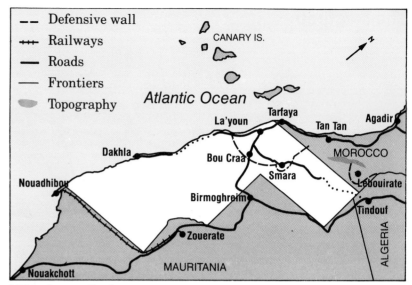

Western Sahara

The erection of a wall (1979) marking off the useful part of the country has turned out to be militarily effective. Since then, four more walls have been erected, covering most of the country.

more and more difficult. There is no military solution to the situation and negotiations are inevitable at some point.

Also in 1988, the five North African states signed an agreement that was intended to be the beginnings of a common market. With the riots in Algiers (1988) followed by harsh repression, attention turned to the rise of Islamic fundamentalism, which appears difficult to eradicate despite the efforts of various political formations recently allowed to express themselves.

Libya, a rich oil state that is very underpopulated, lacks the manpower to fulfill the ambitions of Colonel Qadafi.

The Arab Middle East

As an intermediate zone between Europe, Asia, and black Africa, the Arab world enjoys the advantage of being situated on major transport routes, but it also suffers the vulnerability this gives rise to. Since World War II the strategic and economic importance of this vital area has been continuously at the center of world tensions.

The creation of Israel (1948), a consequence of modern nationalism, anti-Semitism, and the genocide of the Jews, led to Arab rejection of European interference. From 1967, Palestinian nationalism has made its presence felt and raises not only the refugee problem, but also that of the necessity for a separate state.

The Arab world, confronted by an industrialized Israeli nation that possesses a modern army and is supported by the USA, has been mobilized and inspired around slogans of unity and demands for a Palestinian state.

The Arab countries, whose political autonomy was limited until 1952 and even until 1958, progressively built up their strength until, from 1973 onward, they became an economic and financial factor in the world balance of power. Militarily, the neutralization of Egypt (1978) gave a decisive boost to Israeli superiority.

Israel, obsessed with security and enjoying military superiority, has annexed the Golan Heights (which belonged to Syria) and, by multiplying its settlements, demonstrated its determination to retain the West Bank (Judea and Samaria). The number of Palestinians under Israeli jurisdiction is about 2 million (of whom 1.4 million are in the occupied territories), as against 3 million Jewish Israelis.

The "Intifada," the expression of the refusal of the Palestinian population of the West Bank and Gaza to remain under Israeli occupation, began in the autumn of 1987 and has continued ever since. Israel's standing in Western public opinion is not helped by it. The Palestinian national question remains a major source of conflict in the Middle East.

The Arab world has vast mineral resources: more than 50 percent of world oil reserves and 25 percent of gas reserves, a third of the world's phosphate, and an abundance of several vital minerals. The agricultural sector remains weak. Above all, too few concerted efforts seem to have been made to take maximum advantage of the financial resources at its disposal to lay the foundations for real agricultural and industrial development.

Islam, "religion and way of life," proclaims itself to be a social and cultural fact defining every aspect of behavior. It is interpreted today not only as a religion, but also as a national value. Only rarely is it not the state religion. National values have often been given pride of place when modern Arab nationalism has asserted itself. In periods of crisis like today, fundamentalism exercises a growing influence.

Religious sects continue to evoke strong feelings of belonging. In Syria, for example, state power is tightly controlled by the Alawite minority, in Iraq by the Arab Sunni minority.

Baathist Syria, rival of the no less Baathist Iraq, has failed to bring to fruition its plans for a Greater

Syria that would bring Lebanon and Jordan into its orbit, but it was able to improve its positions in Lebanon at the time of the Gulf crisis (1990) and it continues to control part of the Palestinian movement.

Despite the efforts by the Soviets in the past, the United States has succeeded in retaining its predominance in the region. It remains for the United States to reconcile, to the extent possible, the divergent aspirations on the Palestinian problem or the status of Jerusalem, on the one hand of its Israeli ally, on the other of its Arab allies and, first and foremost, Saudi Arabia.

Islam and Religious Sects in the Middle East

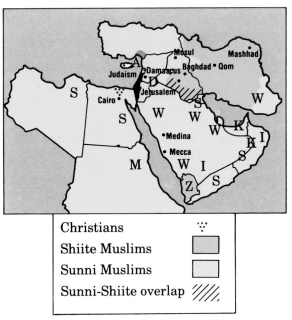

Christians ⋮

Shiite Muslims ▨

Sunni Muslims ☐

Sunni-Shiite overlap ▨

Muslim Sects

Wahhabites (W)

Alawites (A)

Druse (D)

Zaidites (Z)

Sanoussis (S)

Mahadis (M)

Ismailis (I)

Kharijites (K)

The League of Arab Nations: Created in 1945, it comprises all 21 Arab states except Western Sahara (formerly Spanish). It includes one non-Arab state, Somalia. The PLO (Palestinian Liberation Organization) is, in fact, an equal member. Many economic associations reinforce cooperation.

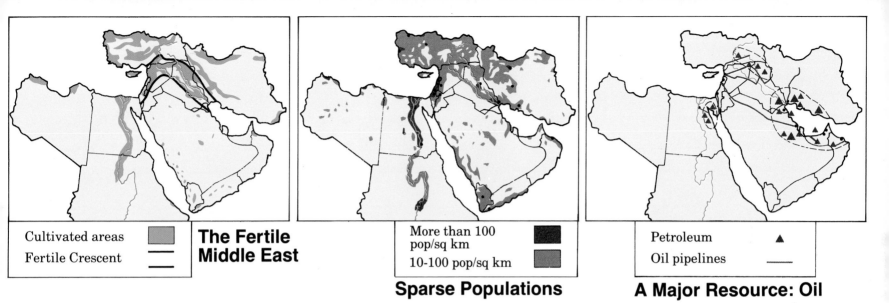

The Fertile Middle East

Cultivated areas ▮

Fertile Crescent ──

Sparse Populations

More than 100 pop/sq km ▮

10-100 pop/sq km ▮

A Major Resource: Oil

Petroleum ▲

Oil pipelines ──

Land and Water	Percentage of Land Under Cultivation	Percentage of Cultivated Land Irrigated
Iran	14	20
Turkey	34	7
Israel	20	40
Saudi Arabia	1	80
Egypt	2.5	100
Iraq	18	50
Libya	2	9
Syria	35	10
Lebanon	27	20
Jordan	11	7
Yemen	7	10
South Yemen	1	80
Kuwait	1	100
United Arab Emirates	5	100
Oman	1	—
Mean	11	24

Petrolium Production

	(% of world total)
Saudi Arabia	8.8
United Arab Emirates	3.0
Kuwait	3.0
Iran	4.6
Iraq	4.5
Qatar	0.7
Oman	1.0
Bahrain	—
Total	25.6

Petroleum reserves: over 60% of world total

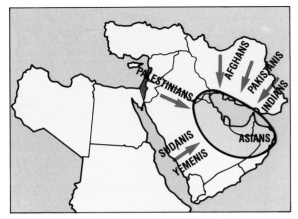

Immigration into the Gulf

Thanks to various means of fuel conservation and substitution, the West has succeeded, in ten years, in reducing its oil consumption by about 25 percent.

Oil production had to be progressively reduced after 1979–1980. In 1983, oil prices fell. Over the decade 1973 to 1983, the percentage of oil coming from the Gulf was 30 percent for the USA, 60 percent for Western Europe, and 70 percent for Japan.

Population of the Arabian Peninsula in the 1980's (millions)

Saudi Arabia	14.5
Yemen	10.5
Kuwait	1.7
Oman	1.5
UAE	1.5
Bahrain	0.5
Qatar	0.4
Total	30.6

Foreign Skilled Personnel and Labor in the Arab Gulf States in the 1980's

	Total Employed	Foreign Employed	%
Saudi Arabia	2,384,000	1,300,000	57
Bahrain	60,000	30,000	50
Emirates	300,000	239,000	80
Kuwait	304,000	211,000	75
Oman	350,000	70,000	20
Qatar	86,000	54,000	80

Origins

Yemenis, Palestinians, Egyptians, Jordanians } 75%

Pakistanis, Indians, Other Asian countries } 25%

The Arabian Peninsula is the most vulnerable region in the Gulf. Five states combined (including those grouped in the United Arab Emirates) do not have more than 6 million inhabitants. It was essentially to guarantee the stability of Saudi Arabia and these five states that the American Rapid Deployment Force was set up. Part of this force can be deployed from Diego Garcia (3,700 km. from the Gulf), with facilities at the air and naval bases at Masirah (Oman), Berbera (Somalia), and Mombasa (Kenya).

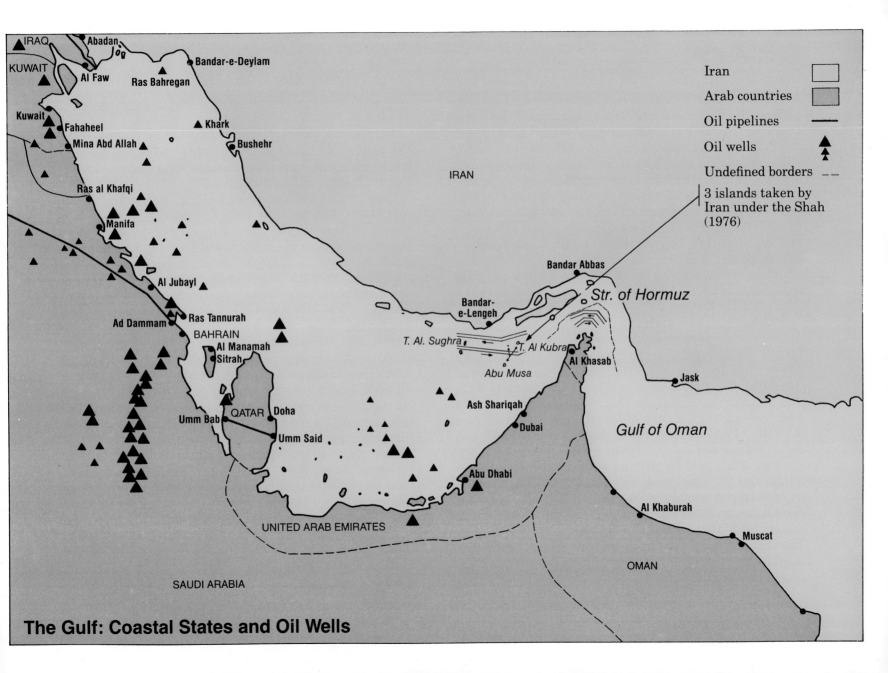

The Gulf: Coastal States and Oil Wells

IRAQ
Abadan
KUWAIT
Al Faw
Ras Bahregan
Bandar-e-Deylam
Kuwait
Fahaheel
Khark
Mina Abd Allah
Bushehr
Ras al Khafqi
IRAN
Manifa
Al Jubayl
Ad Dammam
Ras Tannurah
BAHRAIN
Al Manamah
Sitrah
Umm Bab
QATAR
Doha
Umm Said
UNITED ARAB EMIRATES
SAUDI ARABIA
Bandar Abbas
Str. of Hormuz
Bandar-
e-Lengeh
T. Al. Sughra
T. Al Kubra
Al Khasab
Jask
Abu Musa
Ash Shariqah
Dubai
Gulf of Oman
Abu Dhabi
Al Khaburah
Muscat
OMAN

Iran
Arab countries
Oil pipelines
Oil wells
Undefined borders
3 islands taken by
Iran under the Shah
(1976)

Saudi Arabia

In November 1973, Saudi Arabia reduced its oil output by 30 percent and soon after quadrupled the price. In a year, its GNP rose 250 percent. Since 1974, Saudi Arabia's position, which had already been rising after 1967, has become preeminent. During the previous decade, the Wahhabite kingdom, founded on fundamentalist Islam and enduring tribal structures, had been mainly preoccupied in foiling attempted revolutions deriving from Middle East socialism and Nasserism in particular. Egypt's defeat in 1967, then Sadat's rise to power and the break with the USSR (1972), which it encouraged, enabled Saudi Arabia to go on the offensive as leader of the conservative forces in the Arab Middle East.

Although it has increased its capabilities, particularly its air power (air base at Tabuk, not far from Israel), Saudi Arabia remains a second-rank military power. The leaders of a kingdom that is underpopulated (about 14 million inhabitants), fabulously rich, and sharply stratified, in the middle of an unstable and coveted region, are obsessed with security and stability. Political control is highly centralized and tight, reinforced by the peculiar harshness of Wahhabism. The royal family (which is very large) incarnates the regime, and fears both any significant change in the world market that might precipitate a depression, and the effects of rapid modernization in a society built on traditional religious and tribal values. The occupation of the Great Mosque in Mecca in 1979 was a sign of the relative fragility of the regime. The proportion of immigrant labor is high, although it is split into various ethnic groups and is frequently rotated.

Externally, the Soviet presence in the Red Sea and the pro-Soviet revolutionary center in South Yemen were perceived as serious threats. The southern frontier is strategically vulnerable.

Saudi Arabia is too weak militarily to influence its neighbors, but uses its vast financial resources as a means of foreign policy. Its aid, very large in volume, is used to ensure the stability of friendly neighboring Arab regimes, to help the Arab states generally (in their struggle with Israel among other things), to combat vigorously any Communist influence, and to encourage Muslim states throughout the world (including those of Africa and Southeast Asia) to strengthen the place of Islam in state and society. More ambitiously, Saudi Arabia is attempting as much as possible to maintain the stability of the world market, hence its moderating role in OPEC. In this respect, alliance with the USA is seen as vital, and the interests of the two states converge (except over Israel). In a period when dangers are increasing everywhere, internal, regional, and world stability is at the center of Saudi preoccupations. Saudi Arabia helped Iraq in its war against Iran. Missiles bought from China with a range of over 2,000 miles add a new dimension to the regional equilibrium.

The Iraqi intervention in Kuwait (1990) highlighted the role of Saudi Arabia as an ally of the United States during the Gulf crisis and war (1991).

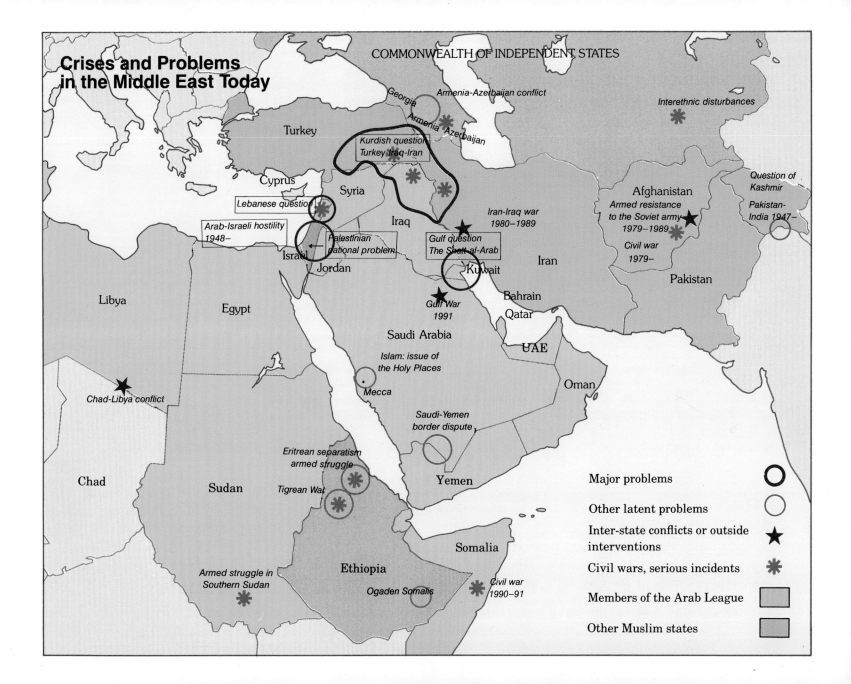

Crises and Problems in the Middle East Today

COMMONWEALTH OF INDEPENDENT STATES

Armenia-Azerbaijan conflict

Interethnic disturbances

Georgia

Armenia

Azerbaijan

Turkey

Kurdish question
Turkey-Iraq-Iran

Cyprus

Syria

Iraq

*Iran-Iraq war
1980–1989*

Afghanistan

*Armed resistance
to the Soviet army
1979–1989*

*Question of
Kashmir*

*Pakistan-
India 1947–*

Lebanese question

Arab-Israeli hostility
1948–

Palestinian
national problem

Gulf question
The Shatt-al-Arab

Israel

Jordan

Kuwait

Iran

*Civil war
1979–*

Pakistan

*Gulf War
1991*

Bahrain

Qatar

Libya

Egypt

Saudi Arabia

UAE

*Islam: issue of
the Holy Places*

Oman

• Mecca

Chad-Libya conflict

*Saudi-Yemen
border dispute*

Chad

Sudan

*Eritrean separatism
armed struggle*

Tigrean War

Yemen

*Armed struggle in
Southern Sudan*

Somalia

Ethiopia

Ogaden Somalis

*Civil war
1990–91*

Major problems ⬭

Other latent problems ○

Inter-state conflicts or outside
interventions ★

Civil wars, serious incidents ✳

Members of the Arab League ▭

Other Muslim states ▭

THE SHATT-AL-ARAB (1991)

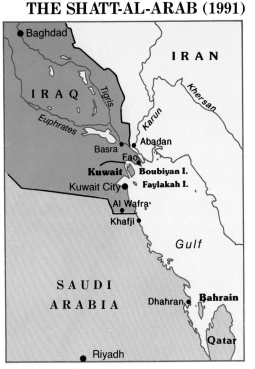

The Gulf and above all the control of the Shatt-al-Arab have been at stake between Iran and Iraq.

Egypt

Egypt is the center of the Arab world: It is the most populous Arab state—one third of all Arabs are Egyptians—and it is also the most ancient and most homogeneous nation in the Arab world, with the largest agricultural population in the Middle East. In spite of very limited resources, Egypt remains, be-

COLONIAL EGYPT

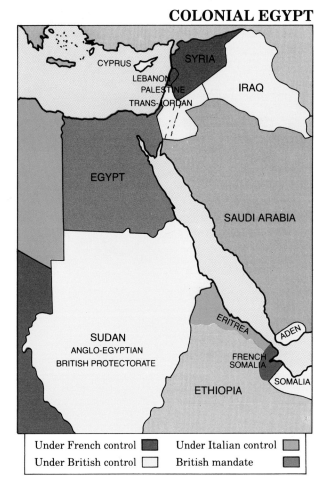

| Under French control ⬛ | Under Italian control ◩ |
| Under British control ☐ | British mandate ⬛ |

EGYPT UNDER NASSER

| Members UAR ⬛ | Suez conflict → |
| Other Arab states ☐ | Lebanon (US interv.) → |

EGYPT'S GEOPOLITICAL LOGIC

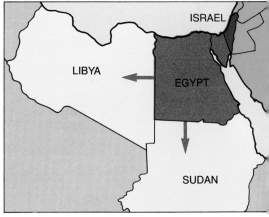

cause of its population, a key factor in the Middle Eastern balance.

In Nasser's time, attempts at Arab unity brought Egypt and Syria together in the United Arab Republic (1958–1961), which in 1963 added Iraq and Yemen. These alliances were short-lived.

Considering its regional geopolitical interests rather than the utopia of pan-Arabism, Egypt should logically direct its efforts in the direction of Sudan (with its fertile, underpopulated lands) and Libya, rich in oil and very sparsely populated.

Today, since the conclusion of the peace treaty (1978) that enabled Egypt to regain Sinai (1982), Cairo has taken up a neutral position in possible future Arab–Israeli conflicts. The American alliance and Saudi aid seem unlikely to resolve the crisis of Egyptian society (in part a demographic one), any more than Nasserite "socialism" did before them. Geopolitical ambitions could in future appear as a solution, if the regional situation allows it.

After some years of isolation, Egypt, partly because of the threat of Iran, has been reintegrated into the official Arab world. The most worrying issues are social and economic in origin, and tensions may become very acute. Egypt enjoys significant American aid and aligned itself with the United States following the Iraqi intervention in Kuwait.

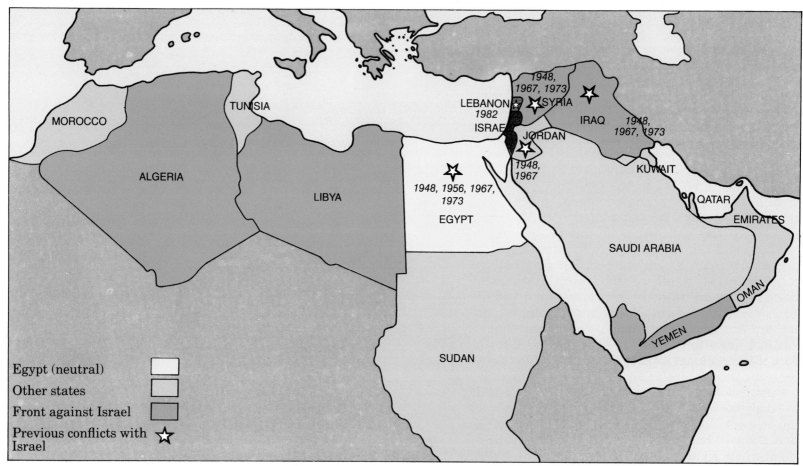

Israel and the Arab World

The agreement among some Arab countries never to recognize Israel, set up in December 1977, includes: Algeria, Libya, Syria, Yemen, Iraq, and the PLO.*

According to UNRRA, there are 2.2 million Palestinian refugees (1988). The Palestinian diaspora is estimated to number 2.4 million.

Jordan	1,050,000
Lebanon	490,000
Syria	290,000
Kuwait	230,000

*Iraq's participation in the 1967 and 1973 wars was limited.

142

Palestine 1947
Jewish Settlements

Tel Aviv
Jaffa
Amman
Beersheba

Jewish State 1947
UN Plan

Tel Aviv
Jaffa
Jerusalem
Amman
Beersheba

Israel 1949

Damascus
Kesar Blum
Haifa
Tel Aviv
Amman
Beersheba
Elat

Israel after 1967
and Occupied
Territories

Haifa
Golan
Tel Aviv
Jerusalem
Gaza
Beersheba
Sinai
Elat

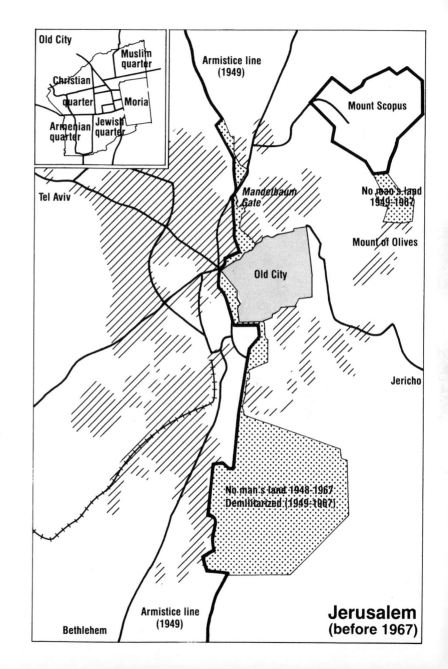

Old City

Muslim quarter
Christian quarter
Moria
Armenian quarter
Jewish quarter

Armistice line (1949)

Mount Scopus

No man's land 1949-1967

Mount of Olives

Mandelbaum Gate

Tel Aviv

Old City

Jericho

No man's land 1948-1967
Demilitarized (1949-1967)

Armistice line (1949)

Bethlehem

Jerusalem
(before 1967)

The existence of the state of Israel (created in 1948 by the United Nations and recognized by, among others, the U.S. and U.S.S.R.), was militantly opposed by the neighboring Arab states (Syria, Egypt, Iraq, Jordan). The Zionist colonization was felt to be a European interference.

The war waged by the Arab states in 1949 was won by Israel, which increased its territory, and created the problem of the Palestinian refugees (about 900,000 at that time). Israel, obsessed with its security, joined the Anglo-French Suez expedition against Egypt after the nationalization of the Canal (1956). In 1967 the Six Days' War gave Israel the control of the Sinai Peninsula (progressively returned to Egypt between 1978 and 1982 after the Camp David agreements through which Egypt had agreed on peace and the recognition of Israel), the Golan Heights (annexed), the West Bank, and the Gaza Strip. The West Bank had been integrated into Jordan in 1949 by the Hashemite dynasty, and Gaza had been under Egyptian administration from 1948 to 1967.

After the defeat of the Arab states in 1967, the Palestine Liberation Organization (P.L.O.), until then without much support, started to organize itself, particularly around Fatah, led by Yasser Arafat. The Palestinian organizations have never been able to go beyond the stage of hit-and-run operations and have used terrorism as a substitute for guerrilla warfare. In September 1970 the Palestinian organizations, which had become a state within a state in Jordan, were crushed by the troops of King Hussein.

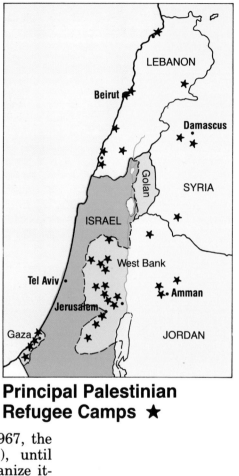

Principal Palestinian Refugee Camps ★

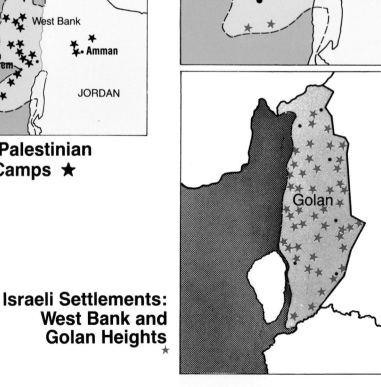

Israeli Settlements: West Bank and Golan Heights ★

144

Lebanon: Evolution of the Situation, 1982–1983

In 1973 the surprise war waged by Egypt led to an Israeli victory on the battlefield. When Egypt made the decision to regain the Sinai Peninsula in exchange for peace and the recognition of Israel in 1977, it faced the hostility of many Arab countries, including Iraq, Syria, Libya, South Yemen, and Algeria.

The Palestinian organizations were hit by the Syrian troops in Lebanon in 1976 and again faced a difficult situation in 1982 during the Israeli intervention there.

In the meantime, the number of Israeli settlements in the occupied territories grew steadily. Since the beginning of the Palestinian uprisings in the occupied territories (September 1988), the situation has become more complex, and the Israeli public —as well as its politicians—are divided on which path to take. What is at stake seems to be the very nature of Israeli democracy: how can it remain a Jewish state if its Palestinian population's growth is faster? How can it remain a democratic state if Palestinians do not have the same rights as Jews?

After the removal of Palestinian organizations from Jordan (September 1970), most Palestinian forces regrouped in Lebanon, militarily the weakest state in the region. Their presence broke the fragile Lebanese communal and political balance. Civil war broke out in 1975 and allowed Syria to intervene (1976), fatally weakening Lebanese sovereignty, which rapidly disintegrated into various spheres of influence. Internal confrontations resulted in de facto partitions.

Israeli intervention (1982) as far as Beirut altered the relations of force inside the country by mandating the withdrawal of PLO forces. The sovereignty of the Lebanese state for the time being is purely nominal, and antagonisms are still very much alive. The laborious negotiations on the withdrawal of Israeli troops from Lebanon enable the much more important problem for Israel—the status of the West Bank and the future of its settlements—to be postponed. Meanwhile, the Syrian grip is becoming tighter and tighter.

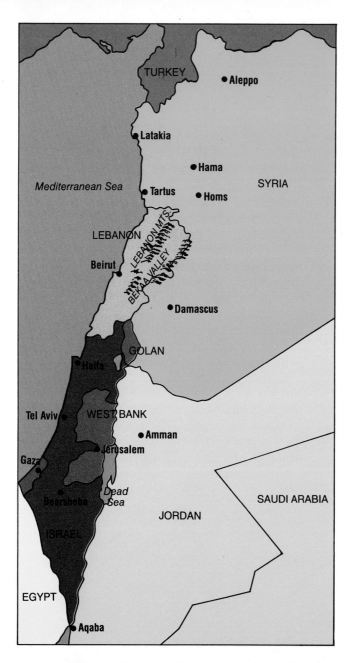

TURKEY

● Aleppo

● Latakia

Mediterranean Sea

● Hama

SYRIA

● Tartus
● Homs

LEBANON

LEBANON MTS.

BEKAA VALLEY

Beirut ●

● Damascus

GOLAN

● Haifa

Tel Aviv ●
WEST BANK

● Amman

● Jerusalem

Gaza ●

*Dead
Sea*

● Beersheba

JORDAN

SAUDI ARABIA

ISRAEL

EGYPT

● Aqaba

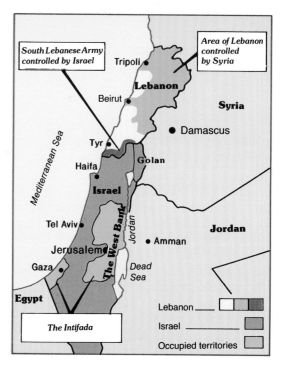

South Lebanese Army
controlled by Israel

Tripoli ●

Area of Lebanon
controlled
by Syria

Lebanon

Beirut ●

Syria

● Damascus

Mediterranean Sea

Tyr ●

Haifa ●

Golan

Israel

Tel Aviv ●

The West Bank

Jordan

● Amman

Jerusalem ●

Jordan

Gaza ●

*Dead
Sea*

Egypt

The Intifada

Lebanon ——

Israel ——

Occupied territories

Israel and Lebanon,
Early 1991

Lebanon and Its Environment

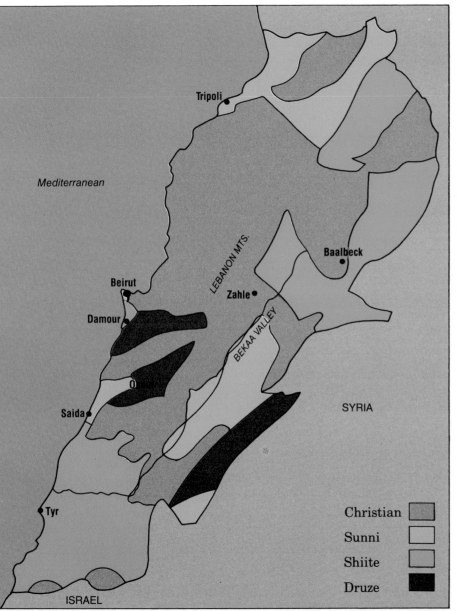

From *Hérodote*, no. 29–30, 1983.

Principal Religious Communities of Lebanon

Shiite	about 600,000 to 650,000
Maronite	about 550,000 to 600,000
Sunni	about 500,000
Greek Orthodox	about 250,000 to 280,000
Greek Catholic	about 200,000 to 220,000
Druze	about 150,000 to 180,000

- The figures given here are estimates. There has been no census in Lebanon in recent years.
- The Shiites are spread out over a good part of the country in scattered settlements. Most are rural people.
- The Sunni are traditionally city people (Beirut, Tripoli, Saida). They occupy rural areas near the cities, as well as the Bekaa Valley.
- The Greek Orthodox and Greek Catholic communities are made up of Arabs Christianized over the centuries. They are traditionally city people, especially the Greek Orthodox group.
- The mountains of Lebanon and other hilly areas have historically been places of refuge for two threatened communities: the Maronite Christians and the Druze (a dissident sect of Islam). The Maronite villages are located on the exit routes from the cities as well as on the mountain routes. The Druze, in addition to the mountains, occupy the Shouf and Mt. Hermon.

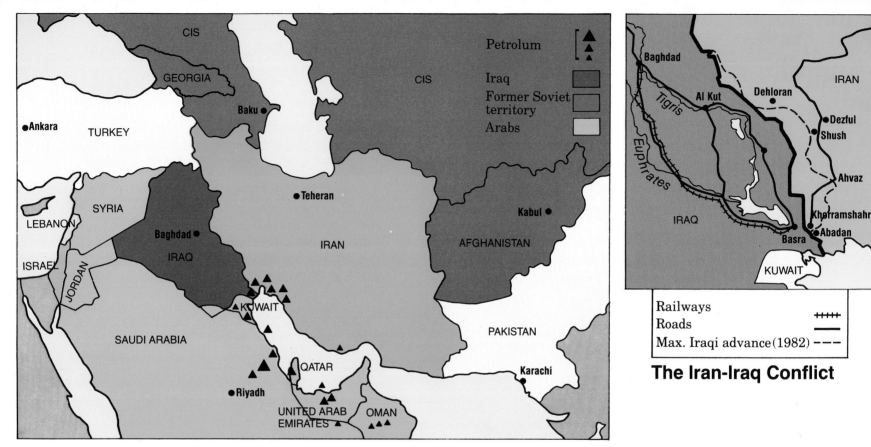

Map legend:

Petrolum

Iraq

Former Soviet territory

Arabs

The Iran-Iraq Conflict

Railways ++++
Roads ——
Max. Iraqi advance (1982) ----

Iran's Perception of External Threats

The fall of the Shah after a popular revolution (1979) deprived the United States of a major ally in the region. None of the forces opposing the government of Khomeini and the mullahs has been able to gain widespread support, and the masses of the population continue to support a regime that seems destined to last, even after Khomeini's death in July 1989.

But hostility toward the United States should not obscure the fact that it was with the former Soviet Union that Iran has a long common frontier, and that its sovereignty was for a long time a matter of dispute between Russia and Great Britain, which even drew up a proposal for partition (1907).

The rivalry between Iraq and Iran (which for a long time supported Iraqi Kurds fighting the central government) was fueled by concessions Iraq was obliged to make to Iran in 1975 (the Algiers agreements) leading to withdrawal of Iran's support for the Kurds, and their eventual collapse. These concessions involved problems of sovereignty in the Shatt-al-Arab and the Iraqi claim to the ethnically Arab Iranian province of Khuzistan.

Capitalizing on the restoration of peace and the considerable increase in oil revenues, Saddam Hussein, the Iraqi strong man in a regime which, since 1968, had devoted itself to building and consolidating the state, launched an ambitious development program in Iraq.

Bound together by Shiism and Persian culture, both expressions of their identity, the majority of Iranians, carried along by revolutionary enthusiasm and/or the climate of "the fatherland in danger," put up a determined resistance to the Iraqi invasion (1980), aided by their enormous numerical superiority (3 to 1).

In 1982, having succeeded in turning the situation around despite logistical and supply problems, Iranian forces entered Iraqi territory. But the massive aid given to Iraq by virtually all states (except for Israel and Syria, both of which supported Iran) enabled Iraq to hold out even when the situation seemed lost (1986). Chemical weapons were used all through the conflict, more particularly by Iraq. To make up for its material difficulties, Iran engaged in high-pressure diplomacy (Irangate, etc.), and it bore fruit. The situation improved after 1987 for Iraq, partly thanks to the presence in the Gulf of the fleets of the United States and its Western allies. The war ended in 1988 in a semi-victory for Iraq. Meanwhile, in both Iran and Iraq, the Kurds who were waging an armed struggle demanding autonomy were harshly put down (use of chemical gas by Iraq against civilian populations at Halabja in 1988).

In 1991, as a result of the Gulf crisis, Iran won back all its territory occupied by Iraq. A new government restored diplomatic and commercial ties with the West.

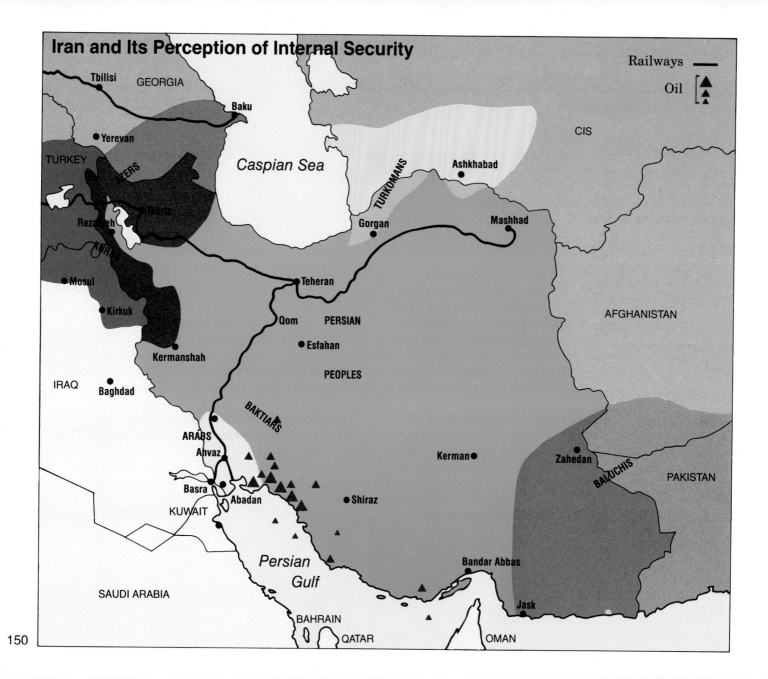

Iran and Its Perception of Internal Security

Railways ——

Oil

GEORGIA
Tbilisi
Baku
Yerevan
TURKEY
AZERS
Tabriz
Rezayeh
KURDS
Mosul
Kirkuk
Kermanshah
IRAQ
Baghdad

Caspian Sea

TURKOMANS
Ashkhabad
CIS
Gorgan
Mashhad
AFGHANISTAN

Teheran
Qom
PERSIAN
Esfahan
PEOPLES

ARABS
Ahvaz
BAKTIARS
Basra
Abadan
KUWAIT

Kerman
Zahedan
BALUCHIS
PAKISTAN

Shiraz

Persian
Gulf

Bandar Abbas

SAUDI ARABIA

Jask

BAHRAIN
QATAR
OMAN

150

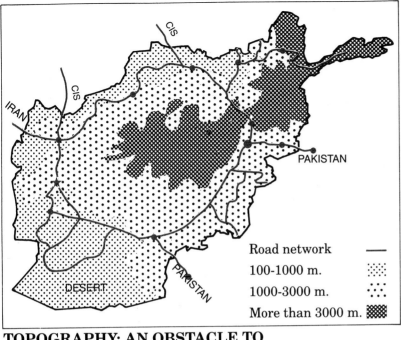

TOPOGRAPHY: AN OBSTACLE TO COMMUNICATIONS

Road network —
100-1000 m.
1000-3000 m.
More than 3000 m.

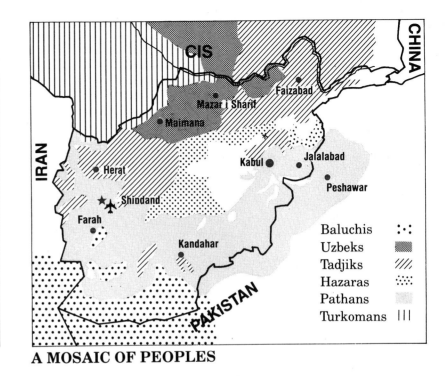

A MOSAIC OF PEOPLES

Baluchis
Uzbeks
Tadjiks
Hazaras
Pathans
Turkomans

Afghanistan

The Soviet intervention in Afghanistan, which began in 1979, was the first Soviet intervention outside the Warsaw Pact countries since the beginning of the Cold War.

The government that emerged from the Marxist-Leninist-inspired coup d'état (1978) rapidly ran up against a massive uprising with many different causes. The Soviet occupation was facilitated by the fact that the two countries shared a common border. The USSR's intervention came on top of Soviet initia-

tives in Angola (1975) and Ethiopia (1977), which took advantage of strategic vacuums and the weakening of American will after the war in Vietnam and the fall of the Shah (1979).

In spite of casualties that approached the millions— and, officially 13,000 dead on the Soviet side—and 4 to 5 million refugees in Pakistan and Iran, the USSR waged a limited war in Afghanistan from 1979 through 1989. Its troops represented about 25 percent to 30 percent of the number of American troops that had been in Vietnam. There was no escalation of the conflict on the Soviet side and counterinsurgency was never seriously undertaken. Occupation on the cheap simply succeeded in strengthening the Party and above all the political police. The withdrawal of Soviet forces was typical of the period of Gorbachev, anxious to present a different image of the Soviet Union.

Turkey

With a thirty-year lead over Nasserite Egypt, the Turks, after the collapse of an Ottoman Empire undermined by national issues, succeeded, thanks to Mustapha Kemal and a military organization based on a traditional state, in avoiding subjugation. Modern Turkey, the first truly independent nation-state in the Afro-Asian world after Japan, was established. But modernization consisted mostly of the external forms of European institutions and not their economic bases, while the nation remained handicapped by a traditional, "backward" society.

Turkey, a member of NATO, the OECD, and the Council of Europe, is the only state in the Middle East linked to the West by a military pact. Turkey seeks to be European and wants to join the Common Market. In the Middle East its imperial past, its peculiarities, and its political leanings isolate it from its neighbors.

It is the only country in the Middle East outside of Egypt to recognize the state of Israel. Traditionally, the main enemy of the Turks is "the Moscof" (the Russian). The Turkish elites have long been aware of the importance their northern neighbor attaches to the vital geostrategic position of Asia Minor. The fall of the Shah of Iran, which deprived the United States of a major regional ally, increased the value of the alliance with Turkey.

During the Gulf crisis (1990) Turkey quickly fell in alongside the United States. It is following the political situation in the Caucasus and Central Asia very closely and has recently rediscovered its Middle Eastern role.

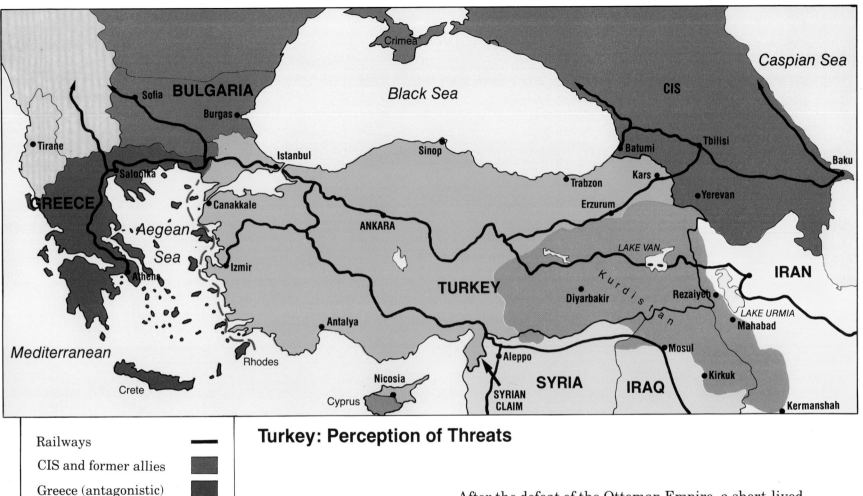

Turkey: Perception of Threats

Railways
CIS and former allies
Greece (antagonistic)
Arab countries
Kurds

After the defeat of the Ottoman Empire, a short-lived Armenian republic was set up and recognized within frontiers laid down by President Wilson (in the years 1915–1917, some 1 million Armenians died during deportations ordered by the Young Turks). The Kurds seemed likely to win autonomous status. The Greeks invaded Anatolia.

153

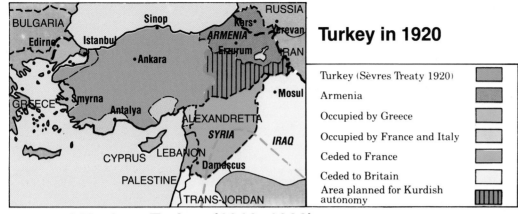

Turkey in 1920

Turkey (Sèvres Treaty 1920)	
Armenia	
Occupied by Greece	
Occupied by France and Italy	
Ceded to France	
Ceded to Britain	
Area planned for Kurdish autonomy	

Birth of Modern Turkey (1919–1922)

Modern Turkey was built on the annihilation of the Armenians and the reconquest of northeastern Anatolia, the expulsion of the Greeks in Asia Minor after their defeat (followed by an exchange of populations), and a process of integration/repression of a large Kurdish minority deprived of all rights as an ethnic group.

Cyprus

Turkish intervention in Cyprus (1974), where the Greek (82 percent) and Turkish (18 percent) communities were fighting each other, revived a multifaceted dispute between Greece and Turkey—both members of NATO. This dispute especially concerns Turkish claims to the continental shelf of the Aegean Sea.

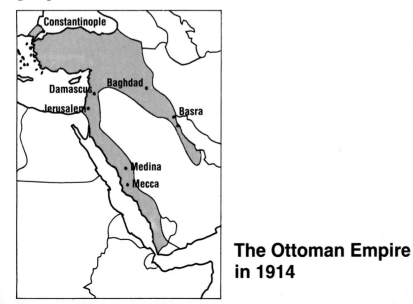

The Ottoman Empire in 1914

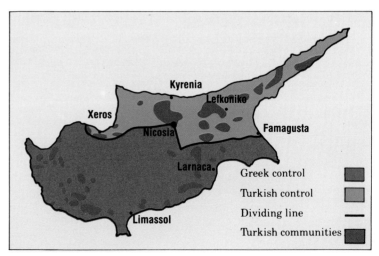

Greek control	
Turkish control	
Dividing line	
Turkish communities	

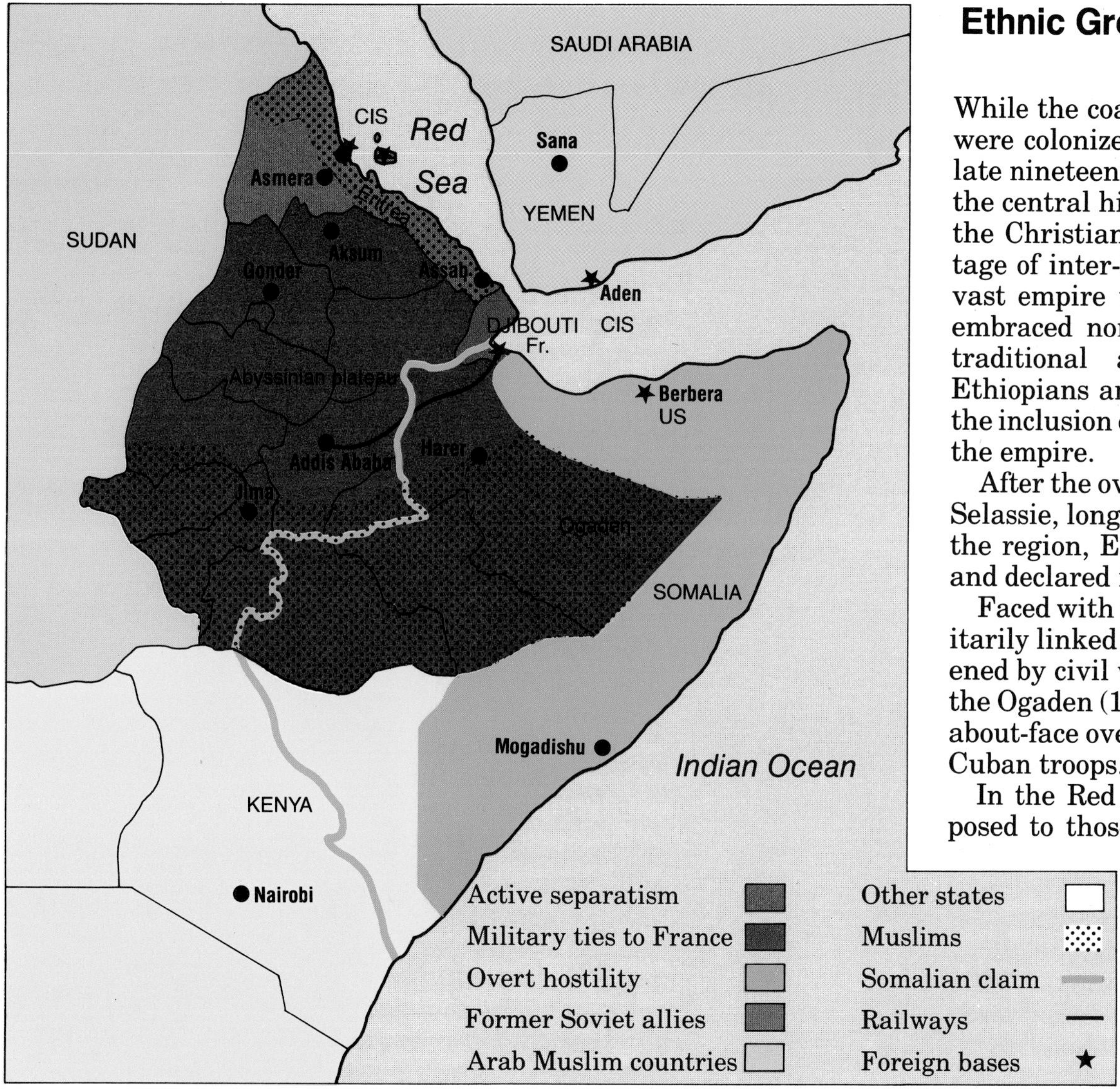
SAUDI ARABIA
CIS
Red Sea
Sana
YEMEN
Asmera
Eritrea
SUDAN
Aksum
Gonder
Assab
Aden
DJIBOUTI
CIS
Fr.
Abyssinian plateau
Berbera
US
Addis Ababa
Harer
Jima
Ogaden
SOMALIA
Mogadishu
Indian Ocean
KENYA
Nairobi
Active separatism
Military ties to France
Overt hostility
Former Soviet allies
Arab Muslim countries
Other states
Muslims
Somalian claim
Railways
Foreign bases

Ethnic Groups in Ethiopia

While the coastal regions of the Horn of Africa were colonized by the European powers in the late nineteenth century, the Ethiopian state on the central highlands remained in the hands of the Christian Amahara. Ethiopia took advantage of inter-European rivalries to carve out a vast empire which, particularly in the south, embraced non-Christian peoples. The already traditional antagonism between Christian Ethiopians and Muslim Somalis was fueled by the inclusion of the Somali-populated Ogaden in the empire.

After the overthrow in 1974 of Emperor Haile Selassie, long the United States' favored ally in the region, Ethiopia moved sharply to the left and declared itself Marxist-Leninist.

Faced with territorial claims by Somalia (militarily linked by treaty to the USSR) and weakened by civil war, it was able to win the war in the Ogaden (1977–78) only thanks to the Soviet about-face over Somalia and the intervention of Cuban troops.

In the Red Sea, Ethiopia's interests are opposed to those of the Arab world, which with

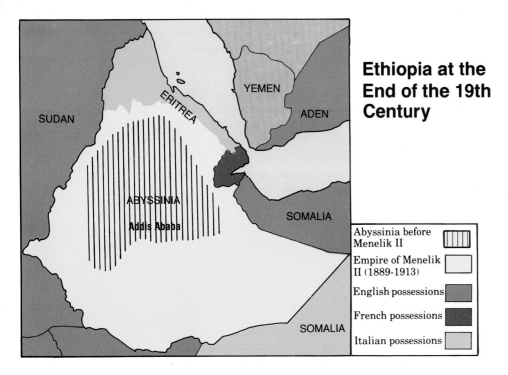

Ethiopia at the End of the 19th Century

Abyssinia before Menelik II	
Empire of Menelik II (1889-1913)	
English possessions	
French possessions	
Italian possessions	

Saudi Arabia in the lead would like to see it transformed into an Arab lake.

Somalia, a member of the Arab League (although non-Arab), has been seriously weakened by its reverses and is in the throes of civil war. The base at Berbera, formerly Soviet, is now an American one that can be used by the U.S. Rapid Deployment Force. In 1988 the Somalia-Ethiopia dispute was settled. Ethiopia now has to face grave economic problems (famine) and a difficult military situation (rebellions in Tigré and above all Eritrea). With the ending of Soviet military aid the situation became untenable for President Mengistu, who fled the country.

Eritrea

Eritrea was an Italian colony until World War II, then was administered by the British (1941–1952). It did not, like the other Italian colonies, win independence. By a decision of the UN, it was attached to Ethiopia as an autonomous territory (1952). Ten years later, the emperor integrated Eritrea as a province. After 1961, a separatist movement developed, Muslim in origin, but spreading to Christians (each religious group having about half the total population) and supported by the Arab states.

The fall of Haile Selassie in 1974 did not alter Ethiopia's imperial character. In spite of Cuban and Soviet aid, the Marxist-Leninist Eritrean People's Liberation Front (EPLF) held out against offensives by Addis Ababa. For Ethiopia, Eritrea represents access to the sea. Although isolated internationally, the EPLF, which is the most remarkably organized armed movement of the last fifteen years, continued to win military successes and captured the country's main towns. The EPLF greatly contributed to the final fall of the Marxist regime headed by President Mengistu.

China and Its Environment

China is a vast country that is strategically isolated. To the north are Russia, with which there is a long-standing territorial dispute, and the new Commonwealth of Independent States. In the era of the unequal treaties (those signed to China's disadvantage by various Western countries have long since been nullified), China ceded to Russia in 1853 2,500,000 sq. km. of territory east of the Ussuri as far as the coastal provinces. Absorbed because of their territorial continuity, these regions (which were not inhabited by Chinese) remained Soviet, but China laid claim to them from the very beginning of the Sino-Soviet conflict.* There was fighting between Chinese and Russians on the Ussuri (1969). After a decade of Sino-American relations, China, disappointed in its hope of obtaining American help in modernizing its military equipment, sought an arrangement with the Soviet Union. A normalization of relations with the CIS would allow it to attend to pressing domestic and economic problems: agriculture, industry, technology, and modernization of the armed forces.

To the south, China is hostile to Vietnamese hegemony over the Indochinese peninsula and would like to see, both in Vientiane and Phnom Penh, governments hostile to the Vietnamese, whose alliance with Moscow is seen as an encirclement. China's only ally in Southeast Asia is a weakened Pakistan. India, beyond the Himalayan barrier, remains hostile.

---

* Underpopulated Mongolia, whose strategic position between China and Russia is obvious, with its 3,000 km. of frontiers, fears the Chinese, particularly for demographic reasons.

Heir to a great civilization that has profoundly influenced its neighbors (Vietnam, Korea, Japan) and conquered a vast empire to the west and north of China's original eighteen provinces, the People's Republic has the advantage of a homogeneous population (92% are Han Chinese) with exceptional abilities, whose initial enthusiasm was largely eroded by fifteen years of political struggles and economic stagnation, aggravated by bureaucratic inertia. For the time being, the status of Hong Kong, like that of Macao, is useful to China's trade. Taiwan remains a secondary problem. As for foreign policy, especially regarding the Third World, after numerous years marked by setbacks, it is today conducted on more realistic lines. It is essentially by relying on its own organizational and productive abilities that China, by managing its security through a prudent and adaptable policy, can hope to raise itself, with great effort, to the rank of a great power, a rank that no state is anxious to see it attain. China's new economic dynamism appears especially in its arms sales. It plays a disturbing role by selling long range ballistic missiles to Saudi Arabia. Practicing *perestroika* without *glasnost* in 1989, the Chinese leadership brutally crushed the people's demand for democratization.

**Cereals: leading world producer (19.5%)
on the basis of seven principal cereals**

Wheat	First in world	17%
Rice	First in world	36
Corn	Second in world	16
Millet	Third in world	13
Cotton	First in world	24
Pork	First in world	—
Sheep	Third in world	—
Soybeans	Third in world	11

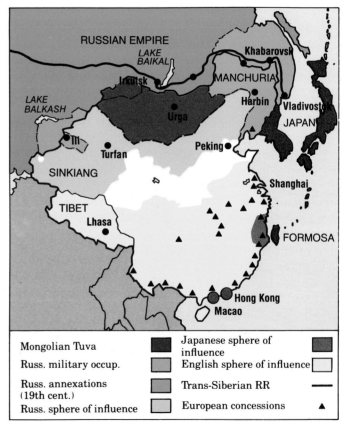

China under Foreign Influence (1904)

Mongolian Tuva
Russ. military occup.
Russ. annexations (19th cent.)
Russ. sphere of influence

Japanese sphere of influence
English sphere of influence
Trans-Siberian RR
European concessions ▲

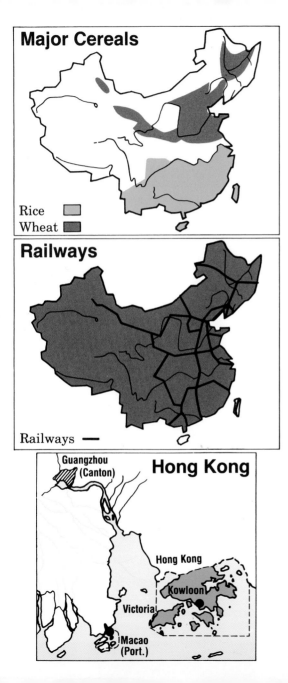

Major Cereals

Rice ▢
Wheat ▧

Railways

Railways —

Hong Kong

Guangzhou (Canton)
Hong Kong
Kowloon
Victoria
Macao (Port.)

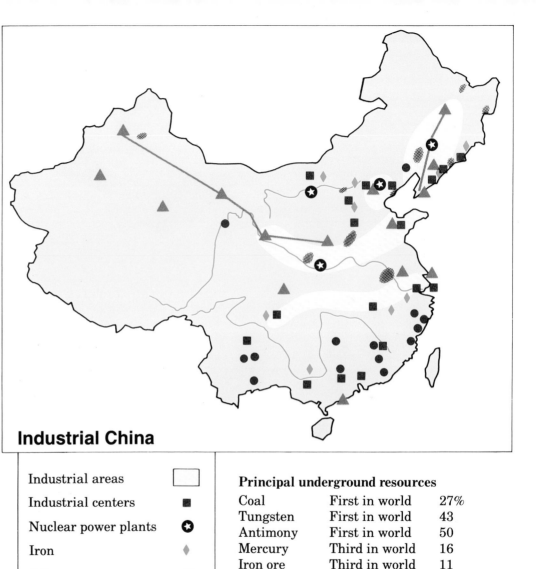

Industrial China

Industrial areas	▢
Industrial centers	▪
Nuclear power plants	✪
Iron	◆
Other ores	●
Oil and natural gas	▲
Coal	⬭

Principal underground resources

Coal	First in world	27%
Tungsten	First in world	43
Antimony	First in world	50
Mercury	Third in world	16
Iron ore	Third in world	11
Lead	Fourth in world	10

No data for many items.

159

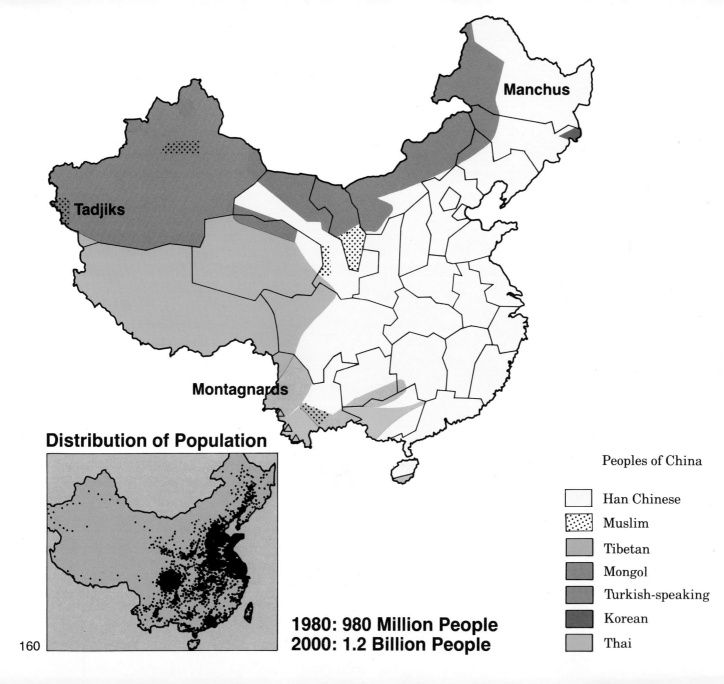

Manchus

Tadjiks

Montagnards

Distribution of Population

1980: 980 Million People
2000: 1.2 Billion People

160

Peoples of China

	Han Chinese
	Muslim
	Tibetan
	Mongol
	Turkish-speaking
	Korean
	Thai

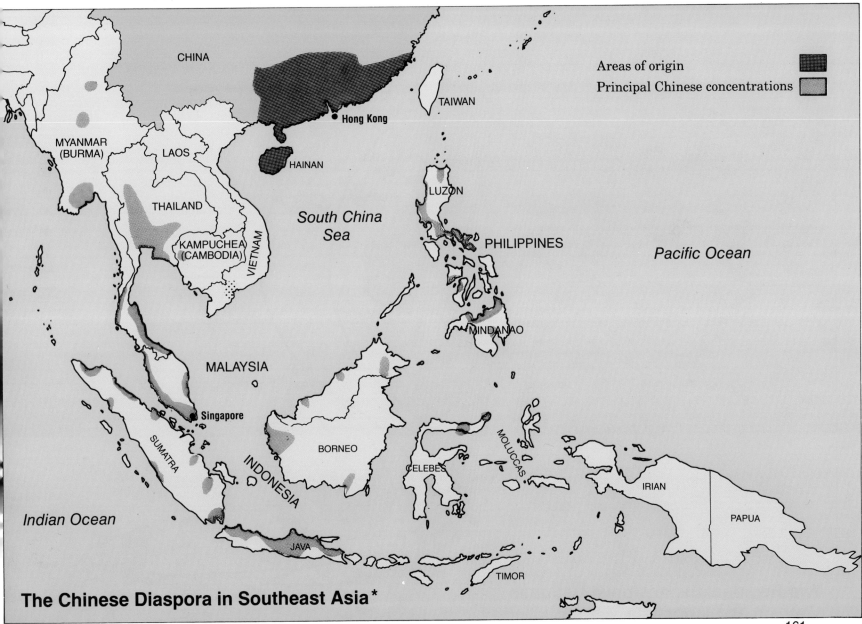

CHINA

TAIWAN

Areas of origin

Principal Chinese concentrations

● Hong Kong

MYANMAR
(BURMA)

LAOS

HAINAN

LUZON

THAILAND

South China
Sea

PHILIPPINES

Pacific Ocean

KAMPUCHEA
(CAMBODIA)

VIETNAM

MINDANAO

MALAYSIA

MOLUCCAS

● Singapore

SUMATRA

BORNEO

CELEBES

IRIAN

INDONESIA

PAPUA

Indian Ocean

JAVA

TIMOR

The Chinese Diaspora in Southeast Asia*

*about 20 million people

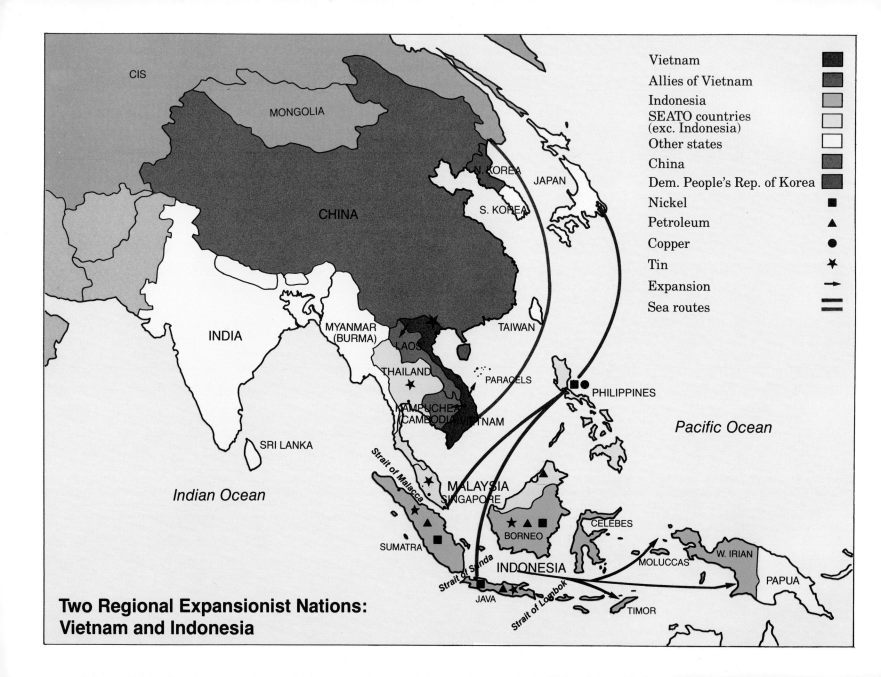

**Two Regional Expansionist Nations:
Vietnam and Indonesia**

Legend:
- Vietnam
- Allies of Vietnam
- Indonesia
- SEATO countries (exc. Indonesia)
- Other states
- China
- Dem. People's Rep. of Korea
- Nickel ■
- Petroleum ▲
- Copper ●
- Tin ★
- Expansion →
- Sea routes =

CIS

MONGOLIA

CHINA

INDIA

MYANMAR (BURMA)

LAOS

THAILAND

KAMPUCHEA CAMBODIA

VIETNAM

N. KOREA

S. KOREA

JAPAN

TAIWAN

PARACELS

PHILIPPINES

Pacific Ocean

SRI LANKA

Indian Ocean

Strait of Malacca

MALAYSIA

SINGAPORE

SUMATRA

Strait of Sunda

BORNEO

CELEBES

INDONESIA

Strait of Lombok

JAVA

TIMOR

MOLUCCAS

W. IRIAN

PAPUA

Southeast Asia

Monsoon Asia is predominantly made up of peninsulas and islands surrounded by sea lanes. Like the whole of eastern Asia, it is an area of high agricultural production (rice) and dense population (except Laos). Without ethnic or religious unity (Hinduism, Buddhism, Islam, Confucianism, and Catholicism), Southeast Asia is characterized by societies that are highly structured, with a national consciousness that is often very old and with considerable cultural depth.

The victory of the North Vietnamese in 1975 and the intervention in Cambodia (1978) signified the hegemony of Vietnam over the Indochinese peninsula, provoking the militant hostility of China. This resulted in an armed Sino-Vietnamese confrontation (1979) and in the support given by Thailand and Malaysia (both members of ASEAN*) to the various Khmer forces fighting the Hanoi-backed regime in Cambodia (now Kampuchea).

The withdrawal of Vietnamese forces, whose military superiority is quite apparent, is out of the question so long as there is no guarantee that Cambodia will be led by a pro-Vietnamese government. Chinese power is perceived as a threat by the Vietnamese, who feel that their hegemony over the Indochinese peninsula gives them a status as a regional power that cannot be ignored.

China in turn has felt threatened by the alliance between the USSR and Vietnam. Despite the existence of chronic guerrilla wars (Myanmar, Laos, the Philippines), no existing regime appears threatened by them. Economically, the most dynamic states are Singapore, Thailand, and Malaysia. But it is interesting to note that the two regional powers that have made territorial advances are Vietnam and Indonesia (Moluccas, 1950–1952; New Guinea, 1961–1962; East Timor, 1976–1977); Indonesia also has designs on North Borneo.

---

* Association of Southeast Asian Nations, founded in 1967. This economic and political organization comprises Indonesia, Malaysia, the Philippines, Singapore, and Thailand.

Population (in millions)

	1950	1980	2000
Indonesia	77	148	216
Malaysia	6.1	14	21
Philippines	20	49	77
Singapore	1	2.4	3
Thailand	20	47	68
Vietnam	30	55	88
Kampuchea	4	6.9	10
Laos	2	3.4	5
Myanmar	19	35	54
Hong Kong	2	5.1	6
Taiwan	8	18	25

East Asia: One of the Rare Third World Regions with Sustained and Rapid Growth

	(annual % rate)	
	1980	1990
South Korea	3.5	8
Hong Kong	9.0	9
Indonesia	9.3	7
Malaysia	8.0	7
Philippines	5.2	4
Taiwan	6.4	8
Thailand	6.3	7

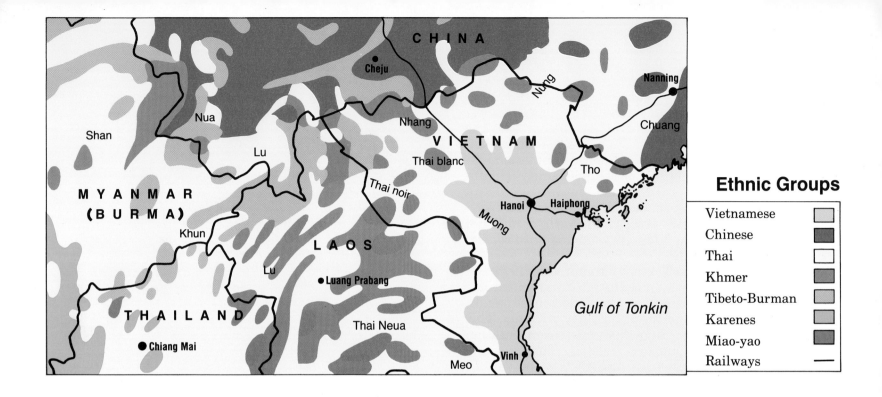

China

Cheju

Nua

Shan

Nhang

Nanning

Chuang

Nung

VIETNAM

Thai blanc

Lu

Tho

MYANMAR
(BURMA)

Thai noir

Hanoi Haiphong

Muong

Khun

Lu

LAOS

● Luang Prabang

Gulf of Tonkin

THAILAND

Thai Neua

● Chiang Mai

Meo

Vinh

Ethnic Groups

Vietnamese

Chinese

Thai

Khmer

Tibeto-Burman

Karenes

Miao-yao

Railways ———

An Area of Geopolitical Fluidity

On the borders of China and several Southeast Asian
countries, the profusion of minorities, their overlap-
ping, and the fact that they are geographically exclu-
sive makes the geopolitical situation particularly
fluid. Political guerrillas that are more or less manip-
ulated by one power or another (China, USA, etc.)
and bands of irregulars engaging in the opium trade
continue to find rear bases or sanctuaries in these
areas.

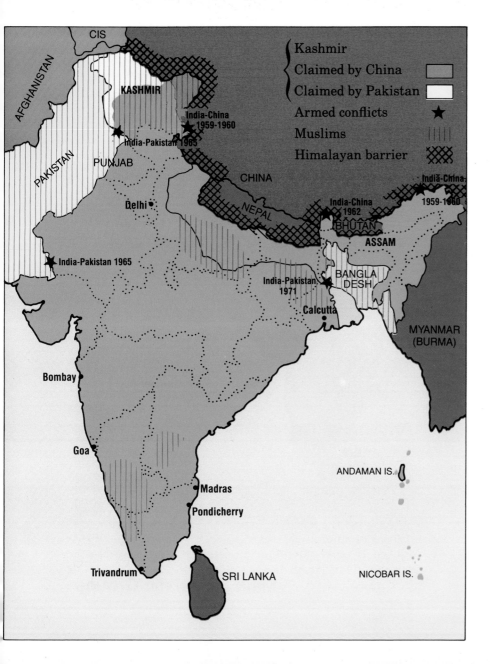

Kashmir
{ Claimed by China ▨
{ Claimed by Pakistan □
Armed conflicts ★
Muslims ▥
Himalayan barrier ▨

India: Its Security Perception

India is, with China, the only great regional power in Asia. India, a quasi-industrial power that belongs to the nuclear club (1974), has more to fear from its internal disparities and distortions, fueled by an almost uncontrollable population growth, than from its neighbors. Its political instability is growing.

India is not a nation, but a civilization. Since independence, the language of administration has been English. In addition to its linguistic and ethnic divisions (especially north–south), there is the problem of its very large Muslim minority (almost 20%). Social cleavages, partly rigidified by the caste system, marginalize 125 million Harijans (formerly Untouchables), despite legislation.

Twice defeated by China (1959, 1962), India has grown stronger since, and China seems unlikely in the foreseeable future to embark on incursions that, in any case, would be logistically difficult to make on a large scale.

Pakistan, which claims Muslim-inhabited Kashmir, is today, after many conflicts, greatly weakened by its defeat in Bangladesh by Indian troops. India always had excellent relations with the USSR (especially in the matter of military supplies) while remaining a model of nonalignment.

The overseas Indian population is numerous throughout eastern Africa, from Kenya to South Africa, as well as in the eastern part of the Indian Ocean (Malaysia, Singapore, etc.).

India is one of the few Third World countries to have the means to carry out its south–south industrial projects. Given its ambitions in the Indian Ocean area, it would seem that strengthening its maritime capabilities, which are already quite considerable, is necessary.

Indian troops were sent to Sri Lanka in 1987 in order to crush the Tamil insurgent movement there. This intervention increased the role of India as a regional power. However, it has had to face violence at home in Amritsar and other cities of Punjab, where the Sikhs want a state of their own within the Union.

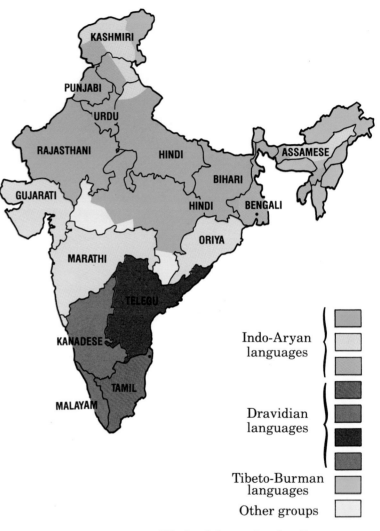

Indo-Aryan languages

Dravidian languages

Tibeto-Burman languages

Other groups

Main Linguistic Groups

Economic India

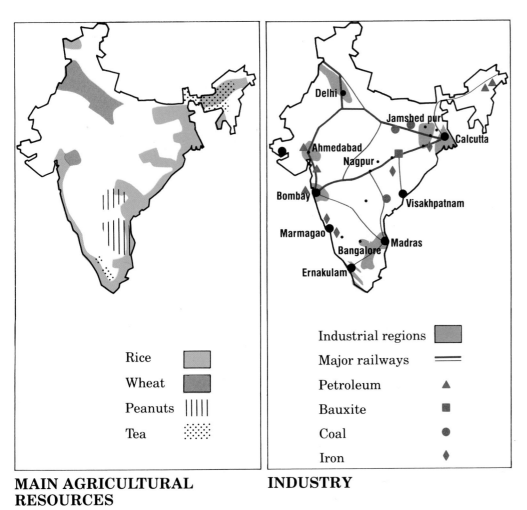

**MAIN AGRICULTURAL
RESOURCES**

Rice
Wheat
Peanuts ||||
Tea

INDUSTRY

Industrial regions
Major railways
Petroleum ▲
Bauxite ■
Coal ●
Iron ◆

Agricultural resources

**Cereals: fourth in world production (10.5%),
on the basis of seven principal cereals**

Rice	Second in world	22%
Millet/sorghum	First in world	24%
Wheat	Fourth in world	10%
Sugar	First in world	10%
Cotton	Fourth in world	9%
Peanuts	—	25%

Mineral and energy resources

Coal	5.5% of world production
Manganese	6% of world production
Chromium	6% of world production
Iron ore	4% of world production
Titanium	3% of world production

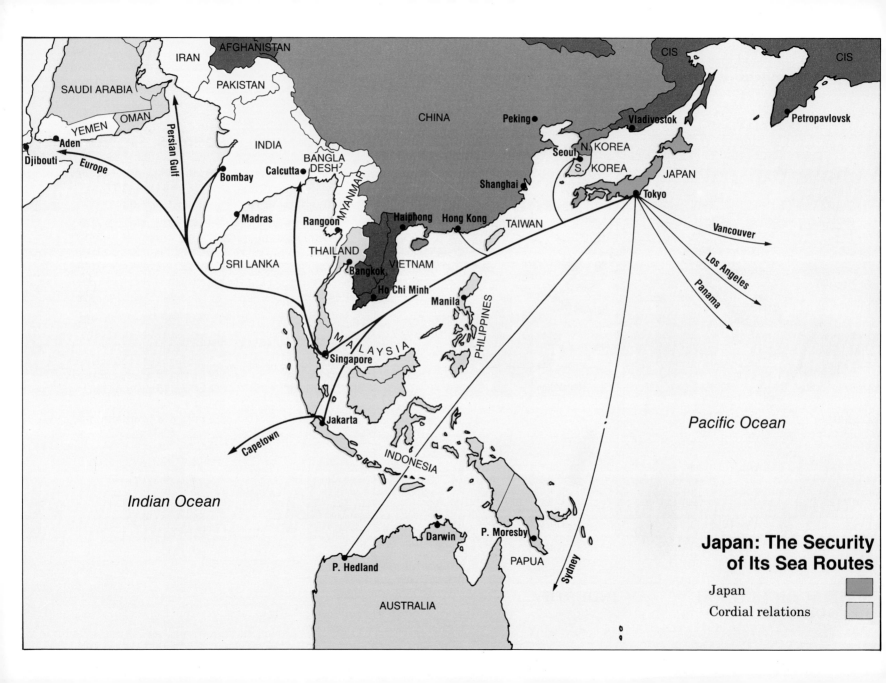

Japan: The Security of Its Sea Routes

Japan

Cordial relations

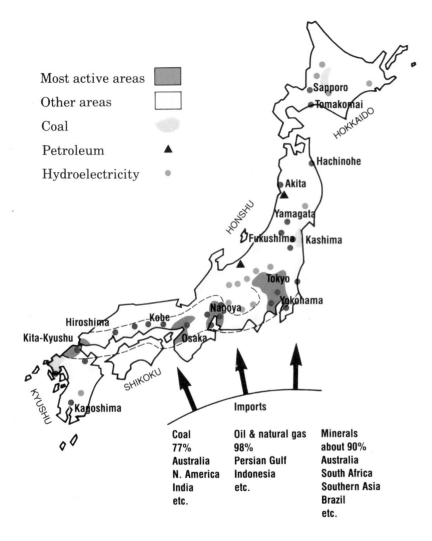

Most active areas

Other areas

Coal

Petroleum ▲

Hydroelectricity ●

Sapporo
Tomakomai
HOKKAIDO
Hachinohe
Akita
Yamagata
Fukushima   Kashima
HONSHU
Tokyo
Yokohama
Kobe   Nagoya
Hiroshima
Kita-Kyushu   Osaka
SHIKOKU
KYUSHU
Kagoshima

Imports

Coal	Oil & natural gas	Minerals
77%	98%	about 90%
Australia	Persian Gulf	Australia
N. America	Indonesia	South Africa
India	etc.	Southern Asia
etc.		Brazil
		etc.

Japan: An Industrial Power

Japan is the only Afro-Asian country that succeeded in responding to the Western challenge and in carrying out an industrial revolution launched in 1868. Since then, it has spared no effort to maintain its independence. At the end of a war in which it had imposed its harsh law on East Asia, Japan suffered nuclear tragedy (Hiroshima, Nagasaki).

Provided with democratic institutions during the American occupation, demilitarized* Japan reoriented its energy, organizational abilities, cohesion (founded, among other things, on a population whose homogeneity has been carefully preserved), and social discipline toward economic and commercial goals. Lacking resources, and aided by a dynamism backed by modern business organization and the consensus of wage earners, Japan has succeeded, in three decades, in outclassing almost all the industrial countries, becoming an irresistible competitor. Militarily, Japan is highly vulnerable, but its economic vulnerability is even greater, given the country's heavy dependence on the world market: A break in supplies of raw materials from the Third World or the erection of barriers in the industrial countries where it sells its products would be serious. Japan's competitiveness tends to provoke protectionist measures in some countries. Japan's security, at the present time, rests on the continuation, as far as it can be done, of free trade.

---

*Japan is linked militarily to the United States.

Having succeeded in controlling its birth rate in the 1950s, enjoying a productive agriculture, engaging in large-scale fishing, and endowed with a hardworking and docile population, Japan has the necessary determination to face all challenges. Its lines of communication—which are vital, especially from the Gulf—are guaranteed by a large merchant fleet. In the framework of new rules of the game to which it has adapted, Japan seems to have realized many of the objectives it had during the years of empire.

Population Density

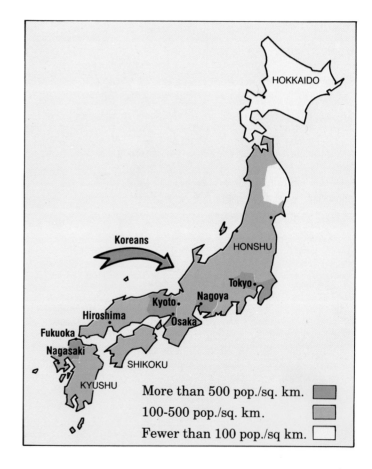

Urbanized Zones in the South

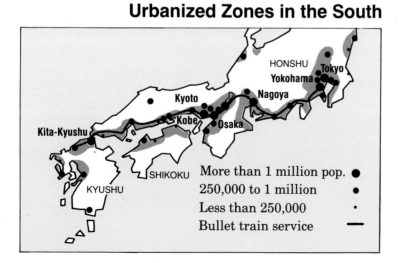

Japan: Vital Statistics

Economic Power

	Japan	U.S.
Population[a] (millions)	121	239
Gross national product (billion $ ppa)	1,468	3,635
GNP per capita ($ ppa)	12,235	15,356
Consumption per capita ($ ppa)	6,751	10,214
Jobs[a] (millions)	58	107
Productivity ($ ppa per job)	25,287	33,921
Unemployment rate[a] (%)	2.6	7.2
Investments[a] (GNP %)	27.5	18.6
Savings[a] (GNP %)	31.4	16.5
Exports[a] (billion $)	177	213
Imports[a] (billion $)	131	345
Research expenditure[b] (billion $)	31	88

Source: OCDE ("ppa" means "purchasing power parity")
a: 1985; b: 1988

Resources Dependency

Imports

Wheat, cereals, produce	25% of needs
Copper	100% of needs
Coal	88% of needs
Oil	99% of needs
Uranium	100% of needs
Iron	92% of needs
Other minerals (except lead, zinc, silver)	90% and more

Main Trade Partners (billion $)

	Exports	Imports	Total	Surplus
1. USA	80.4	29.1	109.5	+ 51.3
2. South Korea	10.5	5.3	15.8	+ 5.2
3. China	9.9	5.7	15.6	+ 4.2
4. West Germany	10.5	4.3	14.8	+ 6.2
5. Taiwan	7.9	4.7	12.6	+ 3.2
6. Australia	5.2	7.0	12.2	− 1.8
7. United Kingdom	6.6	3.6	10.2	+ 3.0
8. Indonesia	2.7	7.3	10.0	− 4.6
9. Hong Kong	7.2	1.1	8.2	+ 6.1
10. Saudi Arabia	2.8	5.2	8.0	− 2.4
11. Singapore	4.6	1.5	6.1	+ 3.1
12. Malaysia	1.7	3.8	5.5	− 2.1
13. USSR	3.1	2.0	5.1	+ 1.1
14. France	3.2	1.9	5.1	+ 1.3
Total Foreign Trade	210.7	127.7	338.4	+ 83.0

Source: The Summary Report, Trade of Japan, 12/1986

Australia

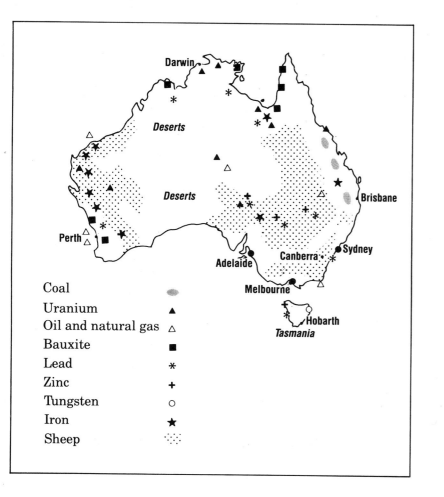

Coal
Uranium ▲
Oil and natural gas △
Bauxite ■
Lead *
Zinc +
Tungsten ○
Iron ★
Sheep

Australia cooperates militarily with the United States in ANZUS (Australia, New Zealand, United States) as well as with Singapore and Malaysia in the framework of the five-nation agreement (Great Britain, Australia, New Zealand, Singapore, Malaysia). It participates in the sea, air, and naval forces detached by the American Seventh Fleet in the Indian Ocean.

Australia occupies an exceptional geostrategic position between the Indian Ocean and the Pacific. As the largest state in the Pacific, it seeks to play a role as a regional power. Its mineral resources are considerable: It has offshore oil; in addition, it is a leading world exporter of grain and cereals.

A close trading partner of Japan, to which it supplies many raw materials, Australia seeks to work with New Zealand, which plays a more modest role.

Sheep	12% (world flocks) 2nd rank	
Uranium	3.5% world prod.	7% reserves
Iron	10.5%	11%
Manganese	7.5%	6%
Tungsten	6.0%	4%
Cobalt	6.0%	11%
Bauxite	28.5%	20%
Lead	11.5%	14%
Zinc	8.5%	10%

Australia: Perception of Its Security

Australia's traditional sensitivity to possible threats from Asia is fueled by awareness of its isolation in the Southern Hemisphere and its low population. Indonesia is often perceived as a potential threat on account of its demographics (the population is projected to be 220 million in ten years) and its closeness: New Guinea is less than 200 miles away.

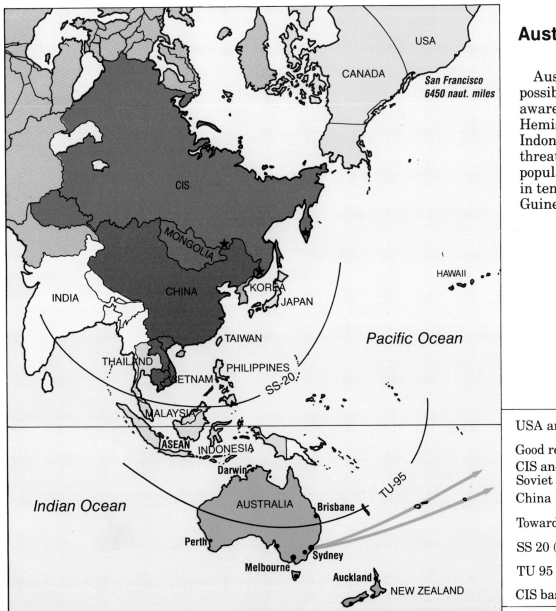

USA and allies

Good relations

CIS and former Soviet allies

China

Toward the USA

SS 20 (range)

TU 95 (range)

CIS bases ★

Latin America

Latin America is economically dominated by the United States, to which it is linked by the Treaty of Rio (1947), an inter-American mutual defense treaty, and by the Organization of American States (1948), from which Cuba was excluded in 1962 at the time of the missile crisis.

The United States historically has defended its geostrategic area: Guatemala (1954), Bay of Pigs (1961), and, following Cuba's move to the left, through the Alliance for Progress, a combination of economic assistance and training of Latin American counterguerrilla forces. [All the Latin American guerrilla movements of the 1960s have been defeated. Since then there have been the coup d'état in Brazil (1964); intervention in the Dominican Republic (1965); destabilization and fall of the Allende government in Chile (1973), and interventions in Grenada (1983) and Panama (1989).]

Basically, the Latin American world is more stable than it appears: In three decades, there have been only two radical political changes—Cuba (1959) and Nicaragua (1979).

Latin America has seen exceptionally rapid population growth: 132 million in 1945; 303 million in 1975; 600 million projected for 2000. The dominance of the Spanish language (except in Brazil) throughout

174

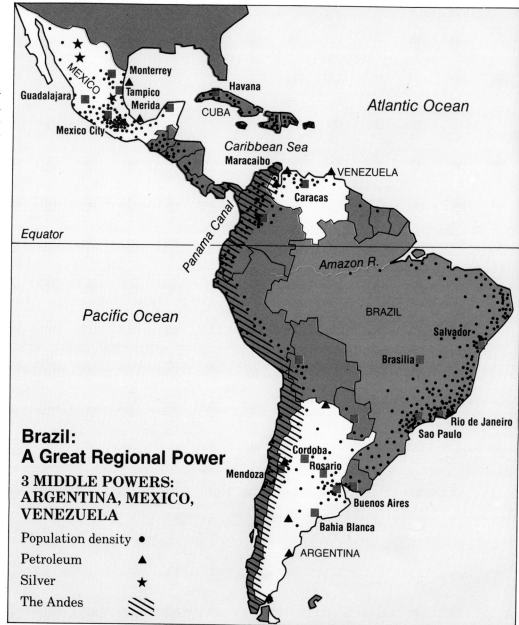

**Brazil:
A Great Regional Power**

**3 MIDDLE POWERS:
ARGENTINA, MEXICO,
VENEZUELA**

Population density   •

Petroleum   ▲

Silver   ★

The Andes   ///

Latin America should not lead one to overlook the existence of large Indian populations (Bolivia, Peru, Ecuador, Guatemala, Honduras, Mexico, etc.), almost all of whom are marginal people in their societies. Outside Brazil, the black or mulatto populations are concentrated in the Caribbean basin.

There has been no integration or resolution of the crisis-laden social distortions, despite strong nationalist feelings and social problems to which the Catholic Church has given expression. Catholicism is a force to be reckoned with; at the end of the century, the majority of Catholics in the world will be Latin Americans.

The continent has substantial resources, although only one country is in a position to export a surplus in agriculture or livestock (Argentina), and only one has really large mineral resources (Brazil). Oil, in modest quantities, is exploited in Mexico, Venezuela, and Ecuador. Peru has five major minerals, but Chile (copper), Bolivia (tin), and Jamaica (bauxite) have only one each. Although backward areas, notably among the Andean countries and in Central America, would seem to have limited prospects, Latin America as a whole is in a much better situation than most of Asia and Africa.

The present crisis and the wars in Central America are perceived by the United States as a test of political will, and it seems that everything will be done to ensure that the Pax Americana prevails in the end.

Three decades ago, Argentina seemed, given its cultural level and its agricultural and cattle wealth, to be destined to become a major power. But neither in terms of development or population nor in its institutions has Argentina lived up to its promise. The failure of the Falklands gamble, underestimating the capacity of Mrs. Thatcher's government to respond, led to the fall of the right-wing military government.

Venezuela, with a small population, can lay claim to the role of middling regional power only because of its oil. Its geostrategic position is linked to the Caribbean as a whole, and its interest lies in maintaining stability there. The 200-nautical-mile limit would allow Venezuela to exercise rights over a significant part of the Caribbean. The drawing of the limits of the continental shelf raises problems with its rival Colombia, which exports a large part of its work force to Venezuela.

Mexico, once considered a rising regional power, demonstrated its fragility in 1982 with the collapse of its currency. Contrary to what it has been claiming for several decades, the Institutional Revolutionary Party (PRI), which has been in power for half a century, has not succeeded in modernizing the country's institutions. Corruption, which is typical of the system, has increased with the oil boom. Today, Mexico is faced with a crisis that may well have serious social consequences. Mexico may soon sign a customs union agreement with the United States.

Peru is facing a serious crisis while economically Colombia, Venezuela, and above all Chile are making progress.

Brazil: South–South Perception

The Organization of American States (OAS), formed in 1948, reaffirmed the cooperation among the American nations (the First Congress of American States, 1889), as did the reciprocal-aid Treaty of Rio, signed in 1947. Members include: the United States; all the South American states except British and French Guyana; Mexico and all the Central American states; and in the Antilles, aside from Cuba, which no longer participates, Jamaica, Haiti, the Dominican Republic, Antigua and Barbuda, Dominica, St. Lucia, St. Vincent and the Grenadines, Barbados, Grenada, Trinidad and Tobago. Different economic alliances regroup some of these countries, such as the Andean group, countries of the Caribbean basin, and the Association for Latin American Integration (ALADI).

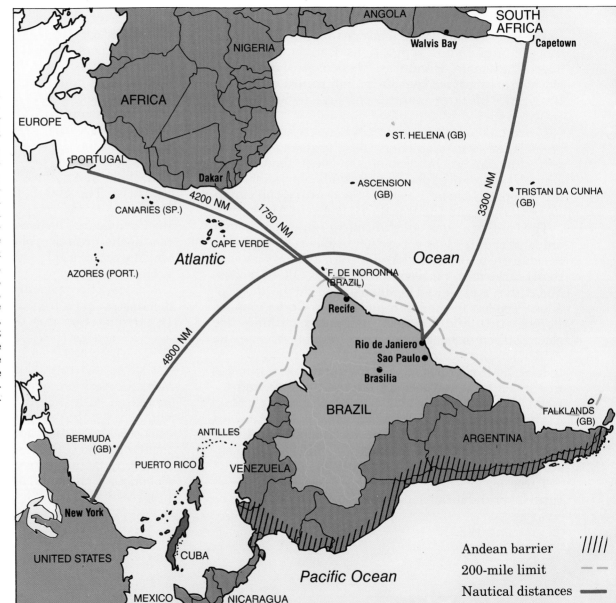

Brazil and Its Resources

Brazil, whose perception of the world is south–south oriented, is like a promontory at the eastern tip of the South American continent, less than 3,000 km from Dakar. It is the only Portuguese-speaking state in Latin America; it is also the most populous and is the only regional power. Moreover, it has considerable ambitions, but the economic base that would enable them to be realized is still lacking.

The development of Brazil depends on the conquest and control of its own territory and its ability, which is currently uncertain, to maintain dynamic growth.

But whatever the difficulties, Brazil is lucky to be able to count on a vast quantity of unexploited resources and is better placed than others to pursue a go-ahead policy.

A multiracial society based on "cordial domination" and mixing may, despite appearances, be the scene of racial problems that are also social problems.

Once tempted to base its African policy on South Africa, Brazil has reoriented its relations toward the Portuguese-speaking states and Nigeria. The creation of a navy suited to its ambitions should be a priority. In the past few years, Brazil has become an arms exporter of some importance, especially to the Third World.

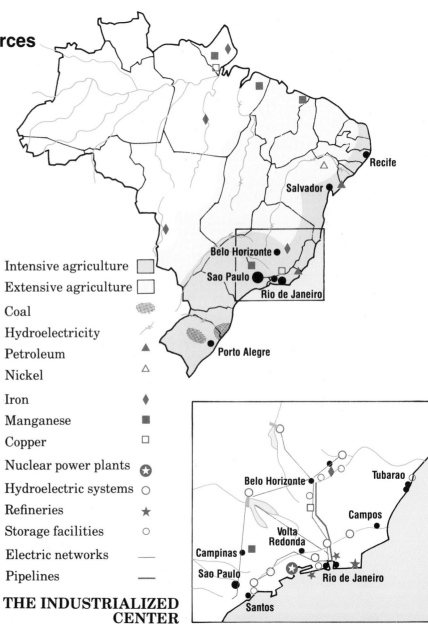

Intensive agriculture
Extensive agriculture
Coal
Hydroelectricity
Petroleum
Nickel
Iron
Manganese
Copper
Nuclear power plants
Hydroelectric systems
Refineries
Storage facilities
Electric networks
Pipelines

**THE INDUSTRIALIZED
CENTER**

Brazil: Occupation of the Land

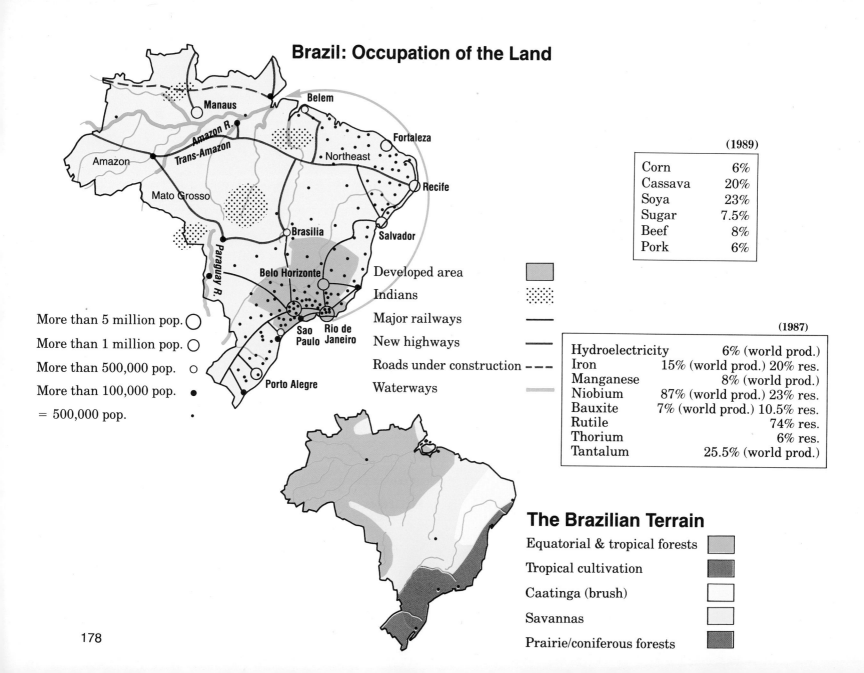

(1989)	
Corn	6%
Cassava	20%
Soya	23%
Sugar	7.5%
Beef	8%
Pork	6%

Developed area

Indians

Major railways

New highways

Roads under construction

Waterways

More than 5 million pop. ◯

More than 1 million pop. ◯

More than 500,000 pop. ○

More than 100,000 pop. ●

= 500,000 pop. ·

(1987)	
Hydroelectricity	6% (world prod.)
Iron	15% (world prod.) 20% res.
Manganese	8% (world prod.)
Niobium	87% (world prod.) 23% res.
Bauxite	7% (world prod.) 10.5% res.
Rutile	74% res.
Thorium	6% res.
Tantalum	25.5% (world prod.)

The Brazilian Terrain

Equatorial & tropical forests

Tropical cultivation

Caatinga (brush)

Savannas

Prairie/coniferous forests

Brazil and Its Geopolitical Aspirations

Portugal and its colonies occupy an enviable situation in the world beyond Latin America that can never be adequately stressed. In both the North Atlantic, where the Azores, Madeira, and Cape Verde constitute unparalleled defensive outposts, and in the south of Africa, where Angola and Mozambique almost mark out a Lusitanian equator right opposite the main power center that we in Brazil represent, and that is without mentioning Guinea, a second Dakar. . . .*

By its prominent situation in the nearest semicircle, which is vital for South America and Brazil's security, this area creates a Portuguese responsibility that we must be ready to take on at any moment.

The Latin world, in its turn, though its ties are looser, must consciously accept a sphere of solidarities that has come to include a large part of the European peninsula and almost the whole of West Africa. And this is because we are a Latin country, by our origin and by our culture, with an outstanding and hard-working population.

(Golbery do Couto e Silva, *Conjuntura politica nacional o poder executivo e geopolitico do Brasil,* Livraria José Olympio editore, Rio, 1981, p. 195; from the French translation by Alain Mangin.)

---

*Written in 1959.

Central America: Zone of Conflicts

Central America, divided into a number of micro-states, is traditionally a geographical area that has been controlled by the United States since the aftermath of the war with Spain (1898); armed intervention in Panama for the first time in 1903, in Nicaragua in 1933, in Guatemala in 1954, and in Panama in 1989 for the second time. In the 1980's the coming to power of the Sandinistas in Nicaragua (1979) led the United States to intervene indirectly, with the aim of both strengthening the Salvadoran state threatened by the Cuban- and Sandinista-backed Marxist-Leninist Far-abundo Marti Front and weakening the Sandinista regime by backing and supplying the "contras". The United States succeeded in containing the revolutionary wave which seemed likely to sweep all before it in the early 1980's in El Salvador and Guatemala. By helping the "contras" it put the Sandinistas on the defensive and forced them into a permanent mobilization that contributed to the regime's economic difficulties. Democratic elections brought the Sandinistas' opponents to power in 1989. But the country's economic situation remains very poor.

Panama: The Canal Zone

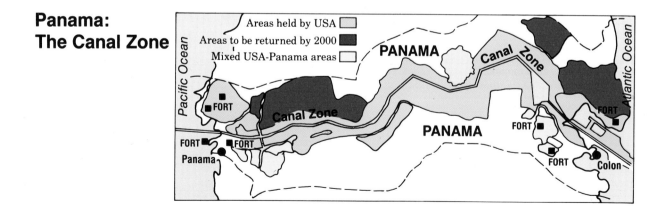

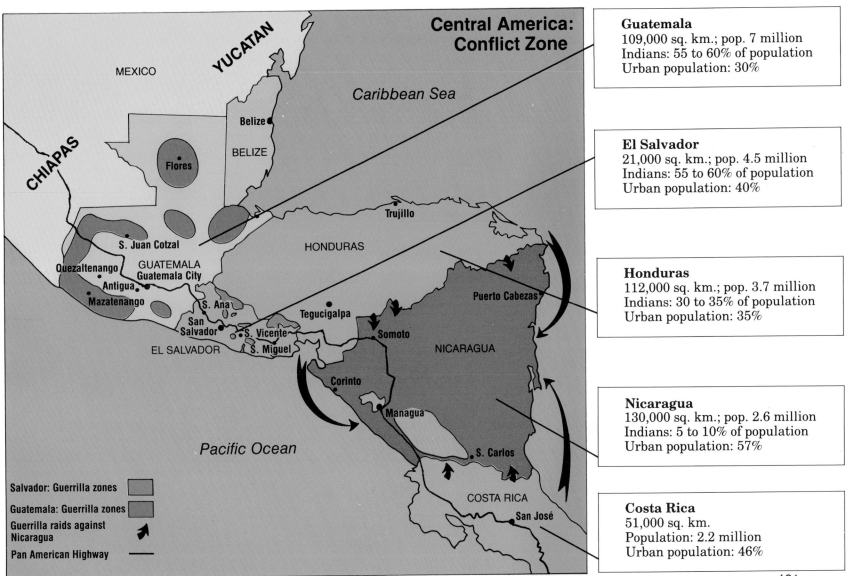

Central America: Conflict Zone

Guatemala
109,000 sq. km.; pop. 7 million
Indians: 55 to 60% of population
Urban population: 30%

El Salvador
21,000 sq. km.; pop. 4.5 million
Indians: 55 to 60% of population
Urban population: 40%

Honduras
112,000 sq. km.; pop. 3.7 million
Indians: 30 to 35% of population
Urban population: 35%

Nicaragua
130,000 sq. km.; pop. 2.6 million
Indians: 5 to 10% of population
Urban population: 57%

Costa Rica
51,000 sq. km.
Population: 2.2 million
Urban population: 46%

MEXICO
YUCATAN
CHIAPAS
Caribbean Sea
Belize
BELIZE
Flores
Trujillo
HONDURAS
S. Juan Cotzal
Quezaltenango
GUATEMALA
Guatemala City
Antigua
Mazatenango
Puerto Cabezas
S. Ana
Tegucigalpa
San Salvador
S. Vicente
Somoto
NICARAGUA
EL SALVADOR
S. Miguel
Corinto
Managua
Pacific Ocean
S. Carlos
COSTA RICA
San José

Salvador: Guerrilla zones
Guatemala: Guerrilla zones
Guerrilla raids against Nicaragua
Pan American Highway

NATURAL CONSTRAINTS

Natural constraints determine the density of human settlement and the eventual exploitation or development of mineral or agricultural resources. They may be obstacles or advantages in times of war and guerrilla activity. Nature, as a constraint and as a resource, is an element of strategy.

Basic Data

World Land Use (%)

	Cultivated Land	Pasture	Forest	Uncultivated Land
CIS*	10%	17%	41%	32%
N. America	14%	13%	34%	39%
S. America	7%	26%	51%	16%
Africa	8%	30%	23%	39%
Middle East	7%	16%	12%	65%
Asia (exc. CIS & Middle East)	33%	4%	40%	23%
Europe (exc. CIS)	26%	19%	33%	22%
Oceania	6%	60%	18%	16%

Forests (in millions of hectares)

Surfaces Covered	1978	2000
CIS*	785	775
North America	470	464
South America	550	329
Africa	188	150
Asia (except CIS)	361	181
Europe (except CIS)	140	150
Japan		
New Zealand		
Australia	69	68
Total	2,563	2,117

* Figures for CIS include Estonia, Latvia, Lithuania, and Georgia.

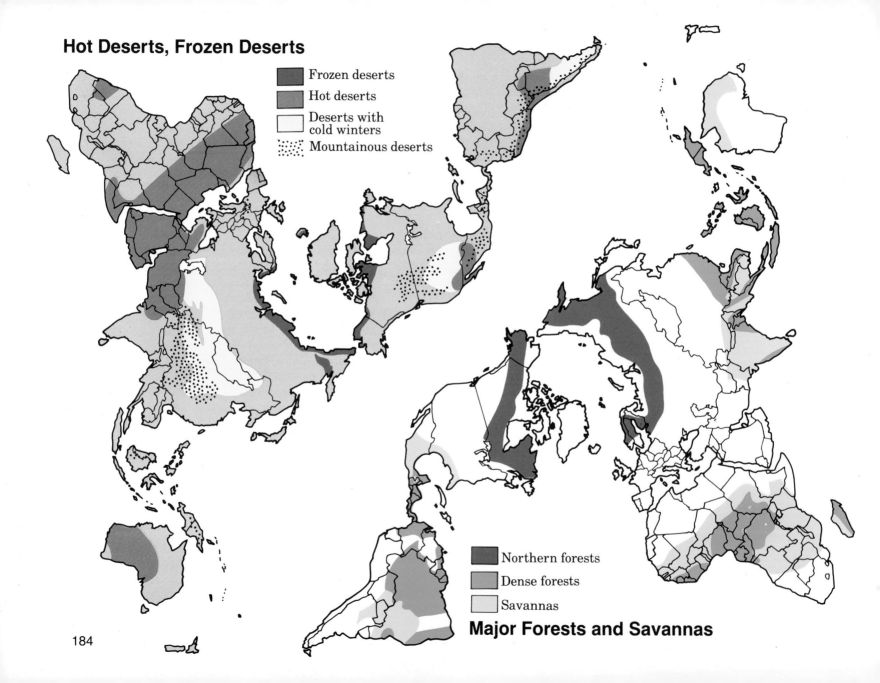

Hot Deserts, Frozen Deserts

Frozen deserts

Hot deserts

Deserts with cold winters

Mountainous deserts

Northern forests

Dense forests

Savannas

Major Forests and Savannas

184

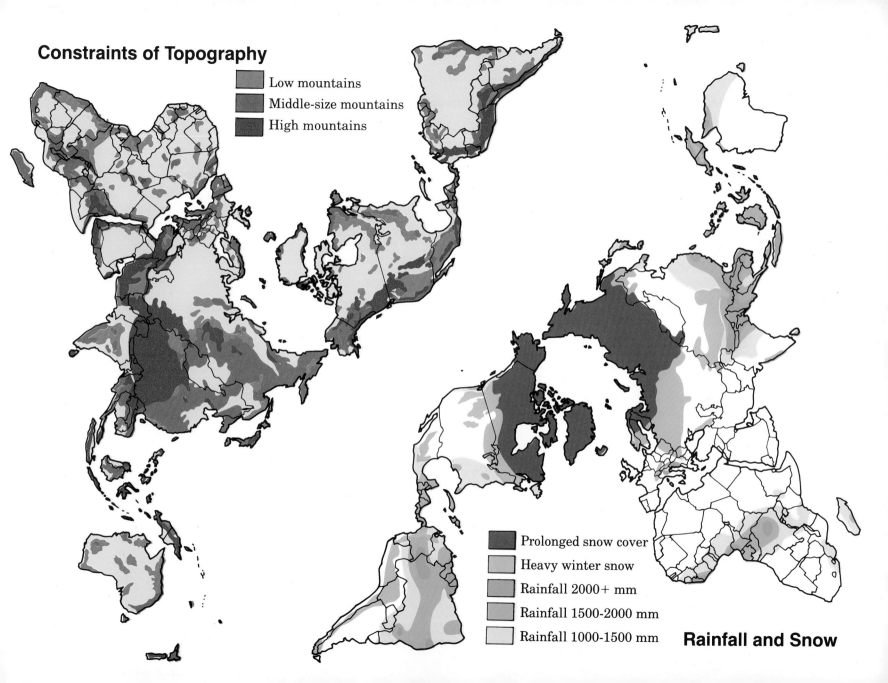

Constraints of Topography

- Low mountains
- Middle-size mountains
- High mountains

Rainfall and Snow

- Prolonged snow cover
- Heavy winter snow
- Rainfall 2000+ mm
- Rainfall 1500-2000 mm
- Rainfall 1000-1500 mm

Availability of Drinking Water

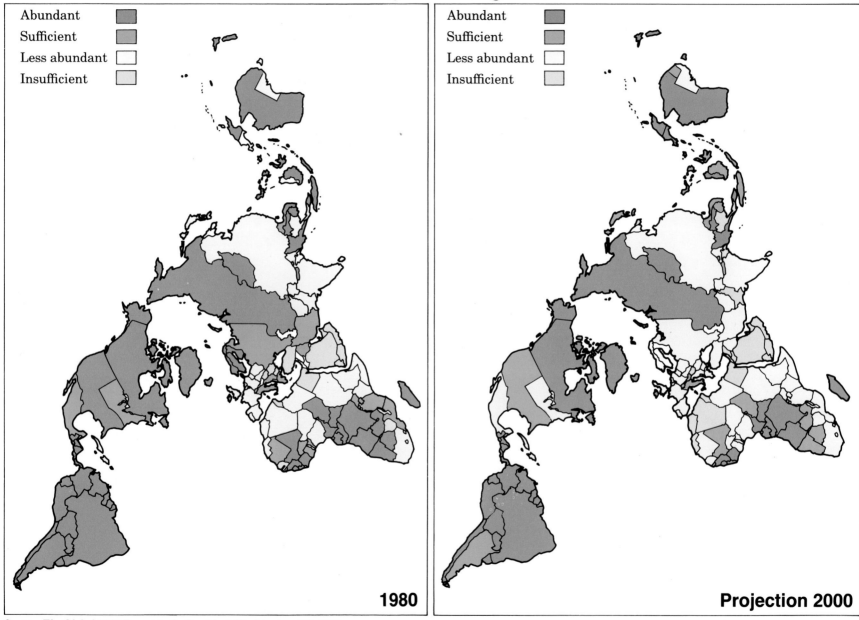

Abundant
Sufficient
Less abundant
Insufficient

1980

Abundant
Sufficient
Less abundant
Insufficient

Projection 2000

Source: The Global 2000 Report to the President, Washington, DC, 1980.

ECONOMIC DATA

Rich and Poor in Minerals

The main areas of mineral production and most known reserves are situated in the great industrial states of the northern hemisphere, in South Africa, and in Australia. Western Europe and Japan have few of them.

Gold production
South Africa   51%
CIS   31.5%
Canada   3%

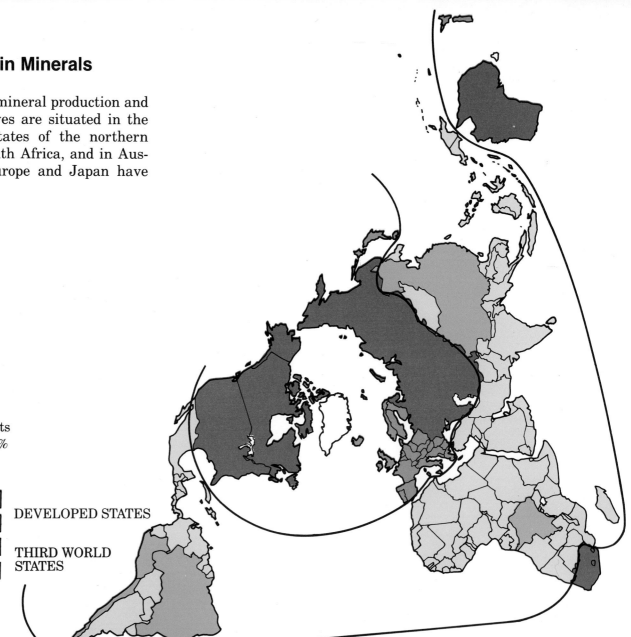

Number of mineral products amounting to more than 5% of world total

More than 6 minerals
Poorly supplied   DEVELOPED STATES

More than 2 minerals
Poorly supplied   THIRD WORLD STATES

Minerals and the Major Producers (% of world total)

	Iron	Cobalt	Chrome	Manganese	Molybdenum	Nickel	Tungsten	Vanadium	Bauxite	Copper	Tin	Lead	Zinc	Silver	Platinum	Antimony	Mercury	Titanium
Major producers																		
South Africa			34	23				30.5							45	16		15
Australia	10.5	6		7.5			6		28.5			11.5	8.5		5			7
Canada	5.5				10.5	26.5				9		10.5	17	10.5				25
United States	8.5				65		6	13.5		19.5		13		10.5		12	14.5	6
CIS/Eastern countries	28	13	37.5	39	11	24	17	30.5	5.5	12	15	17	17	14.5	48	12	32.5	?
Important producers																		
Bolivia							6				10					23.5		
Brazil	11.5			8					5									
Chile					11					13.5								
China	8			6			26	14								18		
India	5.5			6														20
Mexico													5.5	14				
Peru												6	8.5	13				
Zaire		51								6								
Other producers																		
Algeria																	15	
Botswana		5				5.5												
Cuba																		Ilmenite
Spain																	15	
Finland								7										
Gabon				6														
Guinea									16									
Indonesia											13							
Jamaica									14									
Malaysia											25							
Norway																		21
N. Caledonia (Fr.)						7												
Philippines			6															
Thailand											14							
Zambia		9								7.5								
Zimbabwe			6															
Total (%)	77.5	84	83.5	95.5	97.5	63	61	81.5	69	67.5	77	58	56.5	62.5	98	69.5	77	94

* Only production and reserves over 5% of the world total are counted.
• A number of useful minerals (boron, lithium, magnesium, niobium, strontium, tantalum, thorium) have been left out of this table for lack of data.
• Minerals used for fertilizer (potassium, phosphates, etc.) are not included here.
• Titanium: derived primarily from two ores, ilmenite and rutile (incomplete data).

Source: U.S. Bureau of Mines.

Energy and Mineral Resources in the Oceans

Offshore mineral deposits such as deep-sea oil fields are always associated with the continental shelf. Gradually, technological developments are making it possible to operate at greater and greater depths. The number of fields being exploited has increased enormously in the last 25 years.

Since 1950, oceanographic research has revealed the mineral riches of the deep sea, which are in the form of metalliferous mud and polymetallic nodules. The importance of these deposits is promising for the not too distant future.

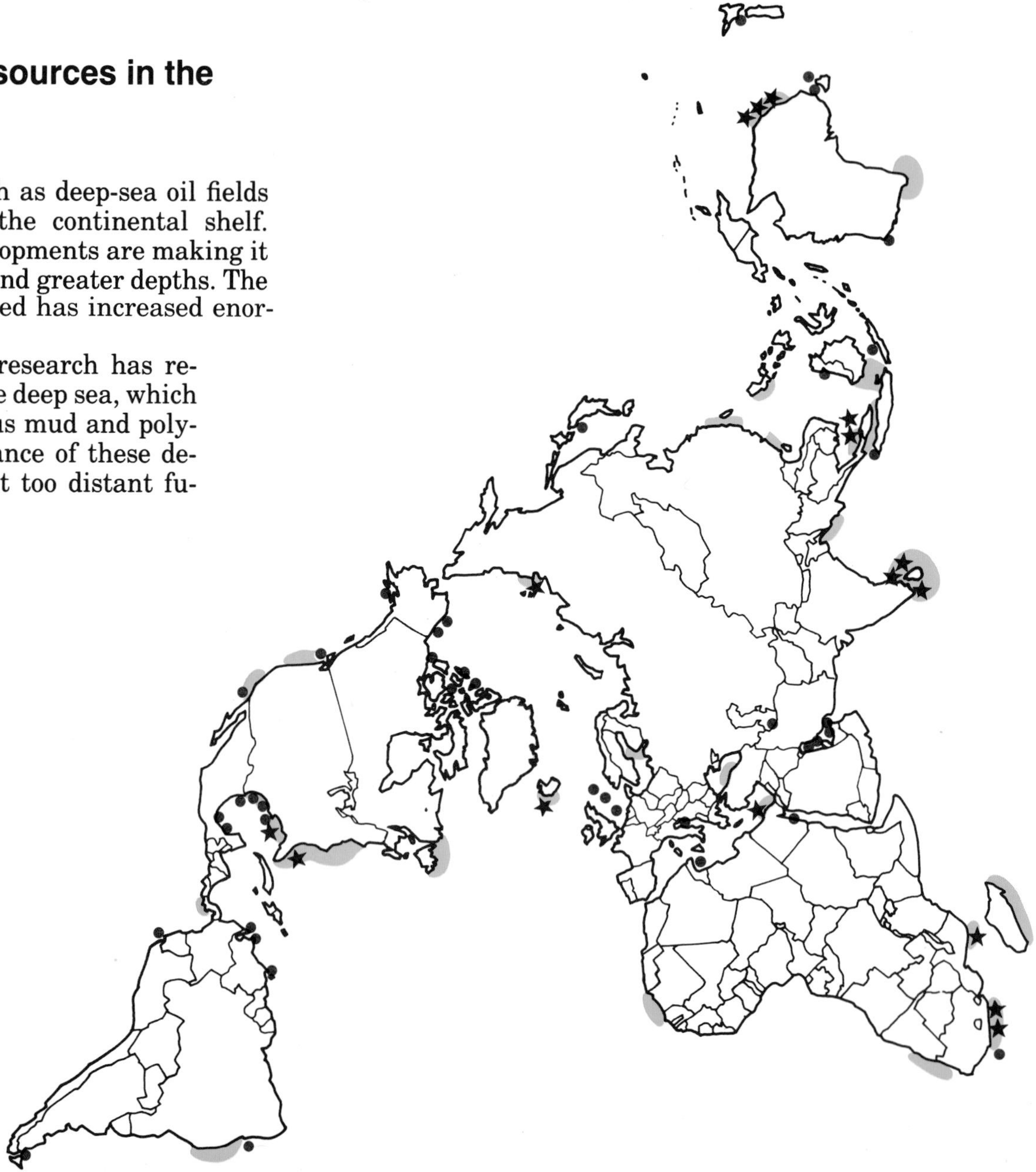

Mineral deposits ☐

Minerals being exploited ★

Oil and natural gas exploitation ●

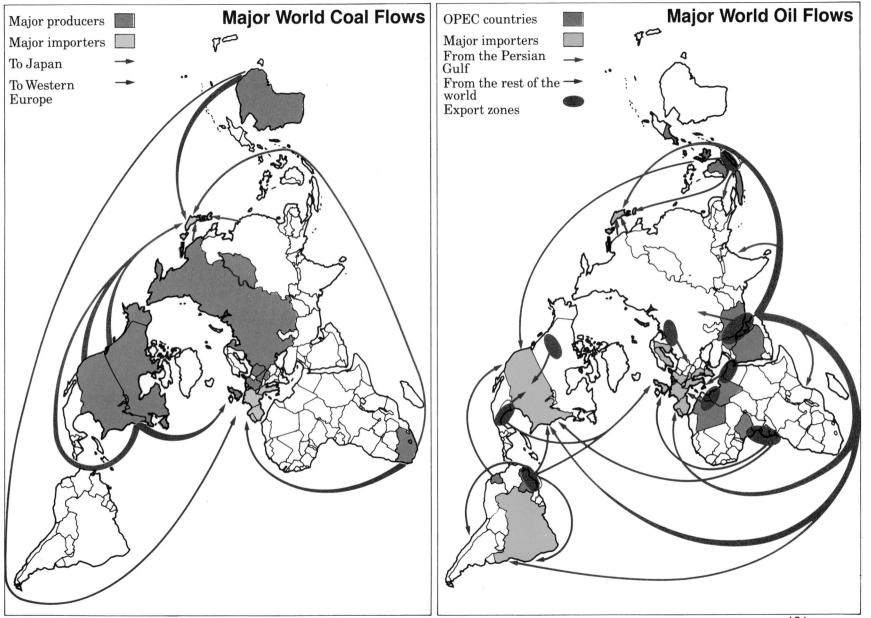

Major World Coal Flows

Major producers

Major importers

To Japan →

To Western Europe →

Major World Oil Flows

OPEC countries

Major importers

From the Persian Gulf →

From the rest of the world →

Export zones

Oil

Since the oil shocks of the 1970s, the demand for oil has slowed down considerably. Western consumption has been reduced by 25% in ten years. Production is now stagnant, at around 3 billion tons. The high-population Third World producers (Nigeria, Indonesia, Mexico, etc.) are suffering a severe recession after a few fat years. Saudi Arabia remains both the vital producer and the market regulator by virtue of its financial power.

World Production

1955	7.72 million tons
1970	2.28 million tons
1978	3.09 million tons
1981	3.05 million tons
1985	2.77 million tons
1989	3.11 million tons

Known Reserves
(90 billion tons)

Middle East	54%
Saudi Arabia	25%
Kuwait	10%
Iran	8%
Iraq	5%
USSR	11%
Mexico	9%
USA	4%

Producers and Reserves (1989)

Production (million tons)		Share of world production	Reserves (million tons)	
CIS	605	19 %	Saudi Arabia	35,000
USA	425	13.7%	Iraq	13,700
Saudi Arabia	270	8.7%	UAE	13,500
Mexico	145	4.6%	Iran	12,700
Iran	145	4.6%	Kuwait	12,500
Iraq	140	4.5%	CIS	8,000

Coal

Production (million tons)		Share of world production	Reserves (million tons)	
China*	900	27.4%	CIS	6,789,000
CIS	600	19 %	USA	2,805,000
USA	600	18.9%	China	1,010,000
Poland	290	9 %	Australia	250,000
India	185	6 %	Germany	230,000
South Africa	175	5.5%	South Africa	85,000

* Coal and lignite together.

Lignite

Production (million tons)

Germany	410	USA	80
CIS	175	Poland	65
Czechoslovakia	95		

Since 1973, the rise in oil prices has given a boost to world coal production, which had been growing slowly since 1955.

1955	1.6 billion tons	1986	3.4 billion tons
1973	2.3 billion tons	1989	3.2 billion tons
1980	3.3 billion tons		

Reserves are enormous, probably 80% of all fossil energy reserves. The appearance of new techniques making it possible to burn coal in the deposits themselves is bound to open up new possibilities.

Members of OPEC (Organization of Petroleum Exporting Countries). Thirteen countries. (Arab countries have formed OAPEC, Organization of Arab Petroleum Exporting Countries.) Initial members included: Iraq, Iran, Kuwait, Libya, Saudi Arabia, and Venezuela (1960). Others followed, including Qatar (1961), Indonesia (1962), Abu Dhabi and the United Arab Emirates (1967), Algeria (1969), Nigeria (1971), Ecuador (1973), Gabon (1975). The 13 states supply more than 50% of the world production of unrefined oil.

Electricity*

Hydroelectricity

	(1980)	(1985)
USA	20%	16.6%
Canada	16%	12.8%
USSR	10%	10.7%
Brazil		4.5%
Japan		4.4%
Norway	4-5% each	4 %
France		2.6%
Sweden		2.5%

Nuclear-powered Electricity**

	(1980)	(1990)
USA	37.5%	28.5%
Japan	11.7%	7.7%
USSR	10.0%	17.5%
France	8.7%	12.8%
W. Germany	6.2%	5.4%
Canada	5.7%	3.2%

*Electricity furnished by power stations using combustible fossil fuels is not included.

**Despite disputes and resistance, the progress in establishing power stations throughout the world is spectacular.

Natural Gas

Production	(1980)	(1985)	Reserves	
USA	35%	26 %	USSR	40%
USSR	30%	36 %	Iran	18%
Netherlands	5%	4.5%	USA	7%
Canada	3%	4.8%	Algeria	4%
			W. Europe	5%

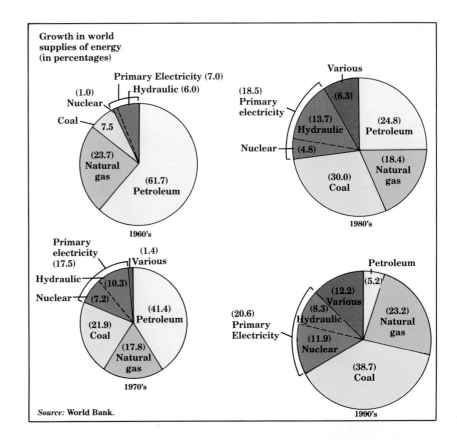

Growth in world supplies of energy (in percentages)

1960's

1980's

1970's

1990's

Source: World Bank.

Energy Consumption per Capita in the Mid-1980's

(In tons of petroleum)

World Energy Production		World Energy Consumption
28%	Third World	14%
(6%)	(including oil exporting nations)	(0.5%)
41%	Developed Western nations and Japan	56%
31%	USSR, Eastern Europe, and China	30%

More than 6 tons
3 to 6 tons
1.5 to 3 tons
0.5 to 1.5 tons
Less than 0.5 tons
North-South line

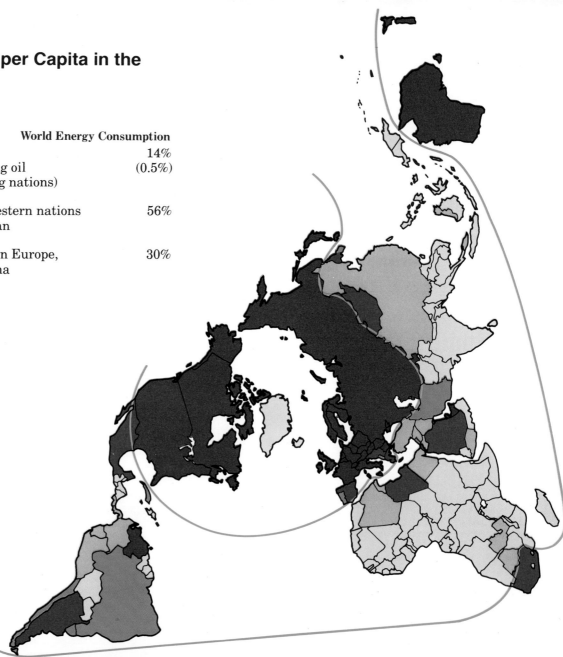

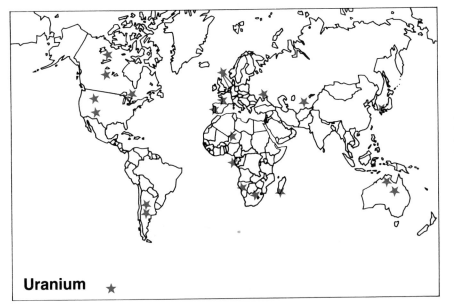

Uranium

Uranium

The states that are big producers and possessors of large reserves* are few and concentrated in North America and the southern hemisphere. There are no reliable figures for China, the CIS, and Eastern Europe.

Production

	(metric tons)	% of world total
Canada	12,000	33
USA	4,800	14
Australia	3,700	11
South Africa	3,500	10.5
Namibia	3,300	10
France	3,200	9.5

CIS—estimated production of 15,000 mt not included in the percentages.

Proved Reserves

Based on 5 million tons; excludes the CIS, China, and Eastern Europe, which have reserves between 3.5 and 7 million tons.

USA	37%
Canada	19%
S. Africa	11%
Australia	7%
Sweden	6%
Niger	5%

Percentage Share of World Industrial Power
(as a percentage of the combined value of mining and manufacturing output)

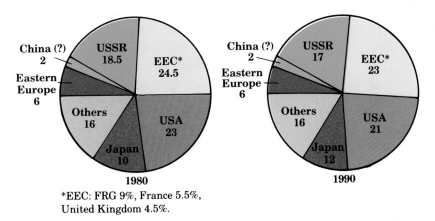

1980

*EEC: FRG 9%, France 5.5%,
United Kingdom 4.5%.

1990

---

*Thorium, occasionally used as a substitute for uranium, is abundant in India (30%), Canada (20%), and Brazil (6%).

World Grain Trade

Major exporters
(% of total exported)

USA	43
France	12.5
Canada	10.5
Australia	6.5
Argentina	4.5

Producers-exporters

Importers

Principal flows →

Chronic malnutrition *

Source: World Bank.

196

LEADING WORLD CEREAL PRODUCERS*

All cereals*

	million metric tons	% of world production
China	363	19.5
USA	284	15
CIS	200	10.5
India	193	10.2
France	57	3.1
Canada	50	2.8
Indonesia	50	2.8
		64

* Calculated on the basis of 8 cereals: wheat, rice, corn, barley, rye, oats, buckwheat, millet.

Major cereals

Wheat

	million metric tons	% of world production
China	90	16.8
CIS	89	16.5
USA	56	10.5
India	54	10
France	32	6
Canada	24	4.5
		64.3

Corn

	million metric tons	% of world production
USA	190	41
China	76	16
Brazil	26	5
CIS	15	3.2
Romania	14.5	3
France	12.5	2.5
		70.5

Rice

	million metric tons	% of world production
China	179	35
India	107	21
Indonesia	43.5	8.5
Bangladesh	26	5.5
Thailand	21.5	4.5
Vietnam	17	3.5
		78

Barley

	million metric tons
CIS	53
Germany	18
Canada	12
France	10
USA	8.8

Fertilizers

Chemical fertilizers are now intensively used in countries with a modern agriculture to ensure high and regular yields, and also to combat soil deterioration.

The major fertilizer producers are the USA, the CIS, the EEC (over half the total), and Canada.

Livestock

The real value of livestock is difficult to compare because of the enormous variety of species and modes of stock-rearing. High-productivity Danish cattle and the livestock of India, for example, have nothing in common.

Over the last two decades, factory farming of chickens and pigs has vastly increased in the developed countries, largely replacing traditional methods of husbandry.

Cattle (million head)		Sheep (million head)		Pigs (million head)	
India	196	Australia	163	China	350
Brazil	137	CIS	140	CIS	78
CIS	119	China	102	USA	56
USA	100	New Zealand	65	Brazil	35
China	77	India	54	Germany	35
Argentina	51	Turkey	52	Poland	20

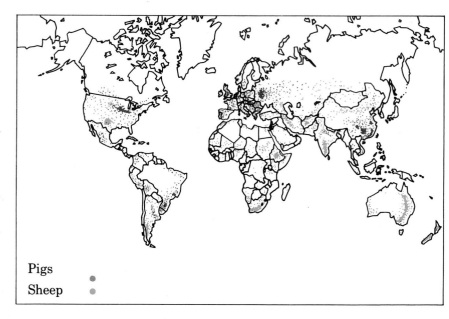

Pigs
Sheep

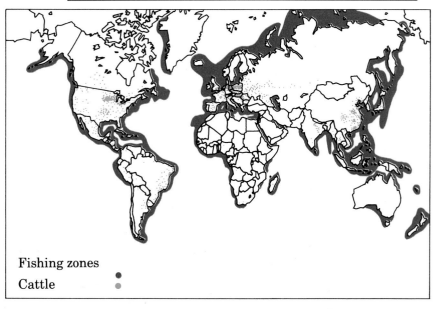

Fishing zones
Cattle

Fishing

Fishing supplies about 10% of humanity's protein requirements. In addition to food, industrial fishing produces a number of products used in industry: flours, oils, grease, etc.

If maritime states extend the limits of their territorial waters to 200 nautical miles, the industrial and deep-sea fishing activities of other states are likely to be severely handicapped.

Japan
CIS
USA   } Major fishing fleets
Chile
Peru
Norway

POPULATION FACTORS

Population by Major Regions in the Second Half of the 20th Century: 1950–1975–Projection 2000

Source: Global 2000 Report to the President, Washington, DC; and the World Bank.

World Population 1800-2000

Year	In millions
1800	900
1850	1100
1900	1600
1950	2600
1980	4400
2000	6100

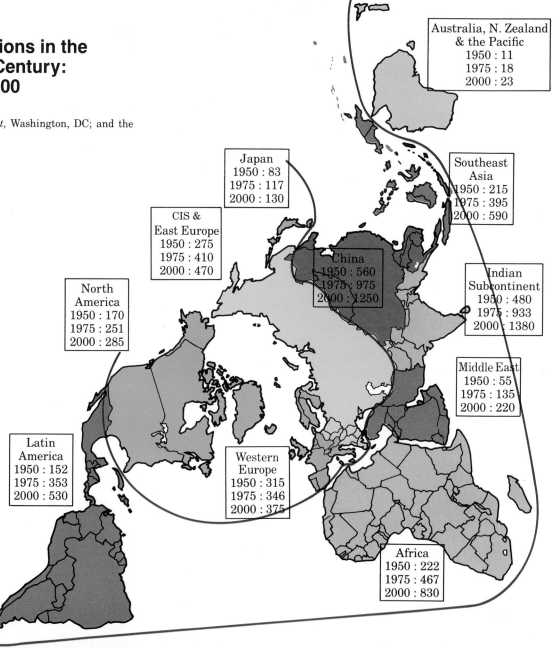

Australia, N. Zealand & the Pacific
1950 : 11
1975 : 18
2000 : 23

Japan
1950 : 83
1975 : 117
2000 : 130

Southeast Asia
1950 : 215
1975 : 395
2000 : 590

CIS & East Europe
1950 : 275
1975 : 410
2000 : 470

China
1950 : 560
1975 : 975
2000 : 1250

Indian Subcontinent
1950 : 480
1975 : 933
2000 : 1380

North America
1950 : 170
1975 : 251
2000 : 285

Middle East
1950 : 55
1975 : 135
2000 : 220

Latin America
1950 : 152
1975 : 353
2000 : 530

Western Europe
1950 : 315
1975 : 346
2000 : 375

Africa
1950 : 222
1975 : 467
2000 : 830

Most Populous States: Evolution of Their Population, 1930 to 2000 (est.)

	1930	1950	1980	2000
China........	430	540	970	1240
India	335	370	673	975
USSR/CIS	160	180	265	315
USA.........	120	155	227	260
Indonesia.....	60	77	146	220
Brazil........	40	53	119	177
Bangladesh ...		40	92	148
Pakistan		35	82	141
Nigeria	19	28	85	161
Japan........	64	84	117	130
Mexico.......	16	26	67	110
Vietnam......	22	25	54	88
Philippines ...	12	20	48	75
Thailand	11	19	46	68
Turkey.......	11	21	45	70
Iran	14	20	38	64
Egypt........	14	21	40	61
Italy.........	41	47	57	61

Evolution of rhythm of world increase (mean annual rate)

1800-1850: 0.55%
1850-1900: 0.57%
1900-1950: 0.83%
1950-1980: 1.87%
1980-2000: 1.65% est.

AGE AND SEX OF THE WORLD POPULATION, 1975 AND 2000

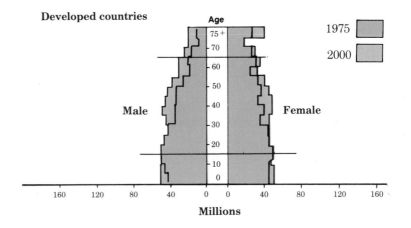

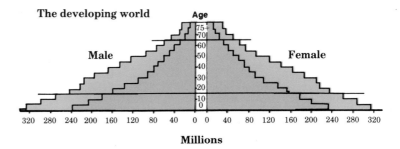

Source: Global 2000 Report to the President, Washington, DC, 1980.

World Urbanization in the 1980's

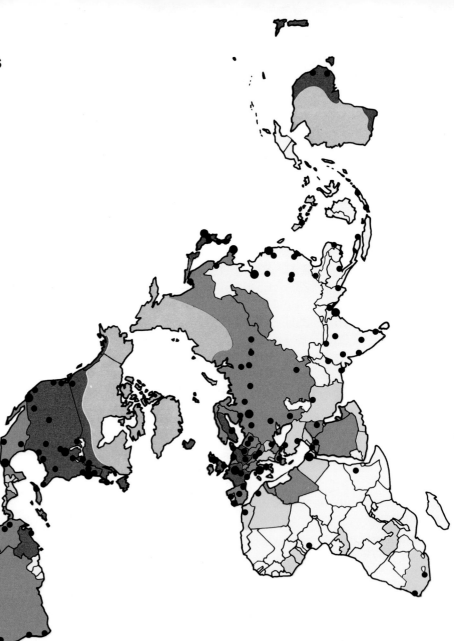

more than 75% urban

more than 50% urban

more than 35% urban

less than 35% urban

Empty regions

Depopulated areas are shown
for the USSR, Canada,
Australia.

Urbanization

The Major Cities or Concentrations of the World

(*In millions of inhabitants; the cities of the powerful industrial nations are underlined.*)

1900		1950		2000 (est.)	
London	6.4	New York	12.3	Mexico	31
New York	4.2	London	10.4	S. Paulo	25.8
Paris	3.9	Rhine-Ruhr	6.9	Shanghai	23.7
Berlin	2.4	Tokyo	6.7	Tokyo-Yokohama	23.1
Chicago	1.7	Shanghai	5.8	New York	22.4
Vienna	1.6	Paris	5.5	Peking	20.9
Tokyo	1.4	Buenos Aires	5.3	Rio	19
St Petersburg	1.4	Chicago	4.9	Bombay	16.8
Philadelphia	1.4	Moscow	4.8	Calcutta	16.4
Manchester	1.2	Calcutta	4.6	Jakarta	15.7
Birmingham	1.2	Los Angeles	4	Los Angeles	13.9
Moscow	1.2	Osaka	3.8	Seoul	13.7
Peking	1.1	Milan	3.6	Cairo	12.9
Calcutta	1	Bombay	3	Madras	12.7
Boston	1	Mexico	3	Buenos Aires	12.1
Glasgow	1	Philadelphia	4	Karachi	11.6
Liverpool	0.98	Rio	2.9	Delhi	11.5
Osaka	0.95	Detroit	2.8	Manila	11.4
Constantinople	0.92	Naples	2.6	Teheran	11.1
Hamburg	0.9	Leningrad	2.5	Baghdad	11

URBAN POPULATION

Source: World Bank.

Developed countries

Countries with medium income

Least developed countries

1950
1950-1975
1975-2000

Billions 0   0.5   1.0   1.5

NORTH–SOUTH

As capitalism introduced modernizing elements abroad, it dislocated the traditional economies of the dominated countries. These distortions lie at the origin of what is called underdevelopment. In fact, the Third World covers very diverse realities, although it is possible to list a number of common traits: preponderance of the agricultural sector, high birth rate, very marked economic and social inequalities. Over the last two decades, the Third World has seen growing differentiations caused by both the level of local productive forces and/or the significance of mineral resources, particularly oil and natural gas. Outside a handful of countries that have seen high growth rates, the majority of Third World countries have made little progress and have generally stagnated or even regressed. In a majority of countries, agriculture, which still employs the bulk of the population, cannot satisfy local needs. Deterioration in the terms of trade that has marked the three decades following World War II continues to weigh heavily. Only the OPEC countries, producers of oil and natural gas, were able to modify the laws of the market during the decade 1973 to 1983.

Population growth, which has since the beginning of the century been consistently high in the Third World, continues at a rate approaching 3%. World population, estimated at 4 billion 15 years ago, will pass 6 billion by the end of the century. At that date, peoples of the Third World will make up 82% of the globe's population, whereas they were only 65% in 1950. The living conditions of the people who live in the Third World have scarcely improved in twenty years, while a third of them are considered to be living in conditions well below subsistence. The reforms proposed by international organizations concerned with development run up against both the unequal North–South system and the political impediments constituted by the ruling strata in the Third World. Up to now, the countries that have recorded notable growth are the oil-producing countries, especially those with small populations, like Kuwait, Saudi Arabia, the United Arab Emirates, and Libya; a handful of countries, such as Brazil or Gabon (underpopulated) that have large mineral resources; and a series of Asian countries where the quality of manpower and business abilities are of a high order: Taiwan, Singapore, South Korea, Hong Kong, Malaysia, Thailand, etc.

Today, there are three categories of countries in the Third World: those few that have a high or relatively high growth rate, some of which already have a significant industrial infrastructure; a sizable proportion of average countries that are developing despite a high population growth; and about fifty classified as less developed countries (LDCs) whose situation is tragic. The current crisis is hitting the Third World very hard. Africa seems particularly threatened in every respect: stagnation, or even regression of growth, galloping population growth, corruption, and the ineffectiveness of the vast majority of ruling strata. In Andean America (Ecuador, Peru, Bolivia, etc.), the situation—and the prospects—are scarcely any better. In Southeast Asia, alongside not insignificant growth and dynamic industrial sectors, there remain, especially in the Indian subcontinent (Bangladesh, India, Pakistan), enormous areas of poverty and malnutrition.

Evolution of GNP by Main World Regions 1975—Projection 2000
(In dollars per capita)

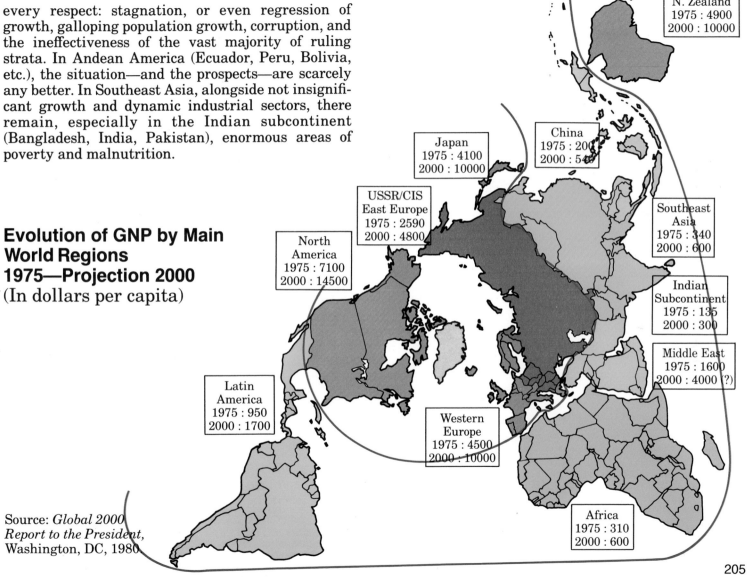

Australia
N. Zealand
1975 : 4900
2000 : 10000

Japan
1975 : 4100
2000 : 10000

China
1975 : 200
2000 : 540

USSR/CIS
East Europe
1975 : 2590
2000 : 4800

Southeast
Asia
1975 : 340
2000 : 600

North
America
1975 : 7100
2000 : 14500

Indian
Subcontinent
1975 : 135
2000 : 300

Middle East
1975 : 1600
2000 : 4000 (?)

Latin
America
1975 : 950
2000 : 1700

Western
Europe
1975 : 4500
2000 : 10000

Africa
1975 : 310
2000 : 600

Source: *Global 2000 Report to the President*, Washington, DC, 1980.

205

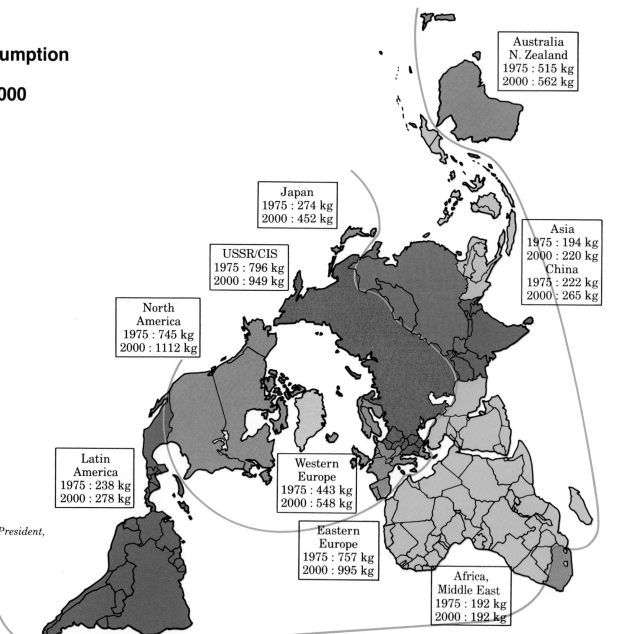

**Annual Grain Consumption
per Capita
1975—Projection 2000**

Australia
N. Zealand
1975 : 515 kg
2000 : 562 kg

Japan
1975 : 274 kg
2000 : 452 kg

Asia
1975 : 194 kg
2000 : 220 kg
China
1975 : 222 kg
2000 : 265 kg

USSR/CIS
1975 : 796 kg
2000 : 949 kg

North
America
1975 : 745 kg
2000 : 1112 kg

Latin
America
1975 : 238 kg
2000 : 278 kg

Western
Europe
1975 : 443 kg
2000 : 548 kg

Eastern
Europe
1975 : 757 kg
2000 : 995 kg

Africa,
Middle East
1975 : 192 kg
2000 : 192 kg

Source: Global 2000 Report to the President,
Washington, DC, 1980.

The Third World: East-West Struggle

The period immediately after World War II was favorable to the Communist forces in Asia: in China totally, in Korea partly. After a long rearguard action waged by the French and the Americans, the upholders of "Marxism-Leninism" won a major success in Indochina, of which Vietnam was the major beneficiary.

Conversely, in Indonesia in 1965, the largest Communist party in Asia was decimated. Over time, the economic situation of the regional allies (Taiwan, Singapore, South Korea, Thailand, Malaysia) of the United States improved.

The recognition of China in 1972 (after a decade of Sino-Soviet conflict), as a result of the Nixon-Kissinger initiative, enabled the United States to engage in a three-sided game advantageous to it.

In the Middle East, compared with the Baghdad Pact (Turkey, Iraq, Iran, Pakistan) period, the West suffered serious setbacks. The fall of the Shah in Iran was a major setback for the USA. But after the long alliance during the Nasser period, the breach precipitated by Egypt (1972) was just as serious for the USSR, whose Arab policy ran into difficulties (Iraq) and was only very partially effective (Syria, PLO) in a situation where, up till now, the United States continues to be in the position of arbiter. Israel, a close ally of the United States, remains the major military power in the region, while Saudi Arabia, whose stability is vital for the West, has played a moderating role among the oil-producing countries.

Russian occupation of Afghanistan, conversely, weakened the United States ally Pakistan, whereas India has succeeded since Nehru in making the best use of the delicate notion of nonalignment.

The Western preserve that Africa had been up to 1975, despite various Soviet attempts (from Guinea, 1959, to Sudan and Somalia in the early 1970s) became an integral part of the East-West confrontation. In Angola (1975) and Ethiopia (1977), the presence of Cuban troops added an altogether new dimension to the Soviet presence. Mozambique was also included among the allies of the USSR. Other African countries sometimes classified as Soviet allies seemed to be in a much more ambiguous situation: Congo, Guinea-Bissau, Madagascar, etc. On the continent as a whole, the West continued to be predominant.

In Latin America, the United States (except during the Carter administration) has essentially maintained its role as policeman: Directly or indirectly, the policy of the "big stick" has been used in Guatemala (1954), without success in Cuba (1961), in the Dominican Republic (1965), in the training of counterinsurgency forces throughout the continent to deal with the guerrilla movements of the 1960s, as well as in Brazil (1964), Chile (1973), Grenada (1983), and Panama (1989).

After the Sandinista victory in Nicaragua, the number of armed struggles increased in the 1980s (El Salvador, Guatemala). These local guerrilla movements, born of particular economic and social situations, enabled the USSR and especially Cuba to challenge Washington in its own backyard, the Caribbean Basin so vital for the geostrategic security of the United States. After a period in which the USSR under Brezhnev extended its presence in Africa and Latin America and stepped up its pressure both in outer Asia and Southeast Asia, the late 1980s saw a new policy conducted by Mikhail Gorbachev that consisted in a withdrawal dictated by economic and financial, if not political, necessities.

After eight years of occupation, the USSR left Afghanistan and Gorbachev succeeded in passing this setback off as a victory for *glasnost*. The settlement of the independence of Namibia, which involved the withdrawal of both Cuban troops from Angola and South African ones from South-west Africa, indicated a disengagement by the USSR from southern Africa, to be seen not only in Mozambique but also in Angola.

Gradually the USSR's disengagement from Central America left Cuba increasingly isolated, and its disengagement from southern Africa indicated a fallback to the periphery where the Middle East represented the major preoccupation of Soviet diplomacy.

Deprived of Soviet support, President Mengistu's regime collapsed in Ethiopia, the military successes of the Eritrean People's Liberation Front having greatly contributed to weakening it.

The Gulf War led to a marked weakening of Iraq and once again raises the problem of a new balance in the Middle East. This will be less favorable to peoples (Palestinians, Kurds, etc.) than to states, notably those that participated directly or indirectly in the victory.

On the Arab side, the new regional security will be assured by the "Cairo group": Egypt, Syria, Saudi Arabia, and other Gulf states. After a long period of deliberate eclipse, Turkey has rediscovered its geographical and historical role in the Near East, while Iran once again occupies the place it is entitled to by virtue of the size of its population, its cultural importance, and its economic potential.

Arms Sales to Third World Countries in the Late 1980's

The leading arms exporters were the United States (37%), the USSR (30%), France (8%), and Great Britain and West Germany (5% each).

The major arms importers were in the Middle East (40%). If members of NATO (12%) and the Warsaw Pact (12%) are excluded, the other importers were Africa (17%), Asia (11%), Latin America (5%). In order of quantity, the main purchasers were Saudi Arabia, Jordan, Iraq, Syria, Libya, South Korea, India, Israel, Vietnam, Morocco, and Ethiopia. These countries (plus Iran*) bought almost a third of the total arms sold in Asia, Africa, and Latin America.

---

* It is difficult to know what place Iran occupies at present.

THE MILITARY BALANCE

The Military Balance

Compiling a balance sheet using tables listing the armed might of the protagonists is only one approach.[1]

This statistical listing, though very useful, is only one admittedly vital factor in a balance in which socio-political factors, attitudes, and will remain of fundamental importance. Traditionally, the listings are measured by experts, but strategies are won with peoples and leaders.

For forty-five years, generalized war has been avoided through the balance of terror. Conflicts have taken place in the framework of indirect strategies, in local conventional wars, or still more often in guerrilla movements or crisis management without overt conflict (Berlin, Cuba).

During the decades after the Cuban missile crisis (1962), the USSR greatly increased its military might in the air, on the sea, and in the nuclear domain.

But strategy is not limited to war—far from it. It aims above all at producing psychological effects on peoples.

For the first time after Brezhnev's escalation using the SS-20 to put pressure on the Europeans, an agreement to reduce medium-range nuclear missiles was reached at Washington in 1987. Over 2,600 missiles were destroyed between 1988 and 1992. Talks concerning arms reduction in Europe are continuing. Western Europe has entered a new era in which it is

A One-Third Reduction in Principle of Offensive Strategic Weapons

	Current Arsenals USA	CIS	Ceiling 1979	Ceiling[2] 1990
Total launchers	2,002	2,503	2,250	1,600
Total nuclear war-heads	14,637	11,694		6,000
of which land-based heavy ICBMs	0	308	308	154
Bombers equipped with Cruise missiles (ALCM)	158	0		150 & 210
Warheads on ICBMs & SLBMs	9,029	10,674		4,900
Warheads on heavy ICBMs	0			1,540
Warheads on mobile ICBMs	0			1,100
Ship-based Cruise missiles (SLCMs)				880

---

[1] In addition, figures are quickly out of date. See *The Military Balance* by the International Institute of Strategic Studies, London, which annually provides figures on the world military balance, nation by nation.

[2] Over 2,600 missiles were to be destroyed between 1988 and 1991.

dependent more than ever on the wills of the two superpowers.

The comparisons reflect only very imperfectly the actual forces, even numerically, as far as air and land potentials are concerned. The American and Soviet tank and airborne divisions have quite different compositions. In fact, no one doubts the superiority of the Warsaw Pact's conventional forces in the European theater.

From the point of view of naval potential, the superiority of the Atlantic Alliance is beyond doubt, control of the seas being vital to the West.

Bush summit proposal shown in white	NATO proposed and 1987 proposal—NATO figures (Note 1)						Warsaw-pact proposal— Warsaw-pact figures (Note 1)		
	NATO now	Warsaw pact now	Each side after cuts	NATO "stationed forces" now (Note 2)	Warsaw pact "stationed forces" now	"Stationed forces" after cuts	NATO now	Warsaw pact now	Each side after cuts
Troops	2.21m**	3.10m**	●	300,000†	600,000†	275,000†	2.98m**	3.24m**	2.60m**
Tanks	22,224#	51,500	20,000	5,121	9,790	3,200	30,690	59,470	26,854
Armoured personnel-carriers	32,475#	70,000†	28,000*	8,500†	13,800†	6,000	46,900	70,330	41,038
Artillery	17,328#	43,400	16,500	850†	4,960	1,700	57,060	71,560	49,928
Combat aircraft	3,977	8,250	3,380	—	—	—	5,450	5,355	4,686
Combat helicopters	2,419	3,700	2,056	—	—	—	5,270	2,785	2,437

Note 1: NATO and Warsaw-pact figures are not directly comparable because the two sides use different definitions of equipment
Note 2: "Stationed forces" are forces stationed outside their own country
* Of these, no more than 12,000 may be fighting vehicles with mounted guns
† *The Economist* estimates

\# Includes equipment in storage
‡ Includes only Soviet and American troops, both ground and air-forces. Cuts would come only from combat forces
● Not in original NATO proposal
** Ground-force troops only

Source: I.I.S.S.

Deployment of United States Naval Forces

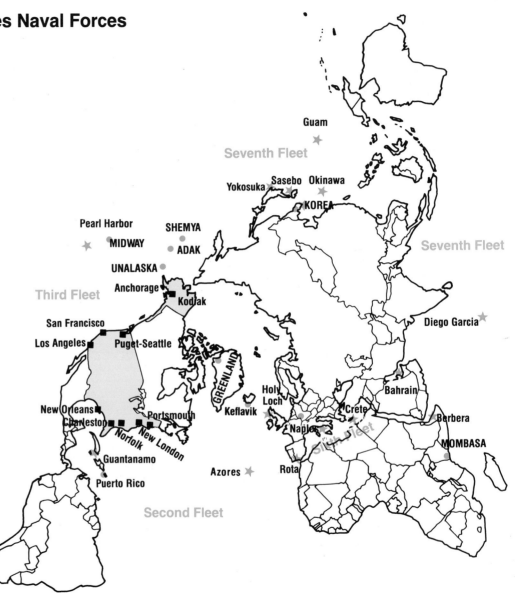

Guam

Seventh Fleet

Sasebo Okinawa
Yokosuka
KOREA

Seventh Fleet

Pearl Harbor SHEMYA
MIDWAY ADAK

UNALASKA

Anchorage
Third Fleet Kodiak

San Francisco
Los Angeles Puget-Seattle

Diego Garcia

GREENLAND

Holy
Loch Bahrain
Keflavik Crete

New Orleans Portsmouth
Charleston Naples Berbera
Norfolk New London Sixth Fleet
Guantanamo MOMBASA

Major bases ★
Supply stations
and other bases ●
Bases in the USA ■

Azores Rota

Second Fleet

212

The Sea and Sea Power

The sea is the most widely used means of communications and trade, and the volume of trade has continuously increased over recent decades. The West—and Japan—depend heavily on freedom of navigation.

As a result of recent technological progress, the sea, a traditional source of wealth from fishing, has become an object of conflict, and disputes over the limits of sovereignty have increased. Offshore petroleum already accounts for a third of world production. But the very near prospect of the exploitation of significant ocean mineral resources is awakening appetites.

The Maritime Convention adopted in 1982 by most countries—but not by the United States, which is the best equipped technologically to exploit undersea riches—stipulates that territorial waters extend 12 miles and that states exercise sovereign rights (especially economic ones) up to a 200-mile limit.

During the 1970s, the rise of Soviet sea power, the result of two decades of effort, was one of the main factors changing the East-West balance, which had previously been almost exclusively limited to the land theater. From 1961 onward, the Soviet fleet progressively extended its presence, and by 1975 it was a worldwide force. In the 1990's, however, American naval superiority remains undeniable.

WORLDWIDE DEPLOYMENT OF AMERICAN NAVAL FORCES

Second Fleet (Atlantic)
Major bases: *Norfolk*, Charleston, Jacksonville, New Orleans, Puerto Rico, Boston, New London, Brunswick (Portland)
• 76 important combat vessels
Units of this fleet are at Guantanamo (Cuba), Bermuda, Keflavik (Iceland), Holy Loch (GB).

Third Fleet (Eastern Pacific)
Major bases: *Pearl Harbor* (Hawaii), San Francisco, San Diego, Whidbey I., Long Beach (Los Angeles), Adak (Alaska)
• 47 important combat vessels

Sixth Fleet (Mediterranean)
Principal bases: Gaeta, Naples (Italy), Rota (Spain)
• 16 important combat vessels

Seventh Fleet (Western Pacific)*
Major bases: Yokosuka (Japan), Guam, Midway
• 23 important combat vessels

---

* A certain number of combat vessels are in the Indian Ocean and the Persian Gulf area.

Note: The headquarters of the fleets are shown in italics.

Military Sites Open to Inspection: Washington Accords (1987)

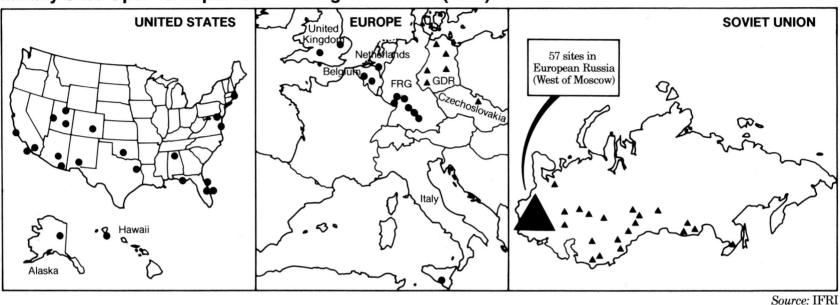

UNITED STATES

EUROPE

United Kingdom

Netherlands

Belgium

FRG

GDR

Czechoslovakia

Italy

Hawaii

Alaska

SOVIET UNION

57 sites in
European Russia
(West of Moscow)

Source: IFRI

United States

22 sites or installations,
11 of them missile
launch sites.

Western Europe

12 sites or installations,
9 of which may be open
to missiles.

Eastern Europe

7 bases which may be
open to missiles.

Soviet Union

77 sites or installations,
53 of which can accommodate missiles.

The USA under the Threat of Soviet Missiles In the 1980's

Distances at which Soviet submarine missile launchers were able to hit the territory of the USA in 1970 and in 1980.

Source: U.S. Naval Proceedings, Washington, DC, 1981.

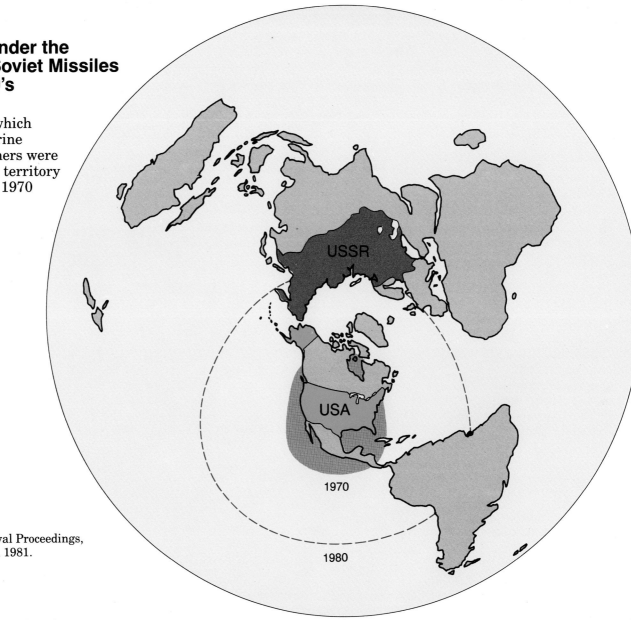

The USSR under the Threat of American Missiles In the 1980's

Distances at which American submarine missiles could hit Soviet territory in 1970, 1980 (Trident I), and 1990 (Trident II).

Source: U.S. Naval Proceedings, Washington, DC, 1981.

Space

Surveillance is currently the most important military application of space. Satellites make it possible to watch enemy missile bases and thus to shorten the warning time. Satellites equipped with cameras move on an orbit that varies between 150 and 500 km high. In the 1980's, the U.S. began the S.D.I. program.

Successful Space Launches

The conquest of space has been largely dominated by the U.S. and the USSR.

Year	1951–1960	1961–1965	1966–1970	1971–1975	1976–1980	1981	1986
USA	31	239	244	135	111	18	6
USSR	9	121	335	413	461	98	91

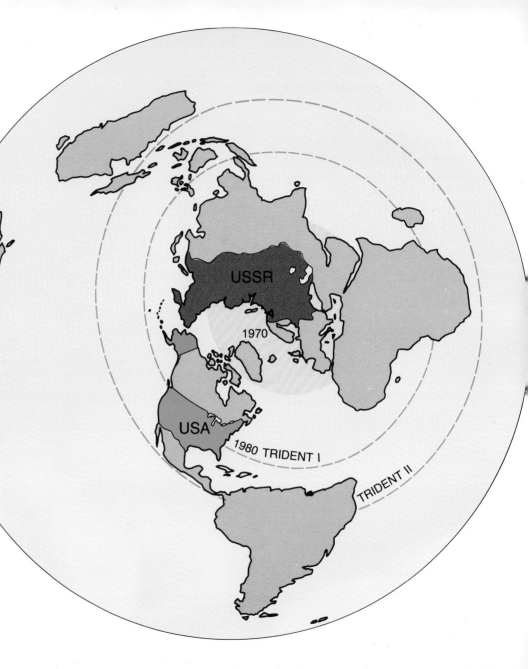

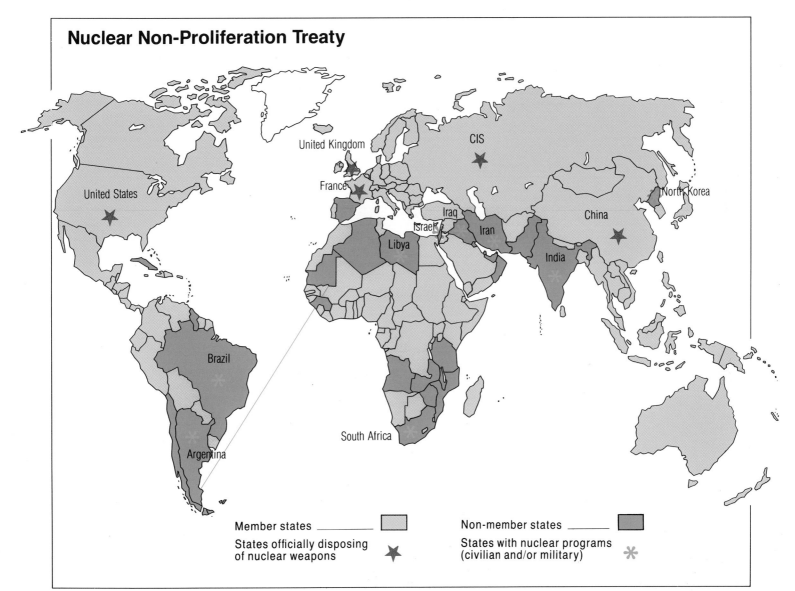

Nuclear Non-Proliferation Treaty

United Kingdom

CIS

United States

France

Iraq

Israel

Iran

China

North Korea

Libya

India

Brazil

South Africa

Argentina

Member states ——————

Non-member states ——————

States officially disposing of nuclear weapons

States with nuclear programs (civilian and/or military)

Chronology: Major Weapons Systems

Year	1945	1950	1955	1960	1965	1970	1975	1980	1983
Politico-military events		Israel 48 / Korea 50 / NATO 49 52	End Vietnam I 54 / Bandung 55	Hungary 56 / Suez 56 / Start Vietnam II 61	Kennedy 60 / Cuba 62	France leaves NATO 66 / Czech. 68 / Six-Day War 67	Bangladesh 71 / Paris Accords 73 / Yom Kippur War 73	Fall of Saigon 75 / Ogaden 77	Afghanistan 79-80 / Vietnam China 79 / Poland 80-81	Falklands 82 / Lebanon 82
Nuclear events	Hiroshima Nagasaki 45	Atomic bomb USSR 49 / Atomic bomb GB 52 / H bomb USSR 53	H bomb US 52 / H bomb GB 57		Atomic bomb Fr 60 / Atomic bomb China 64	H bomb Fr 68 / H bomb China 67	Atomic bomb India 74		

Weapons systems and vehicles

US — Strategic

Year	1945	1950	1955	1960	1965	1970	1975	1980	1983
		(B-47–B-52 51 53)	1st nuclear sub US 54	1st satellite Explorer 58 / 1st SLBM Polaris I 61	Minute Man I 61 / Titan II 62 / Polaris III 64 MIRV	Minute Man II 66 / Poseidon III 71 MIRV	Moon landing 69 / Minute Man III MIRV 70	Space shuttle 81 / Trident IV 80	ACLM 82

US — Tactical

Year	1945	1950	1955	1960	1965	1970	1975	1980	1983
		Honest John 53	Thor Jupiter 59-63	Sergeant 62 / Pershing I 64	FB III 69 / Lance 72				Pershing II 83 / GLCM 83

USSR — Strategic

Year	1945	1950	1955	1960	1965	1970	1975	1980	1983
			Sputnik 57 / Bear 56 / 1st SLBM SSN4 55 / SSN4 57-65	1st ICBM SS-7 61	SS-9–SS-11 65-66 / SSN5 H 64 / Yankee 67		SS-17 (MIRV) 75 / SS-18–SS-19 74 75		

USSR — Tactical

Year	1945	1950	1955	1960	1965	1970	1975	1980	1983
			TV16 (Badger) 55 / Scud-Frog 57 / SS-4 59	SS-5 61			TU 22M (Backfire) 74	SS-21–SS-22–SS-23 78 79 80 / SS-20 77	

Others

Year	1945	1950	1955	1960	1965	1970	1975	1980	1983
				Buccaneer GB 62 / Mirage IV Fr 64	1st SLBM Fr.-67 / Polaris III GB-67 / 1st missile Fr 68-70	Pluton Fr-73	M20 Fr-77	MRBM China-80 / S3 Fr-80	

Source: Pierre Saint Macary, *Conflicts in the Contemporary World*, FNSP, 1982. Revised and expanded by Michel Tatu (1989).

1985	1986	1987	1988	1989
	Reykjavik 86	Washington Treaty 87	Soviet withdrawal from Afghanistan 88–89	
		Intervention of U.S. & Western Fleets in the Gulf 86–87		

Application of the
Washington Treaty
88–

Trident D5
89

MX

Removal
Pershing
GLMC
91

SS-25   SS-24

Removal SS-21–SS-23
Removal SS-20
88–91

M4
(Fr)

The New Economic Centers of Southeast Asia

The Forces in Europe in 1987
before the Washington Accords

	NATO		Warsaw Pact	
	United States	**Allies**	**Soviet Union**	**Allies**
Medium-range missiles (1,000-5,000km)	108 Pershing 2 208 cruise missiles	64 Polaris(G.B) 80 M20(F) 16 M4(F) 18 SSBS-3 (F) (a)	292 SS-20(b) 112 SS-4	
Short-range missiles (500-1,000km)		72 Pershing 1	30 SS-23 77 SS-12/22	
Battlefield missiles	108 Lance 1,000 artillery pieces	55 Lance 44 Pluton (F) 2,000 artillery pieces	350 SS-21/FROG 350 SCUD B 3,500 artillery pieces	215 SS-21/FROG 150 SCUD B 160 artillery pieces
Airplanes	435	1,182	1,765	250
Conventional Forces	Troops: 5 million Tanks: 20,300 Airplanes: 3,200 Ships: 308		Troops: 6.2 million Tanks: 46,600 Airplanes: 7,200 Ships: 126	

Source: I.I.S.S. - London

North America and the Arctic

The U.S. and Canada have initiated the equivalent of a common market, which should be institutionalized by 1998. Together, they represent a huge space. Their combined territorial lands and waters cover about one-sixth of the earth's surface—almost as large an area as the CIS, with a comparable, and much more homogeneous, population.

Talks are under way aimed at establishing a customs union with Mexico. If this were to come about, Mexico would act as a buffer state in relation to immigration from other Latin American countries and suppliers of manpower.

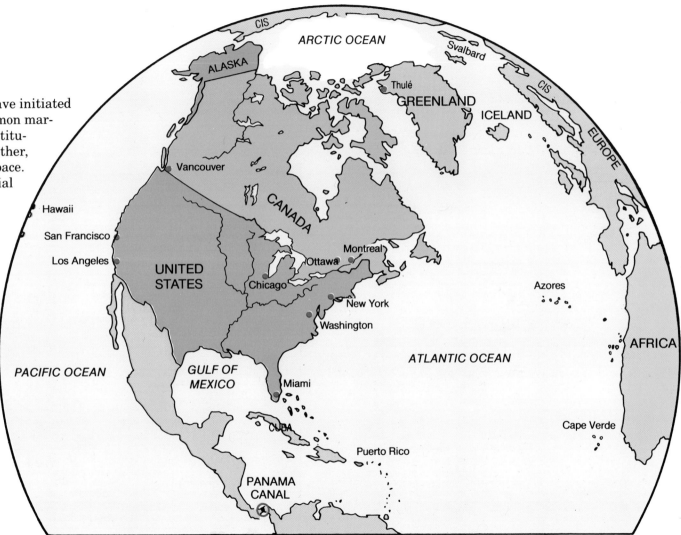

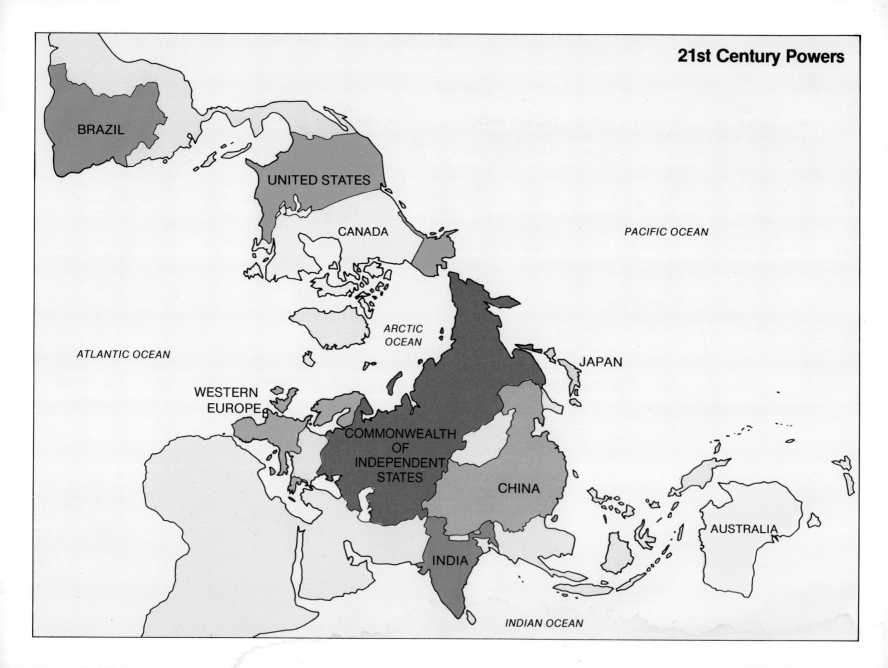

21st Century Powers

BRAZIL

UNITED STATES

CANADA

PACIFIC OCEAN

ARCTIC OCEAN

ATLANTIC OCEAN

JAPAN

WESTERN EUROPE

COMMONWEALTH OF INDEPENDENT STATES

CHINA

AUSTRALIA

INDIA

INDIAN OCEAN

The United States and the Geopolitical Future

The weight of U.S. industrial production in the world economy is less significant today than at the beginning of the century (32% in 1900 and about 20% today).

Nevertheless, despite important domestic problems (education, aging industries and infrastructures, debt, urban problems, etc.), the United States is the overall superpower. No country or group of countries can threaten U.S. security at this time. Japan and the EEC are economic competitors but not superpowers in the global sense. China, despite its size and population, cannot yet be considered a superpower. Like Great Britain during the last century, the U.S. has to ensure an equilibrium of power on the Euro-Asian continent.